Ex Libris

Marion Alicia Sherwood

SIXTH SENSE

SIXTH SENSE

Psychic Powers and Your Five Senses

JENNY RANDLES

ROBERT HALE · LONDON

© *Jenny Randles 1987*
First published in Great Britain 1987

Robert Hale Limited
Clerkenwell House
Clerkenwell Green
London EC1R 0HT

British Library Cataloguing in Publication Data

Sixth sense : psychic powers and
  your five senses.
  1. Psychical research
  133   BF1031

    ISBN 0-7090-2802-4

Photoset in North Wales by
Derek Doyle & Associates, Mold, Clwyd.
Printed in Great Britain by
St Edmundsbury Press Ltd, Bury St Edmunds, Suffolk.
Bound by WBC Bookbinders Limited.

Contents

When
You go
To bed at night

Do
You think
You just put out the light?

Dedicated to the Challenger Seven.

Figures

Introduction

'Much, if not most, of what passes for purely
"sensory" perception contains a large amount of
"extra-sensory material".'
                              Sir Cyril Burt, psychologist

Something must have awoken her. She had been deep asleep in
her Arkansas home. The cares of the world were far beyond her
sleeping mind, as the dark night held the dawn at bay.

Vaunda Johnson was no longer asleep. She did not know why
her mind felt ablaze or why her feet had kicked into motion, as if
guided by some unseen automatic pilot. Yet she stepped from
the sheets and walked into the nursery. Her two daughters were
slumbering as normal in their bunks one atop the other. They
showed no trace of their mother's concern. But, 'without
thinking or wondering why' (as she puts it), Vaunda cradled
Karen from the lower bunk and carried her back to the master
bedroom. The other child, Yvonne, she left undisturbed.

A little while later a scream pierced the night, touching the
echoes of a muffled crash. This time Vaunda leapt up and ran
toward the nursery. Yvonne was fine, but the top bunk had
utterly collapsed. Whispering a silent 'thank you' for her child's
protection, the mother noticed something rather eerie. A
two-inch iron crossbar was imbedded into the pillow, precisely
where Karen's head should have been − indeed, where it *would*
have been, but for that sudden, impulsive, inexplicable act of
taking her from there only minutes before.

She had rescued her daughter from almost certain death. But
how?[1]

The popular naturalist Sir Peter Scott had a famous father.
When his son was only two years old, Scott Senior set off for the

South Pole in a fearsome race across the frozen wastes. The battle was against both elements and Amundsen, his rival to be the first to reach the prize. Catastrophe struck Scott's fateful quest. He and his men arrived at their lonely destination only to taste bitter defeat. Amundsen had beaten them to it. Then the weather set in and their plight became desperate. They never made it home.

Thousands of miles away, baby Peter had no way of knowing this. There was no radio link. He and his mother could only wait for the joyful news that would never come. Then, one night whilst this awful time dragged on, Scott's wife made an entry in her diary recounting how Peter, with that tenuous innocence that flavours childhood, had come to her and said, 'Amundsen and daddy both got to the Pole ... but daddy has stopped work now.'

How did he know about his father's death, far away across time and space?[2]

Yet people do know, and sometimes they can put it to good use.

Bob Cracknell is a psychic detective. Through dark eyes and swarthy complexion he can somehow sense what is going on (or what *has* gone on, or even what *will* go on) at a place where he may never have been. To work this magic, all he needs is a piece of clothing or something that belonged to the person he intends to track.

On 18 April 1977 the body of twenty-four-year-old Janie Shephard was discovered on a common at Wheathampstead, Hertfordshire. She had been abducted, raped and brutally murdered more than two months before. Sometimes Bob Cracknell is asked to help out with cases like this, for his reputation precedes him. On other occasions something supernatural forces him into the fray.

Cracknell picked up vivid images inside his mind. They seemed to connect with the tragedy. Eager to know if they were of real importance, since no details of the crime had been released, he asked a friendly journalist to check them out. 'During the next hour I was in a state of tension and excitement,' this very strange detective explained. 'I was still "tuned in", my whole psyche seemed to be vibrating.' The journalist came back with distressing news. Cracknell's information did not pan out.

'But it must,' the psychic insisted. The journalist could only repeat what the police had told him.

But then there was a knock at Bob Cracknell's door. It was the police. They demanded to know how he had obtained secret and unreleased information. All of it was true! Explaining how he had come by it was little help. Bob has lived a full life and been a down-and-out on the streets of London. There is no doubt he fits the social stereotype some folk have of a murderer or rapist. In any event, the police advised him that he was now a prime suspect!

To try to extricate himself from this tricky spot, Bob Cracknell passed on new material to the CID officers, things that nobody could know. The murderer, he said, was already behind bars. He had been caught for a lesser offence and was serving a short sentence. The officers seemed to exchange startled glances but denied that this could be so.

Officially the story ended here, but Bob Cracknell remains convinced otherwise. He says that the murderer went free, to go back on the streets where, of course, he could have struck again.

The ability to *know* can have its darker side.[3]

Three examples plucked at random from the vast stock of available cases. All are what we might call 'psi-events'*. Many happen every day. Thousands of similar things are never reported, for fear of ridicule, because nobody knows who to report them to, or simply due to a singular difficulty of psi research. The easiest way to resolve any problem is to pretend that the problem is not there. So forget it. Deny it. And hope that it will quietly melt into oblivion.

But disappear is one thing that psi will never do. Mankind has always had its share of mysterious phenomena. Probably it always will. There is little to fear, except fear itself. And the best way to cure fear is to stop such self-denial. We must accept that these things occur, and then we may try to understand them.

We are all potential supermen. The sooner we acknowledge that, the better.

---

* Psi (pronounced as the word 'sigh'): a term often used to describe psychic or undiagnosed psychological phenomena. We shall adopt the word as an acronym for 'Paranormal Sensory Information'.

1. Sensory and Extra-sensory

'Suppose that we were to meet something really
odd – say a new life-form ... could we *see* it
properly?'
Dr Richard Gregory, perception specialist
(*New Scientist*, 30 August 1962)

There have been many books about the paranormal, and I must
justify adding to them. Why should I write this volume and
more, importantly, why do I ask you to read it?

Of course, I believe that I have something relevant to say. For
thirteen years I have devoted much of my life to researching
psi-events, the last eight of them on a full-time basis. In the
course of all this I have learned things which I feel the urge to
share. My views were honed in the workshops of public debate,
which often means wild claims and sensationalism paraded as
fact. From this we are free to choose belief or incredulity. Yet
how do the cautious decide?

I have often had to learn the hard way, fighting through the
mangrove swamps of popular misconception. I have been
surprised to come out with few theories still intact. Yet the
mysteries themselves rarely lose appeal. Whatever their solution
may turn out to be, psi-events *do* happen. That no honest
observer can deny. It is how we interpret these events that
counts. Do we accept the wide-eyed claims of those lurid 'occult'
books? Do we take the line of conservative science and lay the
blame for everything on human imagination? Or is there another
route forward, a better explanation?

It is that better path that I am seeking.

What we call the paranormal is but a commonplace thing of
tomorrow.

So I wish to examine the question of 'extra-sensory

perception' (ESP) and do this from a heretical standpoint. Since it is alleged that these phenomena come from 'beyond our five senses', the first area for exploration must *be* those five senses. Yet, so far as I can tell, it never has been.

I seek to rectify that omission. I will look at what we understand about the five human senses (smell, taste, touch, hearing and vision) and then at what we do not understand. From this we shall be equipped to tackle ESP and pose the radical question: do we need such a concept at all?

Perhaps we shall find that telepathy, clairvoyance and other psi-events do not require extraordinary theories. They may slot neatly into the borderline mists of the five ordinary senses. Possibly we just need more flexibility. If so, ESP will be a myth. But not what ESP reflects.

On the other hand, I must avoid being too sceptical. I am not a scientist, which in this subject tends to be an advantage, but I do have scientific training (in physics and geology). This allows me to steer a course through the middle of the minefield, and mines there are a-plenty.

Nor, I had better put on record, am I a 'psychic'. I rather disappoint journalists and photographers who come to visit and ask to see my tarot cards and crystal ball. Computers, typewriters and casette recorders are not the same somehow! Nevertheless, I *have* had what we might call 'psychic' experiences, and I will mention these when the time is appropriate. My view is that this is nothing special. Psi-events are open to us all. But some of us tend to forget that they have happened.

To be 'psychic' is to be ordinary. Every survey result I have ever seen suggests that. The number of psi-events experienced by people is staggeringly high, and it is no exaggeration to claim that, if it has happened to you, you belong to the majority and not the minority.

It bears repeating that we *each* hold the seeds of the paranormal inside of us. We may be potential supermen (and women), but every 'Superman' has a Clark Kent beneath the multi-coloured costume. We don our suit when we rediscover our inheritance. It lurks within man's genetic structure like a coiled snake ready to pounce. When it strikes, it is easy to be surprised. Once over the shock, the desire is to tame it.

Taming the paranormal, and learning how to use it, is another thing this book is about.

Without further ado, let me take you on a research trip. It was not one I planned, but I made the most of an unfortunate situation, and it turned out rather useful in the end.

In July 1984 I had to enter hospital. Something had gummed up my gall bladder, and the redundant organ had to go. The place where I recovered was pleasant enough, Arrowe Park on the Wirral peninsula. My four-bed ward looked out on green fields and summer skies. Sitting around doing nothing makes me fidget with impatience. So, as soon as I was able, I was wandering the wards on safari for the big game of psychic phenomena, scribbling notes (whenever sister wasn't looking), and I quote from these, since they record what I felt at the time.

I had rather hoped to have an OOBE (out-of-the-body experience) during anaesthesia.[1] By this I mean some conscious awareness of the time when I was supposed to be unconscious. But my mind went out like a candle snuffed into darkness and I woke to find myself back in bed. However, as I recorded, 'during the next twenty-four hours I did notice a very strange feeling which recurred about seven times. I would keep getting a "floating" sensation. I was not actually moving, as my eyes demonstrated. Yet I felt as if I were a balloon rising slowly towards the ceiling. My wits were fully about me and I got very frightened. The thought of "astral projection" [another name for the OOBE] never even entered my head. I just assumed it was an effect of both the lingering anaesthetic and strong pain-killing injections'.

Perhaps it *was* just this, but the experience was a very interesting one, not least because of its parallels with the OOBE. I see the parallels now even if I missed them at the time. I noted about these 'rides', as I called them: 'When I forced myself "back to earth" there was a distinctive "bump" or jarring. That it was not entirely my imagination was seemingly demonstrated by the stab of pain this movement caused in my operation scar ... The first night after the surgery saw me fighting sleep, terrified that if I succumbed I would be carried off towards the sky.'

Associations can trigger memories in the mind, and these events did just that. As a child I had often had similar sensations

on the verge of sleep. There would also be a humming or
buzzing sound that nobody else could hear. I know that because
I called my brother in to listen, and he thought I was potty!
Since childhood I have repressed these things deep into my
mind, but I vividly recall the fear of falling asleep, dreading the
onset of these horrible 'rides'. I do not remember how long
these experiences lasted. Not very long. But they also sometimes
manifested when I was awake, especially in times of fear and
stress (e.g. when a despairing swimming instructress was
dismally failing to overcome my deep phobia of water). My
mind began to fuzz as if filled with sand. The world slowed down
and echoed in a hollow fashion that I cannot describe. But the
picture is still clear in my head, a quarter of a century later.

I have never understood such waking nightmares, or those
strange nocturnal 'rides'. Perhaps this was a test of how I might
react to OOBEs: I may have lost the chance to be a regular
'astral traveller' (This is merely speculation, of course). I know
that I am far from alone. The hummings, buzzings and floatings
that tormented my youth are by no means as unusual as I once
thought.

Without breathing a word about OOBEs or 'rides', when
chatting to a friendly staff nurse I chanced to mention that I was
interested in the paranormal. We each had some free time so she
related her story.

Recently she had been a patient herself in Arrowe Park,
whilst giving birth. Her child weighed over nine pounds, and
partly because of this she was given a light anaesthetic. 'I kept
floating up towards the ceiling,' she told me. 'I had to keep
fighting to bring myself back down again. When I was up there,
all the pain disappeared. I wanted to be free of the struggle.' The
difference between her experience and my own was that she
could *see* her body when she was drifting. It was down *below* her
on the bed. This is the classic OOBE situation and is remarkably
consistent.[2] Millions of people say they have experienced it. But
try telling that to scientists and asking why they do not study it!

A second-year student nurse overheard our conversation and
joined in. Then the sister arrived to advise politely that I was
'scaring the patients with stories like that'. However, she did
reluctantly admit that there were cases of patients reporting such
things. 'It must be a delusion caused by the drugs,' she

suggested. I asked her why this 'delusion' should sometimes happen when people were *not* on drugs, and why it always took the form of floating over your bed. 'Why not imagine yourself back home with the kids or on a desert island?' I proposed. My question went unanswered.

A couple of days later the same student nurse sought me out when she had night duty and we were free of our marauding sister. She directed me to two patients who she believed had undergone a 'ride'.

One of them was a man named Quinn. He had suffered a severe attack after being injected with Heparin, to which it transpired he was allergic. A lung had been blocked and he was suffocating. He had desperately tried to speak but was unable. Then suddenly he was floating above his bed, five feet in the air. His mind was clear. There was no pain. But he was even more astonished by the feeling of peace and calmness that had captivated him. There was also a sort of shimmering haze, as if he was watching through gauze. Through this veil he observed the man in the next bed alert the nurse, and the subsequent rescue.

Everything Mr Quinn said the nurse had done was verified to me. Somehow he had witnessed it when half-way through death's door.

The other case was even more remarkable. It concerned an amazing young woman called Judith, who was a Buddhist although British born and bred. When pregnant she was diagnosed as suffering from multiple sclerosis, and her son was later born with a serious handicap. Despite this he was brought up with loving affection to become a happy child.

In 1983, when he was five years old, the doctors decided that the boy needed a new valve in his heart. Judith explained how on her first visit to him after the operation there was only one question on his mind. 'Mummy – why wouldn't the doctors answer me when they put that thing inside?' After realizing that he did not mean before or after the surgery but *during* it, she asked the boy to explain. 'I was up by the ceiling watching it happen.' To prove his point he gave a graphic description of the valve they had inserted, although he had never seen it. The nurse confirmed to me that he was 'spot on'.

My purpose here is not to try to explain these things. That can come later. But when faced with all these identical stories, perhaps you can see why I take no persuading that psi-events happen. The OOBE *seems* to be an anomaly which fits no conventional theory. Perhaps we shall discover it is less strange than it looks. But it is undoubtedly 'real'. And I need no tarot cards to predict that, if you ask around the members of your own family, it will not take very long to find someone who has experienced this for themselves. The OOBE is one of the most common of all strange phenomena.

This does not exhaust my store of anecdotes from Arrowe Park. There I also met a fascinating woman called Lucia Randles. We are not related, but to share the same name, with the same spelling, in a small four-bed ward, brought us close together.

Lucia was born in Germany and had lived through some terrible times. Amongst them was a night in February 1945 when her father decided to mutiny. 'I am not going on home guard duty,' he declared. Instead he spent the time hiding the household valuables in the cellar and then ordering the family off to the shelters. 'The British will not bomb us,' his wife insisted. But they did. That night, wave after wave of Allied bombers pulverized their city in the single most catastrophic air attack ever mounted (Hiroshima and Nagasaki not excluded). The city was Dresden, and it burned to the ground.

All her father's Home Guard colleagues died that night. But his unexplained action had saved him and quite possibly his wife and daughter too.

Sadly their good fortune ended here. After the destruction they could not find their valuables. They could not even find the road they had lived in. Before that they had spent panic-stricken nights on an island in the zoo lake (the only place where the firestorm could not reach). Here they were safe from the insatiable flames which sucked up the oxygen from the air, but they were terrorized by wild animals, driven crazy through hunger and fear. 'The lions and tigers were too dazed to be a threat,' she remembered. 'The worst problems came from the snakes and crocodiles.'

With the city embers still glowing, Lucia set off on a seventeen-day march towards Munich. Her parents remained behind, as their duty lay in the beleaguered town. As she painfully picked her way across the ruins of her homeland, the young girl had no idea if she was in hostile or friendly territory.

The desperate truth soon became clear. A platoon of war-weary Russian soldiers captured her and several other women. One by one, in a drunken stupor, they raped and beat their victims. Lucia escaped only by hiding under a bed for twenty-four hours, remaining absolutely still. At one point a Soviet invader crashed to the floor and rolled in her direction, his eyes staring towards her. Then they fluttered into unconsciousness, and many minutes later, with the room now deathly silent, she dared to make her exit.

Lucia did reach Munich, but she never got back to her parents. Dresden was captured by the Eastern Bloc and she could not bring herself to face a Russian man again.

I sat awestruck through this stunning tale, pondering that it was the stuff some blockbuster movie might be made of. But the story was far from over. Lucia continued that she moved to Britain, marrying a soldier who had liberated Munich.

They lived in Birkenhead, where he became an office worker. One night in the summer of 1949, after only three years together, she was in the house ironing. A dramatic thunderstorm provided a background accompaniment. Suddenly the phone rang. Instinctively she picked it up with her left hand whilst continuing to iron with the right. It was her husband, sounding faint and distant. 'I love you,' he whispered. She cried out 'Where are you?' But the faltering answer drifted on the wind.

By this point she suspected a prank and switched her mind from the ironing to the phone. Imagine her horror upon seeing her hand cupping empty space. They did not have a telephone in the house.

About an hour later there was a knock at the door. It was a policeman. He bore the tragic news that her husband, having surprised a car-thief on his way from the office, had been gunned down. Her husband had died on the way to hospital about an hour earlier – just when Lucia had received the phantom phone call on a telephone that did not exist. She was devastated by this latest twist of fate.[3]

Three weeks later, still in a state of shock, the night was humid once again. There was no storm this time, but the air was filled with buzzing static. She knew this thanks to her sensitivity to atmospheric conditions (indeed, she predicted a ferocious thunderstorm which struck the hospital whilst we were together).

Deep in her depression Lucia felt the urge to pick up the phone again. This time she resisted, remembering there was no phone. Then suddenly a brilliant flash of light hit the window, and a dazzling, crackling ball was *inside* the room. Her fine hair was attracted towards it, showing how it must have been charged with energy. The ball had no shape, but she 'knew' it was a sign from her husband that all was well. From that day on she recovered her strength.

I can easily explain away this phenomenon as 'ball lightning', a rare and little-understood event.[4] But that is hardly the point. If this *was* ball lightning, the remarkable coincidence of its sudden appearance was enough to alter Lucia's life.

In 1955, still living in Birkenhead, she married again – and acquired the Randles surname. She and her new husband spent sixteen years together, before he died from cancer. A couple of days after his death she claims that he appeared by her bedside late at night and said, 'I miss you so much.' She is sure this was not a dream.

All of this would be enough for any one person, and I was entranced by this silver-haired lady of indeterminate age talking in her lilting Anglo-German accent. Now she was here in Arrowe Park, with the same form of cancer that had claimed her husband.

Lucia had her surgery and was poorly for several days. Meanwhile I was on the mend and was moved to a unit at the far end of the ward, where there was less supervision. I still came back to talk to my friend each day, helping her through the period awaiting news of her health. Had the surgery removed all the cancer, was the main question.

On 5 August 1984, at 9 a.m., she greeted me radiantly. 'My husband came to see me last night!' I searched my memory, wondering if she had told me that she had married a third time. It would not have been too much of a surprise. But I knew this was not so, and her daughter (and son-in-law) were the only ones who came to visit. Then she explained.

At 3 a.m she had got out of bed to put on a housecoat because of the cold. As soon as she got back into bed, she began to feel strange. Time stretched out. Everything went still and quiet. Although we had never discussed it, I knew exactly what she meant. I had often heard witnesses to psi-events describe precisely these symptoms, almost word for word. It is a clue that they have undergone an altered state of consciousness, and I refer to it as 'the Oz Factor'.[5] Lucia knew where she was. She could see the room around her (which, being a modern hospital with open-plan wards, was far from dark despite the hour). In her mind she held the memories of the past weeks: the tests, the surgery and the wait for the results. Then she was aware of her second husband standing beside the bed, silhouetted against the window.

'He was there,' she told me, pointing out the spot. Unconsciously, I edged a little back from the place she was indicating. 'He looked real and solid, but there was a "warm glow" around him. He wore a suit that was his favourite in life. But he was silent.' She felt that he had come to take her with him, but she claims that she told him, 'I am not going.' She explained to me that her daughter was childless but she believed that she would become pregnant soon and she wanted to see her grandchild before she died. With this thought, her husband's 'ghost' smiled and faded away.

Later that day she repeated this story with the same amount of joy to her baffled daughter. I do not think she was making it up for my benefit. But I suggested to Lucia that it might have been a vivid dream, perhaps brought on by our discussion of a few days past. Slowly she shook her head. It was not a dream. She was certain of that. And then I noticed something she herself had never mentioned. The night before had been the one with the ferocious storm. The air was far from cold and doubtless filled with static.

That same mysterious trigger had precipitated another strange encounter. Lucia later received the news that her vision might have presaged. The cancer was gone. She was safe.[6]

How do we know that any of these events 'really' happened? We have only the word of the witness. Could they not have been hallucinations? What is 'real' and 'unreal' anyway, and how do we tell the difference? You have probably come out of a dream wondering for a time if it *was* just a dream, or something more, just as I have.

As long ago as 1905 the psychic researcher J.G. Piddington

was commenting on the importance of such a choice. Indeed, even before then the Society for Psychical Research (SPR) had begun their exploration of the paranormal by taking a census of 'hallucinations'.

Hallucinations of a pathological kind can occur when a person is ill or depressed or under the influence of drugs. All these factors apply to my hospital cases. However, there are other cases where they do not apply and these display features identical with the stories you have met so far. What Piddington did was to compare the pathological cases (as reported by doctors) with data obtained from psychic sources. He found big differences. Medical cases usually occurred on the fringes of sleep, to single witnesses, and involved shapeless, insubstantial images of an almost totally visual nature. Psi-events, on the other hand, happened around the clock, sometimes involved multiple witnesses, tended to be of human figures which were solid in appearance, and interacted with the witness using *all* his senses (although vision and hearing were the most important).[7]

Sixty years later Celia Green and Charles McCreery, conducting psychological research at Oxford's psi-laboratory, also studied 'apparitions' and reached similar conclusions.[8]

A more modern piece of research is the classic 'Ruth' experiment, involving psychiatrist Dr Morton Schatzman. This came about when he was approached by a woman who as a child had been sexually abused by her own father. Years later she found herself in possession of incredible powers of imagery and was 'haunted' by spontaneous hallucinations involving *all* the senses. With the psychiatrist's help, she learned to control the images so that the 'ghost' of her father could appear and disappear at will, although there was always some autonomy. Eventually Ruth was able to create images of other people, including Dr Schatzman, and make them appear in the same room as the 'real' person.

In different circumstances Ruth might have gone to a psychic researcher instead of a psychiatrist. But there was never any doubt that these very realistic images *were* hallucinations. Nobody else could see them, and she knew that, when she was 'seeing' him, her father was decidedly alive and thousands of miles away on the other side of the Atlantic. Nor was he trying to appear. Whatever was allowing this fantastic thing to happen, the secret lay in Ruth's own mind.

Many psychiatrists sceptical of psi would have either sent Ruth packing or endeavoured to 'cure' her. We lose a great deal of our superman abilities by being bludgeoned out of them by society. Fortunately Morton Schatzman saw the opportunity and realized that Ruth could 'get well' by *using* her powers instead of wishing them away.

Working with other doctors and scientists, he placed Ruth in front of equipment which measured brain response and asked her to 'hallucinate'. Some amazing results emerged. If she made her spook stand in front of flashing lights, her brain reacted as if a real person had blocked out the lights and she was not detecting them. Since nobody really was there, common sense suggests that her brain should have reacted to the lights even if she insisted she was not seeing them. In contradiction to all this, if the room light was turned off and Ruth was asked to make her apparition put it back on again, she could do so. The light did not 'really' come back on, but Ruth perceived it as doing so. However, she remained quite unable to read a book in the hallucinated light. She was as much in the dark as anyone else.[9]

Piecing this dramatic research together leads us towards important (if startling) conclusions. What we perceive to be real is a product of our mind, and this is *more* significant (at least in some respects) than what is physically there. The statement, 'It was not real, just an hallucination', is thus seen to be very ambiguous. If our definition of 'real' is based on whether we can read by an imaginary room light, it is a valid argument. If instead we define the term from what has sufficient 'substance' to block the path of light rays to the brain, there seems little difference between a real and a hallucinated object.

What price our real, substantial world now? How can we *ever* be sure that what we see is truly there? We must always fear the gypsy's warning – it might all have been invented in our heads! The UFO that we see in the sky could be from outer space or inner space. The difference seems to be marginal. In the end, it may all come down to this question.

Hilary Evans is a paranormal researcher who is deeply intrigued by these things. He has published an excellent survey of 'apparitions'. He notes how many solo explorers (mountain-climbers, round-the-world yachtsmen etc) have found themselves conversing with travelling-companions who were not 'really' there. The phenomenon has a lot in common with the imaginary playmates children have.

In *Beyond Explanation?* I discussed a mountain climber's ghost on Everest.[10] Evans has since added many others. In 1895, for example, sailor Joshua Slocumb became ill on his desperate lonely voyage and when a storm struck, all hope seemed lost. But the 'ghost' of a mariner materialized and steered his vessel safely through. The apparition explained that he was a member of Christopher Columbus's crew and did not want to see a fellow sailor lose his life. However, Slocumb was interested in the historical voyages of Columbus, so this ghost seems to have been a rather appropriate one to rescue him.[11] This implies that the spectre came from Slocumb's imagination (rather like Ruth's visions of her father).

Researcher Gordon Rattray-Taylor, in a fascinating book about the brain, commented that high-altitude manned balloon experiments had to be curtailed because high above the atmosphere in this very lonely place the solo balloonists began to feel disorientated and light-headed undergoing what I readily spot as 'the Oz Factor'. This doubtless prepared them for imagining experiences similar to those discussed.[12] Our suspicions can only be compounded when we consider that modern lone sea-voyagers do not encounter ghosts from sailing ships but (in the case of yachtsmen John Ridgeway and Sir Francis Chichester) see twentieth-century spooks such as flying saucers.

Maybe the mind, devoid of imput from the senses, is rebelling against the lack of activity. It manufactures stimuli of its own. That seems a very logical solution – at first. But then we pause and wonder *who* saved Joshua Slocumb from the storm? Could he have done it himself?

Look back to the head of this chapter (p.13) and read the words by the perception specialist Richard Gregory. He asked this rhetorical question as man first set off towards the stars and reasonably wondered if we could perceive things we had never met before. There is evidence that natives who had never seen ships (and later aircraft) failed to 'see' them when civilized man first invaded their domain. True we *imagine* alien bug-eyed monsters, but we do so only because of past experience of things like them. All our aliens are humanoid or cobbled together from animals and other familiar forms. We only perceive what is in our minds to perceive. If an alien were *truly* alien (and we had no possible image to describe it), Gregory suggests that we might not see it. He could very well be right.

This is a tough concept to grab hold of. Yet it seems to be part of the reason why our memories of childhood do not begin with a slap from the doctor as we emerge from the birth canal. Our memories *fade in* gradually over the months and years that follow. This appears to be because *everything* we experience as a very young child may be called an 'alien' image. There is nothing in our minds to represent it. So we cannot perceive it until we learn to do so.

Our heads contain a 'mind store' of images from which we build our perceptions. But that 'mind store' is not a part of our genetic structure (at least not the fine details). We have to put things in and stock it up, by way of trial and error, experience and what parents or schools *teach* us to call real. In this way the boundaries between truth and imagination shift until they define along pre-established consensus lines. The world becomes less fuzzy, and we not only perceive it but are able to remember that we have perceived.

A presently unanswered question, fascinating at this juncture, is whether this 'learned' perception is an accurate one. Since it is really the result of what consensus opinion teaches, it is bound to fit the pattern of modern-day concepts. This raises the intriguing possibility that those who undergo psi-events in childhood and, for some reason, are *not* taught to consign them to that wastebin labelled 'fantasy', might learn to put a whole new perspective on reality. Their 'mind store' will contain a stock of images different from those of the rest of us.

The parameters of reality may be personally defined. If we just happen to miss those lectures of life which deal with psi-events, no images to identify them will be in our 'mind store'. In that case, as with Gregory's hypothetical aliens, the supernatural could pop up right in front of our noses and we would simply never *see* it. Richard Gregory also accepts that we 'learn' reality as we go along. He cites visual illusions as an important demonstration of that.[13]

Among all the fascinating illusions that dazzle your eyes, there is one less obvious but which you can test for yourself.

Next time you are on a train with an open front cab that allows
a view of the rails ahead, sit right at the front. On a long, straight
stretch of track, focus your eyes on the metal as it rolls off
towards the horizon. Continue to watch idly as the train rattles
along to the next station. Two or three minutes is ample
observation time. Now, when the train stops, notice what
happens. Something rather odd.

The lines begin to move in the opposite direction, flowing out
from you as if they were alive. It is a peculiar sensation which
lasts for some time. Objectively, the answer is simple. The brain
has become conditioned to expect the lines to move across your
stationary field of vision. When they stop doing so, it
compensates and *presumes* them to be moving in the other
direction. You know they are not. But try altering your
perception so the rails do not melt.

The same effect can be produced by staring at the rotating
wheel in a microwave oven (although this is not so easy on the
eyes). What such persistent illusions show is that our brains *do*
create our perceptions. It is not the information coming into our
senses which constitutes reality. It is what our brain shuffles out
of all this data that 'creates' the world outside.

Colin Blakemore, in discussing other illusions, makes further
points which should be equally disturbing to the well-balanced
mind.[14] For instance, we are incapable of perceiving things
which do not move. Nonsense, you say. I see my TV set on the
far side of the room. That is not moving. No, but your eyes are.
They flick about to create the motion which allows perception.
And when both you and the object are quite still, you 'intuit' the
existence of the object, assuming that, if it was there a minute
ago, it will still be there now. We do an awful lot of 'filling in' –
making assumptions based on past experience. And, of course,
for it to be past experience there has to be an image in that
ever-faithful 'mind store'.

Blakemore describes an illusion not unlike the one involving
railway lines. If you stare at a tumbling waterfall for some
minutes and then refocus on the rocks beside it, the same
compensation effect makes the rocks appear to 'ripple'. We
know from past experience in our 'mind store' that rocks are
pretty boring things. They are lumpy and grey and come in
different shapes and sizes. One thing they do not do is ripple. So

we persuade ourselves that what we 'see' is a false perception, or hallucination. Now consider what might happen if we were to travel to a planet round a distant star with bizarre landscapes and geology. Here they may have rocks that *do* ripple. Our choice between hallucination and reality would now be virtually impossible.

This may well be the problem faced by witnesses to psi-events. They have an anomalous perception which does not fit in, and only *they* can decide how to interpret it.

Psychologists are very much involved with the relationship between perception and reality. The purpose of these seeming diversions is to show that we too must consider it if we hope to understand the paranormal.

Professor M.D. Vernon cautions us that the solid permanence of objects is not a product of reality. Most professors of physics would agree, since their quest for basic building-blocks of the atom has lead them deeper and deeper into a land of

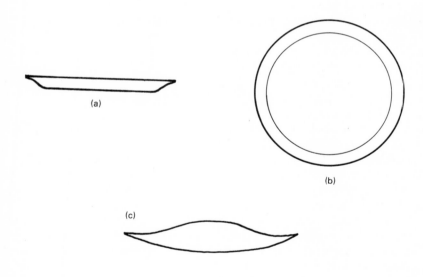

Fig. 1: How we perceive objects at different angles.

make-believe. However, they may not share the opinion of this psychologist that the solidity (which obviously has to come from somewhere) is the product of our brains.[15]

She explains her reasoning by pointing to the importance of context. If we see the shape (Fig. 1a) and are *told* it is a 'plate', we know we must be seeing it edge on, because our 'mind store' has images of plates in different angles, and a plate face 'on' is different (Fig. 1b). If we see a more anomalous shape (Fig. 1c) and are not told what it is, we make assumptions from the context and our past experience. But is this its 'real' shape, or are we again viewing it at a strange angle? It may be a matter of choice.

When we are dealing with the perception of the unfamiliar, the chances of being wrong are high.

An interesting experiment some years ago consisted of showing ambiguous figures to a group of subjects and *naming*

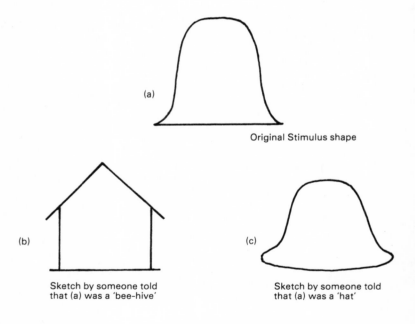

(a)

Original Stimulus shape

(b)

Sketch by someone told
that (a) was a 'bee-hive'

(c)

Sketch by someone told
that (a) was a 'hat'

Fig. 2: Experiment that shows how naming an object affects
memory and perception.

Fig. 3: Children making inferences that alter perception.

them at the same time. The subjects were split into small teams, and each team was given different names for the same figure. They were then asked to redraw what they had seen, after a suitable lapse of time. The teams tended to draw their pictures more like whatever object name they had been given.

For example, the figure shown might have been Fig. 2a. Those who were told this was a 'bee-hive' tended to draw it later as Fig. 2b. Those advised that it was a 'hat' produced very different pictures (Fig. 2c). This experiment comes from an era before UFOs, but suppose it were repeated now and one team was told that Fig. 2a was a 'flying saucer'. How do you think *they* would redraw it?[16]

Vernon shows that the same results apply to classic ink-blot (Rorschach) testing of children in the 9–11 years age group.[17] The meaningless inkblot (Fig. 3a) was shown to them. One child decided for himself that it looked like a hand holding a cane (Fig. 3b), another that it was a duck swimming on water (Fig. 3c). When they later redrew what they believed they had seen, there were differences, as shown in the figures, according to the context placed on the inkblot by the child. One can imagine a child (or even an adult – as this works just as well) looking at the same Figure 3a and interpreting it as the 'Loch Ness Monster'. If this had happened in a real-world situation (not an experiment looking at ink blots), would the percipient have completed a witness sketch that looked like Fig. 3a or Fig. 3d?

We desire pattern in what may well be patternless. The famous 'fairies in the fire' phenomenon and seeing images in random patches of dark and shade on trees are obvious examples.

Not only do we change our perceptions according to what we expect, but we have a habit of forgetting incongruous facts. A recent experiment shows this very well. A twenty-two-minute story about a bank robbery was recounted to groups of seven- and ten-year-olds. Psychologists had seeded into the story actions that were out of character for the familiar people in the plot. James Bond, the Bionic Woman and others took the lead roles, and an example of the incongruity comes when the Six Million Dollar Man fails to lift up a can of paint because he is not strong enough! As a control, the same story was told to other groups of children using different characters who were unfamiliar to them. In this case there were no expectations from the images in the children's 'mind stores' about what the characters could or could not do. All the children were given memory tests immediately and three weeks later.

The aspects of the story which concerned characters known to the children who performed actions that might be expected of them were remembered very well. The incongruous acts performed by unfamiliar characters were also well recalled (with slightly less success: a five per cent error rate at the end of the three weeks). But the actions performed by characters the children knew which *were* out of context with that character's normal behaviour were either forgotten (to a high degree) or changed in memory so that expected acts were performed instead. The children tended to say that the Six Million Dollar Man *had* picked up the can of paint.[18]

A more famous test of the same principle was carried out by Elizabeth Loftus of the University of Washington. She showed groups of students a short film about a car smash and then asked questions about it. One of these was, 'How many of you saw the broken headlamps?' Fifteen per cent said that they had. Which is strange. There were no broken headlamps! She had led them to believe there must have been, by the way she phrased the question, and quite a few changed their perception of the events to fit the newly ascribed expectation. This 'cueing' process was demonstrated a number of times in the experiment.[19]

There is a good reason for this discussion of perception. It is crucial to our understanding of psi. Seeing, or sensing, is not just a question of light rays or sound waves processed by the brain. Many other factors are involved, including past experience to build up a mind store, cultural context, personal belief, cueing by others and visual ambiguity.

This last point is particularly important. If we see something out of the ordinary, our perception of it will *not* be the same as someone else's. Instead it will be heavily influenced by what we think it is – even when this thought is little more than a guess. And guesses can, of course, be wrong.

Since most paranormal phenomena involve something out of the ordinary, we cannot afford to forget these things. There *is* a difference between what we see with our eyes and what we perceive with our mind.

All the problems discussed during the last few pages could affect how we observe a psi-event. I have myself investigated dozens of UFO cases where the 'UFO' was without doubt something remarkably ordinary, such as Venus or the Moon. Yet it has been the catalyst for an extraordinary experience.[20]

What seems to happen is that the false premise, 'It's a flying saucer', has moulded what the mind perceives so that it becomes more like a UFO and less like the star or planet it really is. The same principle is demonstrated by Professor Vernon's work or the ink-blot tests. Optical illusions, the cultural myth of the alien UFO, and cueing (if someone says 'Oh look – flying saucer!', I defy you *not* to look!) are all complicating factors.

However, there certainly seems to be more to it than that. Why do some people find their reality changing so much that an alien abduction or a ghostly vision follows on? How can information that appears to be consistent convey itself from case to case? Why does the 'hallucination' or 'illusion' sometimes alter the course of a person's life? We need more than the pat answers science is offering.

Perhaps the 'outer' experience of a psi-event is merely the reflection of something more dynamic at an 'inner' level. The true encounter happens in the mind, and the UFO or apparition is a side-effect which leaks out into visual perception.

A clue to all this might be what I call 'the Reality Blink'.

Rosalind and Peter Warrington, whom I have known for many years, were on holiday in Western Scotland some time ago. Standing in a car-park at the Kyle of Lochalsh, they were passing the time by eating fish and chips when suddenly they turned to one another and rather sheepishly asked, 'Did you just see that?' Both had. A car, unattended and parked among the rest, had without warning (and quite impossibly) moved sideways! The motion had been short and over in a second. Said car now sat in its 'new' location as if nothing had ever happened. Nobody around them seemed the least bit concerned by this challenge to the laws of nature, as if they had simply not perceived it. Peter told me, soon after the incident, 'We sort of paused mid chip and shrugged. But whilst we both *saw* it, cars don't of course move sideways. So it was a case of "oh" ... and then on to the next chip.'

This weird story has rarely been discussed by any of us because it fits into no obvious pigeonhole. It is not a ghost or a timeslip or some recognizable psi-event. Yet it is very peculiar. The only reason I have taken so much notice of it (when others who were told doubtless forgot it very fast) is that I have experienced similar things throughout my life.

I cannot profess anything as dramatic as a moving car, but a number of times I have been 'idling', with my thoughts on other things, when my attention has darted towards the floor or wall. I find myself staring at a mark or blemish convinced it was not there a second ago. There is a dull realization that it has just popped into existence out of nowhere. Usually I persuade myself that such 'Reality Blinks' are optical illusions. My eyes simply see a mark that I had not consciously noticed before. This is the obvious answer, because things do not materialize out of thin air, do they? But it is hard to escape the feeling that this solution is imperfect.

On one occasion my cat, who was comfortably dozing on the chair arm beside me, looked across at the wall at the same moment I did. So unexpected was this that I scrambled over, wondering if we had been distracted by a spider. But the spot on the wall which formed my 'Reality Blink' *was* just a spot on the wall. It looked for all the world as if it had always been there. Which common sense says it must have been.

Just as I was prepared to dismiss these things as silly little foibles, I discovered that other people go through 'Reality Blinks' as well. On 20 April 1958 writer Somerset Maugham claims that the head moved on a portrait he was looking at. As he described how it remained in its new position as if it had always been there, I knew through mounting excitement just how he felt. He explained that, if he were hauled up before a court and asked on oath about the matter, he would face a problem. Asked to swear if he had seen the head move, he would be forced to say, 'Yes'. Asked if it 'really' had moved he would be bound to answer, 'Certainly not!'

With that shifting, apologetic way one feels about 'Reality Blinks', Maugham passed the comment, 'I suppose it was an optical illusion.'[21]

The famous psychic Rosalind Heywood notes that she also has had this experience. A figure in a portrait 'leant out' and offered advice. 'I use the words "he said" ' she remarks, 'but this is not really accurate, for although the visual experience was an outer one, he in fact conveyed his meaning in ... the more immediate "interior" fashion ...'[22] Indeed I know what she means.

The 'Reality Blink' has not really been considered as a psi-event before, yet it just might be a flashlight that illuminates the answer. Reality seems to be a fluid thing.

I will close this long introductory look at the mysteries we shall confront with one of the strangest cases I have met. It begins oddly and builds into a 'Reality Blink' without parallel.

The participant, Mrs E. Sage, conveyed the story to me a few weeks after it had occurred. I corresponded with her at the time, clarifying points and trying to figure it out. But I have never published details before as it frankly left me stumped.

Mrs Sage lives in Kent, by the Medway estuary. She has three children, two of whom are practically adults and a much younger daughter. To all intents and purposes she is an ordinary housewife. However, she has had at least one UFO encounter.

On 4 August 1980 she decided to visit the shops for a tin of peas. As she set off, her mind was filled with frustration over having forgotten the peas earlier in the day and with a minor tiff she had just had with her son. It was 4.50 p.m. on a fine summer day as she climbed a flight of stone steps leading to an alleyway by the grocery store. She tells me, 'Out of the corner of my eye something in the sky made me jump. It was like a smoke ring going round and round with sort of sparks coming out of the edge of it ... I shouted when I jumped and (as I did) this thing seemed to appear from nowhere in the place where I had seen the smoke ring.'

The 'thing' was like a miniature helicopter, no more than four feet tall and a little longer. It had no rotor blades, doors, engines or windows save a perspex-like bubble at the front. It was covered in green and tan camouflage markings and had a cross-shaped vent at the back. Inside the bubble sat two men, 'identical twins' about five feet eight inches tall and wearing one-piece grey jumpsuits. Their hair was long, down to their shoulders, with curls at the bottom. The only obvious, difference between them was that one man's hair was corn-coloured, the other's was dark. Their eyes were blue and complexions 'olive-skinned'. Other than that they seemed ordinary people.

This object was hovering on top of the roof of a house no more than fifty feet from Mrs Sage. At the far end of the passage she could see the road with traffic on it, but everything was 'muted'. It was, she said, 'as if I was hearing it from inside something ... as if I was inside'. This is a classic description of 'Oz Factor' symptoms. Aside from this indication that the witness was in an altered state of consciousness, she does note that a peculiar mist clung to a picket fence separating the house from the alleyway. It smelt sweet and sickly, and as she passed she felt a little dizzy.

The object now started to float down from the roof so as to hover partly over and partly within some thick bushes that bordered the house. She could 'hear' a conversation between the two men and was able to pick out every word. Although Mrs Sage thought these were spoken words, I am inclined to assume that they were 'heard' in her mind.

The dark-haired man seemed angry and said to his colleague, 'You said it was all right.' His blond co-pilot was trying to soothe him, saying, 'I know. I know.' As the witness continued to walk past the object, at a point where the alley bends, the blond man added. 'It's all right. She thinks we're army.' A flap then came down from the bottom middle side, and there were several 'clicks', which Mrs Sage thinks might have been a camera taking photographs. 'That's it then,' the angry man said. 'All that work wasted.' His companion replied, 'Not necessarily.'

In a bit of a daze the woman went on to the shop, at the end of the alley, leaving the object there. She got her peas, had a conversation about a wedding with a friend and returned homeward several minutes later. She is surprised by these actions but points out that her mind was already hazy about the experience. This is why she thinks she never mentioned it to her friend. On the return journey down the alley she saw no sign of the object and did not expect to. But the fair-haired man now stood in the garden, bending over. As she went by, he straightened up and smiled. The man wore a camouflage (army-type) jacket which he had not had on previously.

From this moment on, Mrs Sage *forgot* all about the incident. It was five weeks later, she says, on 8 September, when she first remembered anything. A neighbour chanced to mention a UFO seen by Scottish policemen, as described in her newspaper. This opened up the door to her mind, and over the next six or seven weeks the entire story came back to Mrs Sage in bits and pieces. During this time she felt sickly and bad-tempered and found sleeping almost impossible.

The story so far is strange indeed and has interesting comparisons with the UFO enigma but it is hardly a UFO sighting in the conventional meaning of that term. However, what happened next is more unusual. Somehow the alleyway changed. It became quite different from the alley she had known so well before.

Logically, there is no way the changes in the alley way *could* have happened. Yet Mrs Sage's perception of it does seem to be different after the encounter. She says, 'The steps are narrower, and the fifth step was wider than the rest, but now all are the same size. The bungalow went further up. So did both gates ... there are thick bushes where there were no bushes before. A tree went from round the side of the garden to the position where I saw the craft. [If it had been there when I saw the object] ... it would have marred my view.' None of these things could 'really' have happened in the time between August and December 1980, when Mrs Sage first wrote to me.

Such cases pose major questions about the nature of reality and whether it might not be a *personal* phenomenon. Most of the features of the world exist because they are common to all our 'mind stores'. Some things on the outer limits of reality may depend on individuals rather more.

2. The Brain

'What we perceive comes as much from inside our
heads as from the world outside.'
William James, philosopher.

Professor M.D. Vernon may again be quoted, putting clearly the
issue that we face: 'We tend to think that a picture of the
external world falls on the retina and is conveyed to the brain,
and that this picture is similar to the picture formed on the film
of a camera. But what in fact reaches the brain is a pattern of
nerve impulses, the frequency of which corresponds more or less
to the brightness of the light reaching the eye.'[1]

In other words, what we experience is at best an illusion of the
truth. The world is re-created inside our heads by that
unfathomable decoding instrument called the human brain.
What we take as the real universe out there is in fact a massive
con-trick perpetuated by our grey matter as a means towards an
end.

Figure 4 is a cross-section through the outer surface of a
human brain, showing the main centres that we believe relate to
different sensory functions. We have learnt these through
experiment, as the brain is largely insensitive to pain. It can be
operated on with the patient conscious, and he can report what
he 'feels' if a certain spot is touched or stimulated. We can also
gather data from malfunctions, when a portion of the brain is
damaged or injured. This helps us understand which parts
control which functions.

But there is much that we still do not know. Indeed we
understand less about the brain than about some of the planets
in our solar system.

The brain surface (cortex) is pinky grey and wrinkled. It is
about four millimetres thick and shrouded by the skull, a

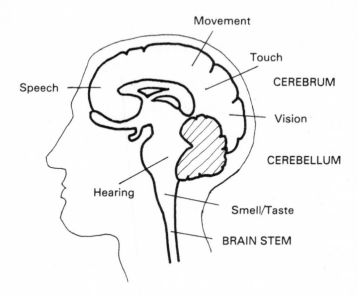

Fig. 4: Cross-section through the human brain

remarkably protective casing. But brain matter slops around in here like a jelly and can be damaged soon enough if struck a blow.

There are two main dome-like sections that have a brain stem leading into them. This ferries bundles of nerve fibres. The dominant upper dome is called the 'cerebrum', and the main sensory functions are located here. Below this, huddled at the back, is a walnut-like and walnut-sized area called the 'cerebellum'. This visually seems less important but acts as a fine-tune mechanism for what would otherwise be crude and unrefined sensations.

Other than this we do not know a great deal about the cerebellum. It seems to control subconscious functions. But there are psychologists, such as Dr Stan Gooch, who believe that it is the most important site for psi-events. He argues that the cerebellum in women is often larger, and they seem to have more psychic abilities then men. He even suggests that its appearance and location might be the source of the 'hunchback' legends and the word 'hunch' (meaning intuition or psychic awareness). He certainly feels that it runs the autonomic nervous system, which is responsible for subconscious motions and the 'automatic pilot' – the phenomenon that might have helped Vaunda Johnson save her daughter's life. (See page 9). However, despite their potential, it is fair to say that Gooch's theories still remain controversial.[2]

We know rather more about the cerebrum. It is split into two mirrored hemispheres. Because of the way nerves cross over from the sensory organs to the brain, the *right* sensory fields are controlled by the *left* cerebral hemisphere, and vice-versa.

Linking the right and left hemispheres is a Clapham Junction of 200 million nerve fibres called the corpus callosum. This is very important because when severed it isolates the two hemispheres. Normally feedback through here lets one half of the brain know what the other is up to. When the corpus callosum is cut, such feedback is seriously reduced, with quite extraordinary consequences that we shall consider later.

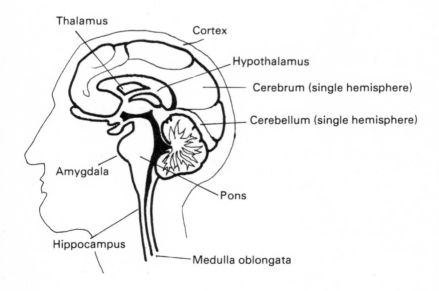

Fig. 5: A cross-section of the brain showing the main areas.

Figure 5 shows a slice through the middle of the brain (as depicted in Fig. 4) and names the major areas inside the cortex. It would be easy to get lost in a maze of technical terms, but there is no real need to remember them all. Just refer to this figure if you find yourself lost.

Each area has a distinct function. The 'pons', for example, seems related to consciousness. If this (deep-seated and well-protected) area gets damaged, a sort of on/off switch is thrown and the person enters deep coma. Similarly the 'amygdala' seems to control anger and arousal. When it is removed from wild animals, they usually become docile, leading to the daring suggestion that removal of the human amygdala might be a way to 'cure' vicious criminals.[3]

It is possible to localize dozens of functions in various parts of the brain.[4] But as biologist Dr Steven Rose warns us, 'Describing the properties of the brain in molecular terms is not the same – as seems sometimes feared – as explaining away these properties.'

I have spoken of certain areas in the cortex controlling aspects of human behaviour, but it is possible that the brain simply *channels* the control from some other source. In a hi-fi system we have base, treble, and volume operations which may be similar to different parts of the cortex. We call them controls, because tuning them seems to produce desired effects. However, the real essence of the sound (on the tape, record or radio station) is unaltered by whatever setting we put these 'controls' onto. They make no difference to the music – only to the way we perceive it.

Studies of human evolution show that we are virtual new-comers of very minor consequence to the history of the universe.[5] We owe our status as rulers of the Earth to a remarkable explosion in the growth of the brain. Its size has quadrupled over two million years. This has lead to speculation that such unexplained development might have been induced by an external (even alien) intelligence. Doris Lessing expresses this very well in her five novel *Canopus in Argos* series.[6] And the vivid scene from the Arthur C. Clarke inspired movie *2001: A Space Odyssey* depicts what might have been the moment when it all began. An extra-terrestrial teaching device provokes a sub-human ape to use a bone as a tool, and man's rise to dominance becomes assured.

In real terms brain volume has increased from 400 cubic millimetres two million years ago to approximately 1,400 cubic millimetres now. Our evolutionary progress has been at an amazing and exponential rate, with all that has occurred in the past 10,000 years swamping the remainder into utter unimportance.[7]

Whilst Darwin's theories of growth by natural selection and survival of the fittest struggle to encompass mankind, science does consider that he must have got it basically right. Our brain appears to have developed in three stages. There is an 'old brain', not unlike that of a reptile, centred on the brain stem and relating to primary senses. But around it has grown the 'mid brain', which has a lot in common with less advanced types of mammal. Senses such as smell function here, and it is interesting that many mammals (e.g. dogs and cats) have a far better smell sense than we do, as if we have grown beyond the need for great reliance on this area. Surprisingly it is also very important for emotions. The 'new brain' is centred on the cerebral hemispheres, and it is here that all the higher senses seem to locate. Vision, hearing and logical thought, as well as language, separate man from the other animals. Our 'new brain' is the reason.

The philosopher Arthur Koestler has suggested that this three-stage development is the root cause of the world's evils. War, violence, crime etc are all aspects of animal behaviour from our older brains. So rapid has been the growth of the 'new brain' that we cannot contain these primitive urges, and global suffering is the result.[8] Will mankind survive or become one more evolutionary cul-de-sac?

The cerebellum has also evolved, but in a different manner. Its role is subconscious, intuitive and possibly psychic. It is quite fascinating that the cerebrum and cerebellum reflect two totally distinct ways of coping with sensory input. One uses logic, rational thought and science, the other intuition and mysticism. In *Beyond Explanation?* I devised a two-mode concept of reality that dovetails very neatly with this. Normal reality mode is of logic and the cerebral hemispheres. Synchronistic reality mode is of the cerebellum.[9]

Each human brain has a fantastic number of nerve cells, called neurons. The total is believed to lie between 10 and 15 thousand million – although nobody has actually counted them, of course. A single neuron consists of a stem body (called an axon) and strands or feelers that look like branches of a tree and so earn the name dendrite. These dendrites transmit sensory information around the brain and link up adjacent neurons across gaps called synapses.

In real terms the synapse is a minute distance, but on the scale of the neuron it is like the English Channel. Chemicals control whether or not the channel is traversable. Hormones, such as serotonin, are particularly important. The electrical impulses conveyed through the neurons produce chemical ions (usually of sodium or potassium) which may, or may not, be able to bridge the gap. Like a regulating valve the synapse is thus either open or closed. The pattern of open and closed synapses controls the flow of an electro-chemical signal around the vast array of neurons in the brain. You can doubtless imagine that, if there are thousands of millions of neurons in a single brain, the number of different patterns that can be formed by linking them together is nothing short of enormous – as it must be, for each different pattern corresponds to a different tiny aspect of human behaviour.

In fact, incredible as it might seem, there are more possible links than the total of every single atom in the universe! Small wonder that life is such a complicated business.

It would be easy to get lost in a mass of mathematics, but all that really counts is this basic system, which I have very much simplified in the last few pages. Sensory impulses come from the sense organs to the brain stem. Here they trigger a neuron into action, and it stimulates chemicals to flow. If a synapse is open, it transmits the data across the gap. If it is not, the data must find another open route. Each unique stimulus corresponds to a different pattern of linked-up neurons, in a fantastic web of millions of connections. In crude terms, 'I see something which is blue' would create a pattern of transmissions very different from 'I see something which is red'. Eventually (and a finite amount of time is always involved) the impulse reaches the cerebral areas, where it is sorted and processed into our mental perception.

It is interesting to see what happens if this chain reaction goes wrong. Might it lead to an anomalous perception? Some brain physiologists think that the sensation of *déjà vu* (which we all get from time to time) may be a product of faulty neuron transmission. It is the feeling that something we are experiencing has already happened to us (it literally means 'already seen' in French). It is possible that a similar pattern of neurons is being triggered to one which was triggered in the past, and our sensation is simply a response to this familiarity. Or that part of the impulse arrives subconsciously (in one part of the brain) before it arrives consciously in another. The foretaste may be a matter only of milliseconds, but a feature of *déjà vu* is that we cannot time the experience. All we know is that it seems to have happened somewhere, somehow, before.

A more serious consequence of neuron transmission is epilepsy. This is not a disease but a symptom resulting from several potential causes. It can be thought of as an out-of-control chain reaction, like one domino knocking down a whole line of them in a self-propelled motion. The brain tends to respond to this overload of random impulses by producing a period of unconsciousness.

There are two main types of epileptic attack. The *petit mal* and the *grand mal*, the former being less serious and more common. In a *petit mal* the chain reaction is transient, and the brain 'switches off' for just a few seconds. The sufferer may simply stop doing what he is doing (e.g. talking to someone), stare blankly ahead for a few moments and then resume behaviour once the normal flow of consciousness returns. Very likely he will not know what has happened to him. But if he has a dream or hallucination in this period it is theoretically possible that he might consider it to have been a real (and anomalous) experience. If the hallucination were of a strange light in the sky, he might remember this as a psi-event.

The *grand mal* leads to more prolonged periods of unconsciousness, at least fifteen minutes is not unusual. Convulsions of the muscles and nerves are also accompaniments to this state, which is less dangerous to the victim than it appears to a frightened onlooker. Upon waking, the sufferer can feel dizzy, disorientated, confused and nauseous and have a headache. A study of witness reports to close encounters with psi-events will quickly show that these are commonly related after-effects from their ordeal.[10]

About one in a hundred people suffers from epileptic attacks of one sort or another, although there are reasons to believe that many more may have occasional experiences without necessarily knowing it. Migraine headaches are very like the aftermath to an epileptic attack and seem to have a direct correlation with chemical changes in the brain. Whilst there are certainly differences, there may also be unsuspected relationships. It is of much interest that psychic researchers have learned by accident that many people who regularly experience psi-events also tend to be migraine sufferers, and less often epileptic.

On the night of 9–10 March 1979 thirteen-year-old Nina E of Shipley, West Yorkshire, suffered an epileptic attack. She was used to these and went to bed to rest. However, this proved rather difficult. At about 1.30 a.m., approximately $2\frac{1}{2}$ hours after the attack, she heard the floorboard creak in her bedroom and leapt up to see a weird figure coming towards her. It was literally a little green man!

According to the report by Paul Bennett of the West Yorkshire UFO Research Group, the 'man' was about twenty inches tall and glowed with a vivid aura. The most prominent features were large, piercing eyes, and arms way out of proportion for its size. It continued from the end of the bed for about ten seconds, at which point Nina jumped out and put the light on. The figure then vanished immediately.[11]

There are no green midget burglars in Shipley, and the suspicion has to be that this was a hallucination. A connection with the epileptic attack must at least be considered. Nevertheless, this type of psi-event is very common. It even has a generic name: 'the bedroom visitor'. Among such appearances, small 'men' with odd colours and out-of-proportion body features make up more than their fair share.[12]

The witness interprets what he sees in many ways. It could be a 'ghost', or a 'demon', a 'religious vision' or an 'alien'. Each of these has been more prevalent in different eras. This artificial segregation of the evidence means that researchers in one field often do not know that the exact same phenomenon is being reported elsewhere. This not only hinders efforts to find a solution but imposes answers upon researchers which could be quickly seen as inadequate if they knew the full facts. Obviously, if these figures appear in all these disguises, chances are the phenomenon is not really any of them. Even worse, some researchers dismiss the evidence as not fitting in and make the error of the scientist by dismissing this as 'just a dream'.

It is too consistent to be 'just' a dream. Whilst it may very well be hallucinatory in nature, this alone does not constitute a satisfactory answer. It remains a psi-event. Sometimes it can be a very repetitive one. Dr Michele Clare from the Sheffield Society for Psychical Research has relayed to me work that they have done on 'bedroom visitors' seen by a lady in that city whom they just call Mrs P.[13]

The events tended to occur around 5 a.m. Mrs P would 'feel' someone nudge her or the heavy pressure of a person lying down on top of her bed. She was alone whilst these things happened. One day in early 1984 a figure entered the room. 'It was headless and like white see-through plastic,' Mrs P explains. It climbed onto her bed, not surprisingly resulting in a scream and mad dash out of the room. A few days later there was a thunderstorm (remember the Lucia Randles' stories?). It was 6 a.m. and still winter, so absolutely dark outside. Suddenly a white ball the size of a football appeared on her bedroom door and drifted in her general direction. Once again Mrs P fled in panic.

Other than these encounters the woman has heard a buzzing noise in her bed at night. If you recall, when telling you of my childhood adventures, I explained that this was common. Without getting drawn too far into speculation, it is worth noting that both this buzzing sound and the apparent existence of an electrical field surrounding the witness might be significant clues. The brain transmits information by electro-chemical impulses. So can a strong external field produce psi-events in certain types of people?

Mrs P has tried to resolve her problems by visiting both a doctor and a priest. The priest told her she was seeing demons and had better stop drinking tea, coffee and alcohol and presumably pray for absolution. The doctor prescribed some sleeping-pills and suggested she was having nightmares. In other words, neither was much help. The Society for Psychical Research could not assist a great deal either. The trouble is that *nobody* has a foolproof answer to a dilemma such as this – not when we see the world in such black-and-white terms and insist that something is either real and natural, and can thus be driven away, or unreal and supernatural, and so subject only to the laws of magic.

For the sake of Mrs P and the thousands like her, there has to be a better answer.

In its struggle to understand what goes on inside our skull, science has employed many analogies. At first it saw the brain as a giant telephone exchange. But it soon rejected this when it found the impossibility of handling so much data. Then computers were invented and became popular symbols for the brain. However, someone must programme a computer. Who programmes us? The answer, 'God', has little appeal to the rational scientist, who demands that 'He' should turn up at the laboratory for experiments!

In any case, the computer analogy does not work. Individual circuits in a computer house individual bits of data. The brain is just not like that. Whilst there are areas, as we have seen, that are important control points for specific functions, the load is also spread in a remarkable way. If you cut out a lump of brain, you do not necessarily remove everything connected with one sense (such as vision), or one emotion. Amputation of a brain area tends to reduce the quality (not always very significantly), but it rarely destroys the capability altogether. This seems illogical mechanics. But the brain is not a machine.

There are some people who suffer from a disease called hydrocephalus and have practically no cerebrum, with only tiny amounts of brain cortex, less than many 'dumb' animals. Now that we can take photographs of the brain of a living person, colour-coded to show what is going on, there is no doubt about this, and it has shocked many scientists. The question, 'Is our brain really necessary?' has even passed a few lips, because these people have huge chunks missing that ought to control key functions such as vision and logical thinking. But they are not blind, nor are they zombies. In fact, they have normal IQs and live ordinary lives. At least one has a university degree.

Surprises such as this have provoked speculation about a hologram model for the brain, certainly in the way memory is stored. A hologram is a late-twentieth-century invention which contains whole image encoded into *all* of its parts. If it is photographed onto a sheet of glass, and the glass is then smashed into a thousand pieces, we end up with a thousand smaller versions of the original hologram, each less bright than the whole one but complete in every detail. There are good physical reasons to explain the hologram. The theory actually preceded the invention. But whether this turns out to be yet another misleading analogy, only time will tell. Certainly it has the edge on those preceding it, so far as current knowledge goes.

As for the storage of memory, a few scientists are beginning to question if this happens in the brain at all. They wonder if the brain is not just an instrument which 'tunes in' to the memory signals encoded in an energy field that permeates the body. This would be rather like a radio set tuning into a radio-wave field, although in biological language and coming from scientists it sounds strangely like mysticism.

One thing they are agreed upon is that the principle function of memory is to *block out* things rather than to let them in. Anthony Smith describes this with the motto 'Memory must be defective to be effective.' If it did retain everything, we would soon be swamped with every scrap of information we have ever recorded and, amazing as the brain is, the overload would drive us crazy.

However, there is evidence that we *do* retain an awful lot of this data at a subconscious level. I have been intrigued by 'dream flash-backs', which I am sure are not unique to me, although I have never seen them discussed anywhere. What this means is that at some point during the day, when I am doing something quite different and have no reason to think about dreams, I will get a sudden 'flashback' image of a dream that happened a long time ago. It is always a different dream, and this happens dozens of times a year. Sometimes the dreams that flash back occurred weeks ago. Sometimes I do not recall exactly when, but I know they were years into the past. The experience is brief, not unlike *déjà vu* in the strange feeling it brings, but undeniably real.

The dreams themselves seem of no obvious consequence and had certainly *not* been remembered consciously. I do retain in my mind a constant stockpile of some dream memories (particularly the more vivid or recent ones). But 'dream flashbacks' are of neither vivid nor recent dreams. I can only assume that the explanation is, as with *déjà vu*, one of association. Some sensory input entering the brain is similar to the sensory track left in the neurons when that long-forgotten dream was first recorded. The associative familiarity precipitates the flashback, as a sort of action replay.

This leads me to conclude that somehow I have access to every dream I have ever dreamt. And presumably so do you. What is curious is that the same process does not appear to happen with input memories from the external world. I do not get 'reality flashbacks' of scenes from my childhood that I had forgotten. This suggests that the dreams are stored in a different location, or that access to them is by a route which does not normally open to external events. Possibly the route is subconscious, or psychic. Perhaps the location is synchronistic reality. And it must be important that the flashback is an *image*. Synchronistic reality and the subconscious *use* images and symbols in the same way the brain and normal reality shuffle facts and figures.

Psychologists agree that memory serves to select data input and retains only a limited amount on permanent access. However, far more is available through the subconscious mind. The phenomenon of 'cryptomnesia' is believed to be a possible explanation for supposed 'past-life' memories. And there is no question that there are cases where the origin of material woven into a story of a past-life has been traced back to the 'mind store' of the claimant. They did not know their story was a fabrication. Under hypnosis the route to that hidden memory source was somehow prised open and they simply recounted images of scenes from the past (out of books and films) when they were lead to do this by the hypnotist.[14]

A good way to search for paranormal material is to keep a dream diary. Most often the surprises are psychological in nature. You see first-hand the wonders of how the brain works. But it remains the easiest path towards psychic self-understanding.

Once I recorded a complex dream into my diary and only much later, on reading back through earlier notebooks, did I realize that I had dreamt the *exact* same dream several years before. I had consciously forgotten this, but not subconsciously. However, the story does not end here. In my second diary entry I had somehow described the dream in *exactly* the same words, over several sentences. The diary entries were almost identical. Presumably the explanation for this remarkable experience is similar to cryptomnesia. In the half-awake state as I wrote out my second diary entry I must have accessed the 'mind store' and repeated the original description. If I ever doubt the power of the brain, I just have to look at those notebooks. (The dream, incidentally, was about the discovery of treasure buried underground. A psychologist would recognize this as symbolic. Our subconscious mind can hide great riches of information, like buried treasure.)

My parents explain that before I was one year old I was already reciting nursery rhymes, counting up to twenty and replaying any story that was read to me as if I were a tape-recorder. I also used to perform scientific experiments with hot-water bottles and nod at startled passers-by.

I do not remember any of this, but I suspect some esoteric sect might try to convince me that it proves I had a past life, perhaps as a scientist. Perhaps I did. But this *cannot* be proved by my experience. All that it shows is the gulf between what the brain is actually capable of and what we all tend to be satisfied doing with it. By no stretch of the imagination was I a child prodigy. Educationally I was no smarter than most. But my teachers were concerned about my 'peculiar' behaviour and when I started nursery school urged my parents to put a stop to it.

Mozart is alleged to have been able to recall entire symphonies note for note. An Edinburgh professor showed his prowess at dividing two numbers to forty-seven decimal places in under half a minute. Computers have only recently bettered that feat.

Koestler called the brain nature's only 'luxury organ', because it has so much unused potential. Fear of the unknown can stifle development and we have no idea what the brain is ultimately capable of.

Certainly our research into this wonderful structure leaves us ever more amazed. There is room for many fantastic things. Psi may just be one of them.

3. The Mind

'There is a consciousness field that permeates the
universe, in some way which we simply don't yet
understand.'

Edgar Mitchell, astronaut

It is perhaps appropriate that Arthur Koestler, who was very
interested in the paranormal, left a large sum of money to
establish a chair of parapsychology at a British university. The
Prince of Wales, on behalf of the University of Wales of which
he is chancellor, emphasized his own belief in the importance of
psi by attempting to persuade them to take up the offer. The
university staff refused. Like my teachers, scientists run scared
of the paranormal. It was left to Edinburgh University to take on
the challenge.

One of the phenomena that fascinated Koestler was
coincidence – things which common sense suggests to be mere
chance but which strike us intuitively as something more. Of
course, there are *some* things which are no more than chance. A
careful distinction should be drawn. But I do believe that
coincidence (or synchronicity, to use the scientific name coined
for it by the psychologist Carl Jung) touches the heart of all
strange phenomena. When a psi-event occurs at a subconscious
level, one of the most common ways it seeps out into 'reality' is
in the form of an apparent coincidence.[1]

Let us start by analysing a typical example. It occurred in
December 1985, the week I write this chapter, and is no more
special than being the most recent personal experience I can
relate.

Things started on 13 December, when I was Christmas
shopping in Warrington. On impulse, and for no obvious reason,
I bought a copy of George Gershwin's *Rhapsody in Blue*. I

certainly have a good collection of cassette tapes, but no more than a dozen that are classical. I have nothing by Gershwin, I had never seriously considered buying anything of his, and this was not a new recording. My purchase seems peculiar only when examined in retrospect. How often do we all do things on the spur of the moment? Anyhow, I listened to the tape that weekend and found my mind idling over a daft idea. Perhaps I could suggest a radio series based around the most influential piece of music from each decade of the twentieth century. I had contacts in the field of radio and I seriously thought of drafting a proposal, until I concluded in the end that the series would go down far better in 1999!

In the ten minutes or so of my mulling the idea over, I was scanning my mind for music that would be the equivalent of George Gershwin's *Rhapsody*. I got hung up on the seventies, trying to decide between Mike Oldfield's *Tubular Bells* and *The Snow Goose* by Peter Bardens and Andrew Latimer. Later I played *Snow Goose* and made my decision in favour of that.

A couple of days later, on 17 December, I received a manuscript from my publishers, Robert Hale. It was a book about the psychic experiences of animals by journalist Dennis Bardens.[2] It was several years since I had last been asked to do a 'reader's report' on a submitted manuscript, and happily this book proved enjoyable and easy to assess. But I realized immediately that Dennis Bardens was the father of composer, Peter, although we had never met or corresponded.

None of this seemed peculiar at the time. Just one of those things. But as soon as I finished my report, I did decide to write to the author and ask him about his son. Since he had parted company with the group Camel, after a previous spell with the even better known 'Fleetwood Mac' whom he had helped to form, I had lost track of what the keyboards man was up to. But I knew him to be highly creative and was sure he had to be doing something.

My letter was timely, as it caught the journalist about to leave the country for a spell abroad. In view of this, he telephoned me on 22 December to chat about his son's music and our own experiences as writers on the paranormal. I said nothing about the sequence of events, insofar as, frankly, I never gave them a second thought. But then Dennis spontaneously remarked that he often wondered how Peter would ever follow the *Snow Goose* composition. 'I always think of it as the equivalent to George Gershwin's *Rhapsody in Blue*,' he told me emotively.

I was too surprised to say anything to this. But that one phrase had turned an apparently chance situation into something much odder. If it were a unique event, I might well have continued to dismiss it as pure coincidence. But this kind of thing happens far too often now I know what to look for. Something else is very often involved. Sadly, many of us sweep synchronicity under the rug and don't recall the many instances when they happen to us.

Notice how I bought the tape 'on impulse' (just as Vaunda Johnson has no idea why she went into the nursery). I also chose the time to write to Dennis Bardens, and I happened to know he was Peter's father. There was nothing in the manuscript that suggested this. All these things relate to the subconscious mind, emphasizing my belief that there is more to this than chance. But who passed the Gershwin analogy to whom?

The best answer seems to be that our minds were temporarily 'in tune' at a subconscious level. We shared a common interest in the psychic world and Peter's music. This, plus the bond through his manuscript and Robert Hale the publishers, may have produced an undercurrent of information exchange which neither of us knew about consciously. The way this crystallized into the real world was as a series of coincidences, which were manipulations of our own behaviour, goaded by the subconscious.

In a rational, normal reality sense there was no cause-and-effect relationship between these events. But there has to be some relationship. So this must be found in synchronistic reality. There is no answer to be learnt from our study of the physical brain – which leaves us needing the concept of mind, without restrictions of time and space.

This is just one of the reasons why some scientists accept the existence of mind. Brain alone cannot explain many of the anomalies of mental life. It is apparently possible for scientists to dismiss these things out of hand as if it makes no difference. They have no need to understand the basis of love, or how coincidence works, or why we can imagine things that are not really there. Yet like the rest of us they live their lives and let them happen.

The brain/mind paradox is probably the greatest hurdle science has yet to clear. Is mind a separate, abstract concept which resides inside the brain like a ghost in the machine? – to use a phrase often spoken in this context. Or is it simply a by-product of the brain's behaviour? We feel instinctively a sense of identity, and that this unique, individual 'I' has got to be more than just the 'jelly' of the brain. But scientists do not regard instinctive feelings as sufficient evidence to believe in anything.

There are analogies we can use for both positions. Those who say that mind is an illusion, and the brain is all-conquering, go by the name 'monists'. They suggest we think of a car, which is a machine but which can have abstract qualities like 'speed' and 'performance'. These are quirks that distinguish it from other models but they are not real things you can get a mechanic to show you. They are like moods or feelings in a brain. If you smash the car to bits, it will no longer have any 'speed' or 'performance', even though they do not 'really' exist. In the same way all our subjective experiences are wholly dependent on our brains. It is nonsense to talk of mind as if it could exist on its own.

Ranged in opposition are scientists called 'dualists'. They can see the mind as a separate thing, co-operating with the brain to produce our experience. When you tune in a radio to a local station and switch it on, out will come all kinds of experience (music, chat, advertising jingles etc). The different 'experiences' which emerge have nothing whatsoever to do with the radio set. It matters not what transistors or circuits you use in the design, the radio station's output is independent of them. This is because the station output is really an electro-magnetic field drifting through the air. The radio set simply acts like an energy transformer, turning the signals from an invisible something which humans are not equipped to detect, into another form of energy (sound waves) which are directly accessible to our sense organs.

We know this because we understand electro-magnetism, but a time-traveller from two centuries ago would inevitably assume that the radio *made* the sounds that came out. And he could even prove it. If he started taking bits and pieces out of it, things would go wrong. The sound possibly would not vanish altogether, although quality would diminish. Then a point would come where the removal of enough parts, or one key part, would stop the radio operating. How would you then persuade our baffled time-traveller that, despite all appearances, the radios output *was* still there, even though the radio set no longer functioned?

Many physical scientists used to be monists because they dreaded having to accept an ephemeral substance called 'mind', even though they have been forced to accept a number of these in the past hundred years, including radio waves, X-rays and nuclear radiation. Brave and honest modern physicists take the point, and monism is definitely on the wane.

The debate goes on, however. Where is this invisible 'mind' for which there is no physical evidence, one side demands? Show me where you locate 'mind' inside the brain, the dualists counter? Whilst both the analogies just offered have superficial plausibility, neither one view nor the other has reigned supreme. When that sort of situation drags on for years, the perceptive scientist begins to suspect that it is not the two answers which are right or wrong but the question that was incorrect in the first place.

Psychiatrist Dr Raymond Moody created quite a storm several years ago when he began to collect accounts from patients who had 'died' for a few minutes and then been resuscitated. Of course, none of these people had actually died (if by death you mean that state from which one never returns to life – it *is* a very tricky area to define!).[3] However, they were 'beyond life' in most normal respects and quite clearly in an altered state of consciousness. Although the brain was *not* dead (so the cases tell us nothing about whether life can exist without the brain), they are the best we can do to approach this question.

Moody's book was a best-seller and has been followed by a number of imitators and sequels.[4] This by itself shows the dramatic importance ordinary people put on this matter, even if scientists prefer to spend their time elsewhere. He tabulated dozens of examples and was so objective in his presentation that he received an unusually fair hearing from his peers. Research into the NDE (Near Death Experience) is now one of the rages of modern paranormal investigators. One of the most fascinating things to have emerged from that study is the close correlation the NDE shows with other 'psychic' phenomena, such as the OOBE and UFO encounter of the fourth kind (an alien contact).

One case I followed up concerned a man from Gloucestershire who suddenly found himself unable to swim in a pool. After a few moments fighting, he began to feel ridiculously calm and light-headed and no longer attempted to rescue himself. 'It no longer mattered if I lived or died,' he told me. Vaguely he became aware of somebody hauling him from the water and administering the kiss of life, but he was quite uninterested. He seemed to be floating upwards towards a funnel-shaped thing like a giant telescope, and he saw scenes from his memory whizzing by. 'It's amazing,' he remarked. 'There is this story that your entire life rushes by when you are about to die. It's no story. It happened to me.' This compression of so many events into what can only have been a few seconds is another characteristic of the 'Oz Factor', again pointing out that this was an altered state of consciousness.

You will doubtless have noticed the similarities with the out-of-the-body stories I described in Chapter 1. His return to 'life' was again identical. He came back with a 'jolt' and suddenly felt all the pain and terror that had deserted him during the experience. This account has many of the things which Moody discovered from his patients, although I investigated this story *before* his book was published. Moody also noted that there did not seem to be a cultural bias. Regardless of religious opinions, and across different continents, the NDE was very similar.

My Gloucestershire case, Moody's examples and the OOBEs we met in Chapter 1 are matched by what happened to young Gaynor Sunderland. She also floated up into a tunnel ('like a speck of dust into a vacuum cleaner' were her descriptive words). She lost all fear, became unusually calm and had a visual encounter with 'beings' (as do quite a number of the extreme Moody cases). Gaynor regarded her 'beings' as aliens, however, and her story was reported as a UFO encounter.[5]

There are too many near-identical reports for anything but one conclusion: this is a *real* and quite common, experience. It happens close to death only because this situation precipitates the same set of conditions which sometimes happen in less critical cases. The one thing common to them all is the distinct switch in the state of consciousness. So these are psi-events happening inside the mind. But are they a result purely of changes in the brain chemistry, or an illustration of the mind almost disentangling itself from the brain? One possibility must be correct. And if the experience is a result of chemical changes in the brain, it is hard to understand why it is so repetitive in detail. Human mental experience is a fantastic and varied affair. It would be curious if the exact same changes *always* happened in these situations and manifested as the *exact* same pseudo-phenomenon.

The answer *may* be that the psi-event is 'real', at least so far as mind is concerned. But we must never underestimate the risk of such a view. It is not far short of accepting life after death!

One of Moody's patients was asked if the experience might not have been a hallucination. He replied, 'It was nothing like a hallucination.' He had suffered these in hospital when taking drugs, but 'This experience was nothing like [them], nothing like them at all.'

In December 1976 I was also under the influence of very strong pain-killing drugs after major surgery. I 'lost' two days in a world of delirium and had quite a few strange hallucinations. I am able to contrast these with my one brief OOBE and have no qualms about echoing these words. The hallucinations were blurred and my mind felt dull. The OOBE was completely vivid and extremely lucid. I *know* I was awake and my mind was razor sharp.

It does appear that we need the concept of mind to explain altered states of consciousness like the NDE. It is not difficult to see why American astronaut Edgar Mitchell said what he is quoted as saying at the head of this chapter. He had a 'mystical' experience whilst viewing the Earth from Space. Temporarily entering a different state of consciousness, he was able to sense the unity of all things at the level of mind. This is something many wise religious teachers have discovered before, throughout the ages. Can they all be wrong? Certainly Mitchell has no doubt about the need for the concept 'mind'. And he is equally sure where twenty-first-century science should be headed.

But we must return back to Earth in search of evidence that scientists cannot dismiss, as they may choose to dismiss psi-events or mystical experiences. In the last chapter we saw how the corpus callosum carries nerve fibres between the right and left cerebral hemispheres, and how when the connection is

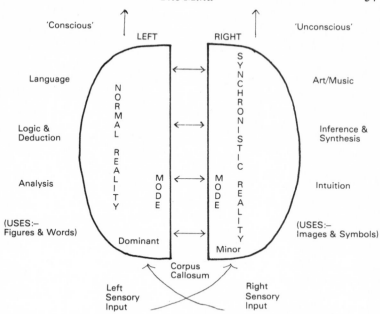

Fig. 6: Differences between the two hemispheres in the cerebrum
of a right-handed person.

severed very strange things happen. This can sometimes be useful to limit severe epileptic attacks to just one hemisphere. But split-brain surgery, as it is known, does a great deal more than that.

As Figure 6 shows, the two hemispheres perform different functions. In most right-handed people this makes the left hemisphere 'dominant', as it is termed. This means that the left has *more* (although not total) control over conscious expression, language, analysis, deduction, mathematical thinking and so on. These are the stuff of rational science, the essence of normal reality mode or the everyday 'real' world. The opposite hemisphere seems far more related to a quite different set of functions, which should be simple to predict. These are unconscious expression, intuitive processes, music, synthesis and artistic ability. Whilst (for a right-handed person) the left hemisphere speaks in facts and figures, the right talks through images and symbols. They are opposite one another in almost all respects.

In a series of fascinating discussions with leading psychologists, Jonathan Miller talked about left-brain/right-brain division with Professor Norman Geschwind. The neurologist described one of the first cases which brought the problem to light, published in 1908 by his colleague Kurt Goldstein. A woman had come to the hospital because her left hand would occasionally try to strangle her own neck. She claimed to have no conscious control over this. It was found that her corpus callosum had been seriously damaged and, as Geschwind points out, this produced a brain split. Only the left hemisphere could talk. Whatever happened in the right hemisphere (which controlled the woman's left hand) was at an unconscious level and was not being transferred across the breach. Yet this internal reaction *was* real, and the right hemisphere expressed itself in the way it knows best. This is not language but emotions, symbols and images. It made its views very clear by threatening to choke the poor woman![6] Of course, had the woman been left-handed, the picture would have been quite different. Dr Stan Gooch would certainly be interested in a situation such as this, since the right-brain/left-brain split is an important justification of his arguments. Indeed, when Gooch and I first corresponded about this, we were involved in a bizarre psychic link.[7]

Norman Geschwind is also a psychologist and worked at Harvard and MIT. Just before his recent tragic death, he published some astonishing work on the differences between left-handed (right-hemisphere-dominant) and right-handed (left-hemisphere-dominant) people. These showed a definite link between left-handedness and genius. It may well be that the increased importance of the right hemisphere, with its intuitive (and perhaps psychic) abilities, is a key factor in the improved performance of such people.[8]

It used to be thought that this division of labour between hemispheres was total. Recent work has disproved that. The relationship seems more akin to that between the cerebrum and cerebellum, with the dominant hemisphere having the majority of abilities such as reading and talking, and the other one (usually the right) acting as a 'fine-tune' mechanism with only limited abilities in these areas.[9]

By the mix-sixties, after successful experimentation on cats,

Roger Sperry began to conduct split-brain surgery on humans, severing the corpus callosum gateway. It was done sparingly, of course, but scientists were still very surprised at how little difference the operation made, except for aiding the epileptic problems.

The worst effects were noticed with artistic people. For example, one or two who were musically gifted claimed to have lost appreciation of the music, even if they could still technically play it. But appreciation is an abstract concept. How do you lose that? The monists use such a report to defend their view that brain and mind are equivalent. By isolating the two halves of the brain, a major feature of the mind has also been cut off from conscious awareness. However, these patients can still appreciate other things, so just what is it they have 'lost'?

The problem grows even more complicated in other experiments upon split-brain patients. Show them an object so it is visible only to their left eye-field (and thus detected by the right hemisphere) and then ask what the person is looking at. He *can* see the object, as you can demonstrate yourself if you wear spectacles, by blacking out half of each lens. But anyone who has had their corpus callosum severed is unable to describe the object. It is almost as if there is a struggle between two minds inside one brain. The right hemisphere allows the person to draw it, or pick it from an array by shape or feel, but this data has not bridged the gap to the left hemisphere, which controls language and speech. So there can be no verbal description.

Psychologists have had some fun using a nude photograph as the object. The person (speaking through his dominant hemisphere) says he has no idea what he is seeing. But he *is* aware of it subconsciously, because his other hemisphere has recorded the observation. This subconscious information can seep out into the external world (remember the woman trying to strangle herself!). In this case the result is not so dangerous. The patient normally just smiles or chuckles, for reasons he cannot consciously explain.

Such results have been rather fancifully portrayed as proof that mind *is* brain. In fact, all it highlights is the distinction between conscious and subconscious levels of the mind, and how different parts of the brain are related to each. Since we know areas of the brain control specific mind functions, this is not a surprising development. It can be answered by the dualists in the same way as they explain other 'control zones', if mind is a consciousness field being decoded by the brain. If you consider the radio-set analogy, it is not unlike cutting off power to the external speakers and connecting up a headphone circuit instead. Then you know what is going on only if you attend to the headphones. But even though to outside appearances the radio is silent, in truth the signal remains unaffected.

It would be very interesting indeed to see psychic researchers working with split-brain patients. Could information detected subconsciously get transmitted to the outside world as a psi-event? I would guess that the answer may be yes. Indeed, its chances of happening might be greater than before because the normal route to consciousness is blocked. It is possible that people with a severed corpus callosum are potentially very good psychics.

There have been cases where the dominant hemisphere has been not merely isolated but totally removed! Now if brain was simply mind, the outcome of this would presumably be disastrous. The majority of logical, rational thought processes. speech, language and so on would be decimated by this catastrophe. No person could survive this as much more than a robot. But that is not what happens at all.

As we saw with sufferers from hydrocephalus, it is quite possible to live a fairly normal life with half your brain (or even more) gone for ever. When the loss occurs early in life, the other hemisphere seems to learn most of the functions of the previously dominant hemisphere, and the resultant effects are minimal – none of which would make a great deal of sense if brain were the equivalent of mind. It is not hard to see why Roger Sperry is a dualist.

Suppose then that we accept the mind as separate from the brain: which of the two is superior? The question is crucial because it decides whether brain (as a physical, biological instrument) *uses* mind, or this hypothetical consciousness field has the upper hand on brain. From the expression 'mind over matter', the answer is quickly suggested. There is no saying 'matter over mind'.

I am not discussing the complex subject of spoon-bending or psychokinesis (moving objects without any physical force).

These are too controversial to use as evidence here. But all doctors are in a sense faith healers because they use the power of placebos.

A placebo is a harmless and ineffective substance given to a patient as a substitute for a real drug, which might have unwanted side-effects. If the patient does not know about the switch and *believes* the drug will work, it often does! He can be cured by a substance that ought to do nothing. Of course, it cannot be the neutral substance which does the curing. It must be the patient's belief in its efficacy. His mind has controlled the body functions and rid the disease from its organs. This has been demonstrated even in quite extreme cases.

Gordon Rattray-Taylor reports how a group of women took part in a three-month experiment to see if they could increase their breast size just by *wishing* to do so. There was an astonishing eighty-five per cent success rate, and real breast tissue was involved, not fluid or fat.[10]

Hilary Evans has been researching this area too and rightly wonders why, if it *is* possible for wishes to come true, he is not driving around the South of France in a Porsche! 'It may be that there is a stronger wish, working inside of us,' he suggests. By this he means that the real influencing comes from not just the mind but the subconscious mind.[11]

One presumes that there must be limits. There are certainly reports of remarkable cures from terribly disfiguring diseases, often employing hypnosis to trick the mind into altering its state of consciousness and freeing those subconscious desires. But there do not seem to be any reliable claims of somebody regrowing a severed limb. Certain animals can do this (e.g. the starfish), so we may wonder why it seems to be impossible. Perhaps it is impossible only because none of us has tried hard enough.

However, the use of mind over matter is recognized as valid even in illnesses as serious as cancer. Sandra Levy (a psychologist) and Ron Heberman (an immunologist) work at the National Cancer Institute in Maryland. They issued a report claiming that fighting the disease definitely does increase a patient's chances of survival. Emotion is important. People who get angry or distressed tend to last longer than those who calmly accept their fate.[12] This will not really come as a shock to doctors. They are all familiar with the patient who gives up hope and fades away.

This all seems to be like those cases of witch doctors and voodoo practitioners willing an enemy to death. It is not so much how the person acts on the outside but his subconscious choice between life and death. If the mind within gives up on hope, Hilary Evans' 'stronger wish' may well precipitate the end. Perhaps curses work in a similar way.

One quite remarkable story comes from psychiatrist Dr James McHarg at the Royal Hospital in Dundee. He had a fifty-seven-year-old woman patient who complained of beasts in her left ear eating into her brain. These symptoms were considered psychotic by the doctor, and as the patient became more and more disturbed he sought desperately for a basis to attempt a cure. No origin could be diagnosed. This was in September 1963. At the same time, unknown to either the doctor or his patient, a man was admitted to the hospital complaining of pains in his left ear. He was not diagnosed psychotic and was released; since no physical cause could be isolated, it was assumed that the pains were imaginary.

This coincidence would never have been discovered had it not been for the tragic sequel. In 1969 the man returned to the hospital. This time the pains he reported in his ear were unquestionably real. A tumour was found here and it was pressing on his brain. There was nothing to be done and the man died. Now the real mystery emerges, for the man turned out to be the brother of the 'psychotic' woman, although the two had been estranged for many years. Beasts in the left ear eating at the brain is not a bad symbolic reflection of what was happening to the man. It is exactly what we might expect from subconscious, intuitive or synchronistic reality.

There are three ways of interpreting this story. Two involve cause and effect, in simple physical terms. Author Christopher Bloom, who researched the case, suggests that the woman detected the undiagnosed condition in her brother and was driven to insanity by the message seeping into her mind. It is possible to take a more gruesome line. Could the woman's psychotic fantasy about beasts in her ear have transferred to the brother and produced the physical trauma? These two options involve mind over matter. The third would be to accept the affair

as a real-world externalization of an inner-world event. The
sharing of information at the level of consciousness manifested
in the universe as a synchronicity or coincidence – not unlike the
incident at the start of this chapter involving Dennis Bardens
and myself.

Whichever way you look at this story, it seems impossible to
explain without a very powerful and dominant mind superior to
the physical brain.[13]

We can also demonstrate this superiority of mind by reference
to optical illusions, which we considered earlier. That illusions
fool us is no problem. They simply mess up the perceptual
processes on route to the brain. A monist would then just say
that, with the brain being fooled, the mind is fooled in tandem.
This *seems* to happen when an illusion baffles us completely. But
in that case we have no 'mind-store' image to choose the truth
from.

However, there are many cases when we *know* something is
an illusion and yet the illusion persists. This is no subconscious
knowledge: it is full and complete. So why does the illusion

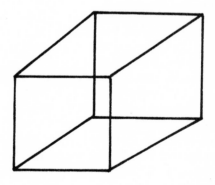

Fig. 7: The 'Necker' Cube. Which way is it facing?

remain? Surely our knowledge of the truth should now extend to the brain (as well as the mind), and the true situation would be perceived.

Figure 7 is another good example. Look at the cube and decide whether it has a front face at the bottom left or top right. You will decide upon one but probably realize that it could be either. If you do not see the illusion immediately, it takes little effort to view the cube as if it were in *both* three-dimensional orientations. What is more exciting is that we can make the cube reverse its positions. Using our mind, we can flip it from a cube angled down to a cube angled up, as often as we like. We *know* this is an illusion, but it goes on happening. It is almost as if our superior mind, accepting the limitations of the brain with which it has to work, has fun with its perception system and juggles the illusion at will.

Theories which state that mind *is* brain have no answer to this simple but alarming riddle.

In just the same way rational science can only stutter in the face of psi-events. I will close the chapter with one case reported to me. If we accept the existence of a separate mind, it is possible to understand what is going on. If to you there is nothing but a physical computer made of 'jelly', I would be interested to know your solution to this story.

It happened in early 1983, when I had a radio series on the paranormal with a Merseyside station. A lady from the seaside resort of Southport wrote to me, saying, 'It is very difficult to put an intangible down on paper,' but she tried. She explained that there was a sort of empathy, or perhaps a telepathic link, with her husband. Every now and then she would get a strange feeling that he wanted to talk to her. It was 'like a liquid surging to fill an empty space'. This built up over a period of a few hours, and she knew then beyond doubt that he was thinking about her. On every occasion this had occurred she claims that she *did* hear from him, in such a way that the timing of this sensation was precise. When it happened, she knew where he was and what he wanted.

You may perhaps be a little confused. A wife knowing that her husband wants to talk to her hardly seems paranormal. But they were not together. Like the brother and sister at the Dundee hospital, they had been estranged for some time. During the year these telepathic messages arrived, followed by confirmation by her husband's real contact, they communicated only four times. All four were accompanied by this strange experience.

The psychic knowledge may have been a blessing to the woman, but it was very awkward for me. You see, her husband was a wanted man, on the run from the police! His crime does not appear to have been too serious, but I was forced into a consultation of my investigators' code of ethics. If I accepted her story as genuine, where did my duty lie? One clause told me to co-operate with the police, that withholding evidence was a criminal offence in its own right. Another explained that, if a witness requested confidentiality, I owed it to her to keep that promise.

Of course, I had no real evidence. I did not ever know where the man was. And common sense prevailed in this crisis of conscience. I could not imagine myself strolling into Southport police station and offering to assist them to find a man on the run – not when the assistance would be to advise them of this supposed telepathic link between the man and his wife. My mind was rather on psychic Bob Cracknell and what had followed his decision to help the police with their enquiries!

4. Smell and Taste:
The Taste of Survival – The Smell of Death

'The results surpass all expectations. Our dogs
(using smell alone) found iron ore at depths of 7–13
metres, in dry soil and in swamps.'

Professor Izot Litenetsky,
in the Soviet science journal *Sputnik*, May 1983

There is a very old joke which sees one man say to another, 'My dog's got no nose.' 'How does it smell?' he is asked. And the reply is, 'Terrible.'

This quip masks a truth that is strangely different. It is we, not the dog, who possess a 'terrible' sense of smell. Indeed canine proficiency is quite amazing. It is *one million* times better than our own.

As can be seen from the quotation above, the USSR is hardly behind the times when it comes to using this fact. Very often that nation treats what we call paranormal 'bosh' as no such thing. They perform scientific experiments at some expense and show that it is neither bosh nor paranormal.

Professor Litenetsky has spent months trekking the wastes of Karelia with his pack of trained dogs sniffing out rare minerals. In essence this is not much different from our use of the same animals to hunt for drugs, which no human nose could ever detect. It only takes a readjustment in our terms of what is possible. What is paranormal about these skilled Russian beasts? Why should we draw a line at substances with an obvious smell, when possibly most things have a characteristic odour?

Our purpose in this book is to hunt for the elusive 'sixth' sense which supposedly allows psi-events to occur. The Karelia dogs are our first chance to find it and show that what seems to be psi need not necessarily be very strange.

The paranormal seems on the surface to cover many things. But was it psi that enabled Yorkshire dog Mick to rescue his friend Percy, the chihuahua?

Percy was owned by Christine Harrison of Barnsley. In the same month Professor Litenetsky was publishing his results (May 1983), the poor animal was hit by a car. It seemed that he had gone to that great kennel in the sky, and his limp body was buried in a sack beneath the garden of his grieving owner. She explained that there was no heartbeat and his eyes had glazed over.

Mick was a fond playmate of the chihuahua and seems not to have accepted that his chum was dead. He frantically pawed away at the garden and dug up the sack, dragging it all the way towards the house. On seeing the commotion, Christine Harrison found that her dog, far from having died, was now alive again. He was in a rough way from his ordeal, but he happily pulled through.

No human sense had earned Percy his reprieve. Somehow Mick had 'smelled' the difference between life and death.

It is not only dogs whose sense is that acute. A male moth can smell a female almost a mile away. In view of the sizes involved, that is really a phenomenal distance. A honey bee can tell the difference between a friendly and unfriendly newcomer simply from its smell. And even we respond in unexpected ways to pheromones – incredibly diluted body smells which are crucial to the sex drive. There would be no prosperous perfume industry but for this.

Though smell in man is pathetic by comparison with that of most other animals, it may not be easy to convince Helen Cramer and Barbara McCauley of Macy, Nebraska.

At 9 a.m. on 6 January 1977 they were together at the McCauleys' grocery store when something most unusual happened.

It began when Helen smelled something burning. Before she could mention this, Barbara commented on it too. They searched the building and went outside but there was no sign of a fire.

Barbara's husband, Edward, was several miles away at his

father's farm, having gone there to pick corn. At 9.45 a.m. he returned unexpectedly with the news that his father had suffered an accident when falling from his harvester. This had occurred at 9.a.m. just as the burning smell had manifested in the shop. As he was pouring petrol into the engine, the heat caused a spontaneous ignition. The fierce flames had sent him crashing backwards.[1]

Immediately we see the same question before us. Was this a psi-event? That is certainly how it was reported to *Fate* magazine, which records many anecdotes just like it every month. But perhaps it was nothing more than an enhanced sense of smell. No eyebrows would be raised if Helen, Barbara and Edward were the names of three moths.

Smell and taste will be examined together for two main reasons. Together they represent the poorest development of the human senses and are very old. They are also very simple. But more importantly, they tend to be coupled with one another. Our experience of food, for example, relies on both taste and smell, which is why we rarely enjoy eating when we have a cold.

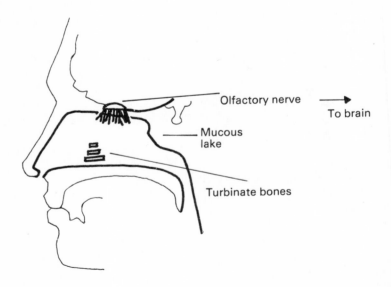

Fig. 8: Main parts of the nose.

Our smell-detector (the nose) is shown in Figure 8. It is unique among the sensory organs in that it has nerve cells directly exposed to the air. This is because air is what carries smells, and there would be no sense of smell in a vacuum.

The nasal cavity traps a sample of air and brings this into contact with a lake of mucous substance. The olfactory nerve leading to the brain has hair-like cilia which are rather like reeds in a swamp, attracting the sample. An important consequence is that for something to be detectable it has to be soluble in this mucous. When something does not dissolve, we call it odourless, which only means that *we* cannot smell it. It does not mean that it has no smell, and it is perfectly possible that another animal could detect it.

There are some drawbacks from this simplicity. There are odourless and colourless substances that can be deadly. Solids are also impossible for us to detect, because our crude system requires volatile molecules suspended in the air. That can apply only to liquids and gases.

When we breathe in and out, the turbinate bones in the nose create eddie flows which wash the molecules towards the mucous and the cilia, just as waves are crashed against the seashore. The cilia then grab in a bundle of molecules. There are millions of exposed nerve cells which then react and 'detect' the smell. But we do not fully understand how.

Do substances all have a unique inherent smell? If so, is it caused by the rate of vibration of the molecules in the air? Is it atomic structure that counts? Can life and death and other abstract concepts have a smell? Is the stimulation of the nerve cells entirely chemical, or electro-chemical like the transmission in neurons?

Whatever the truth about all these things, once detected the impulses travel up the olfactory nerve by a very circuitous route to reach the limbic area of the mid-brain. They do *not* feed into the cerebrum. All of this implies that smell is an ancient sense, and part of our animal heritage. Some scientists suggest that this complex routing implies that smell was once a more important sense than it now is. That matches the superior abilities of animals and suggests that the feats of dogs and moths may once not have been beyond us.

Could Neanderthal man smell a tiger many miles away? Did

he follow his nose to find home base in the dense trees? It is quite possible. Smell has certainly been relegated to the third division of the human sense table. Seen in this light we might wonder if the events at Macy, Nebraska, were examples of a newly blossoming sixth sense or a throwback to a very ancient one.

Turning to taste, this, if anything, is even worse. It is harder to test for comparisons in animals. But it is thought that what little sense of taste we do have is of significance only when coupled with smell.

The nerve cells in the tongue are embedded into the surface at the front, back and sides. There are none in the middle, but a few on the walls of the throat and the tonsils. They are called 'taste buds' and come in varieties that allow four different taste sensations: acid, sour, salty and sweet. Of these the last two are very insensitive. We can detect only one part diluted in 400 and 200 respectively. This is partly because both these tastes are part of our diet and are not normally reflective of any danger substances. The other two *can* be, suggesting that food is bad or poisonous, for example. Because of this we can detect one part in 130,000 when the sour taste buds are triggered, and one part in two million when the taste is acidic or bitter. Again the substance must be soluble in water. This once more can make certain substances (even dangerous ones) undetectable, and explains why poisoning has been such a long-standing favourite of would-be murderers. We do know (at least in the case of salty and sour tastes) that the method of transmission is electro-chemical, just as in the neurons of the brain. Changes in the ions 'create' the taste.

The final way in which smell and taste are closely alike is with the routing of the nerve paths to the brain. Once again there is a very complicated pathway which seems out of context for the importance of the taste sense. In fact, *three* separate routes exist, twisting and turning all over the place until arriving in an old part of the brain. This is the medulla on the brain stem.

From these descriptions it should be clear that smell and taste are senses that developed early in human evolution but have since gradually atrophied. They are probably far more significant in the lives of less advanced animal life. However, as with all senses the actual experience of the sensation occurs inside the brain and not in the nose or tongue. These do nothing more than gather the basic sensory input.

A very great deal can happen to the nerve impulses on the way to the brain. But just how they are turned into the sweet taste of ice-cream or the rich, dark aroma of coffee remains very much a mystery. Since these sensations spend most of their time as electro-chemical impulses winding down long and complicated pathways, the brain is best considered as a transformer which changes the electro-chemical energy into another (far more subtle and thus more intangible) energy field.

So much we still do not know. And I said these were the simplest senses!

When the Florida psychiatrist Dr Berthold Schwarz studied the activities of the Free Pentecostal Church in southern Tennessee, he observed some very strange goings on there. Acolytes were seen tasting substances, with apparent ease, which would undoubtedly have killed the rest of us.

Schwarz watched in astonishment as two 'saints' from the movement helped themselves to a double dose of strychnine sulphate dissolved in a small glass of water. They reported no weird tastes, and absolutely nothing happened to them. He took the residue away for analysis by chemist William Lane of the Schering Corporation. Lane discovered 35 milligrams of the deadly poison in the solution and admitted that it ought to have caused severe convulsions at the very least. How this control was achieved is quite baffling. But then so is the sense of taste.[2]

Anomalous taste and smell impressions certainly occur. For instance, if you connect the end of a battery to someone's tongue, they can 'taste' the electricity. I would not recommend you try this, as saliva conducts the current. But those who have tried it under controlled conditions (myself included) describe a 'tang' which is very hard to put into words. To say it feels like electricity is the best they can do. And if that makes no sense to the uninitiated, I can only point out that we lack the words to describe things such as this.

There is obviously an explanation for this phenomenon. The nerve impulses which create the 'taste' *are* electrical. However, we have far more trouble with the claims of Dr Leon Smith, of a New Jersey medical centre. He believes that he can 'smell' diseases!

To Smith gangrene is like rotten apples, typhoid similar to freshly baked brown bread and so on. Is this a genuine faculty? Do diseases have unique smells? Or is the answer one of association? To a doctor there must be many subliminal clues which suggest these illnesses from the appearance or behaviour of the patient. Dr Smith may merely substitute the apparent smell for these clues, picked up on a subconscious level by his mind. 'Having a nose' for something is a common expression. Perhaps, as it implies, there is a tendency to regard instinct as a smell.

Those who investigate paranormal phenomena inside people's homes often come across the claim that a strange odour was involved, regularly a sweet or sickly smell. UFO researchers have noticed this as well, although they more often deal with a tangy, electrical smell (and occasionally taste).

One case I investigated concerned a landing in Wallasey, Merseyside, which involved an elderly lady and a figure that appeared in her garden.[3] But there were other features to this case which I did not record at the time. The woman had undergone poltergeist phenomena around the house, with objects vanishing and later reappearing in unexpected places, and pools of water materializing on the floor out of nowhere. She had also noticed a pungent smell (a bit like lavender only much more powerful), and there seemed to be no natural origin for this.

Brain malfunctions can produce smells which are not 'really' there. Epilepsy, for example, might scramble the neuron impulses and generate a pseudo-smell. As a sort of hallucination a suitable image from the 'mind store' is then extracted to represent it, and the smell is given attributes that match it with something known. In memory it probably then becomes more like the genuine smell, and the person believes that he smelled lavender, flowers or perfume. Of course, whilst this is most interesting in the wake of earlier speculations about the epileptic/psychic link, there must presumably be a reason for the 'attack' in the first place.

In 1985 TVS, a British television channel, produced an experimental 'smelly-vision' programme. Viewers were given cards that when scratched released molecules of a certain smell into the air. The idea was that they should guess what the smell was, with no other clues to go on. Then, when this had been done for several different smells, the truth was revealed. Also visual images of the substance appeared on screen so the smell could be linked with those. I was one of many thousands who took part. As others who did so may recall, it proved surprisingly easy to guess some smells, much harder to detect others. The visual clues certainly made a big difference, and reliance on smell alone proved very rudimentary.

Are we saying that peculiar smells in connection with psi-events are not necessarily real at all? At times I think we must be, if by real we mean external to the mind. There is every reason to suppose that very convincing smell sensations can occur thanks to a false neuron transmission. There *will* be a trigger for this transmission, but it need not be an object in the outside world passing information to the nose.

What applies to smell and taste may very well apply right across the board with all our senses.

There will be times when a person simply has a temporary disfunction of the brain, which, as we saw with epilepsy, can happen to many people for no obvious reason, even when they do not consider themselves ill. In that case the entire experience (visual, auditory, smell etc) *might* be an internal event caused by these false neuron transmissions. There need be no external source, although there could be an internal one of some interest. Cases like these would probably be demarked by a dream-like or fuzzy appearance.

However, I am equally sure that on some occasions a *real* external phenomenon can be the cause. If it has an electrical field associated with it, or discharges ions, or certain chemicals, it is quite feasible that it could precipitate the faulty neuron transmission, leading on to hallucinated senses. In UFO research there is a phenomenon called the UAP (Unidentified Atmospheric Phenomenon) which seems to be exactly what we are talking about. It radiates considerable energy.[4] The way this can effect animals is discussed by Tributsch in a non-UFO context, and it is interesting that he considers the anomalistic behaviour of dogs during earthquakes to be due to their acute smell sense picking up ions released by the stresses in the ground. He argues that serotonin hormone can be stimulated, leading to strange reactions. Serotonin, you may recall, is a key element in the transfer of impulses across the synapse link.[5]

Smell, despite its relative unimportance, may indeed hold vital clues to our understanding of psi-events.

Linda Pezze of Torrington, Connecticut, had an interesting story to tell. On 4 December 1970, the first anniversary of her mother's death, she found the gas light on her stove turning itself on when she did not touch it. Her mother had always been fussy about leaving this on and the danger it might bring, so Linda immediately associated her experience with the return of her mother's 'spirit'. The next day Linda returned home to find all the gas rings on and a lily of the valley smell all over the kitchen. This had been her mother's favourite perfume.[6]

It is easy to interpret this as a straightforward spooky tale, but it is also possible to counter with an associative explanation. Perhaps, with her mother's death on her mind, she had left the rings on herself without consciously realizing it. Our subconscious can play little tricks like that if it feels it has to get a message across. To remind her of this, the familiar smell of her mother's perfume might then have been extracted from Linda's 'mind store' as a sort of replay. Had someone else been in the kitchen that morning, would they have smelled it too?

Researcher H.B. Greenhouse adds a new dimension to the problem. He was staying in a New Jersey motel which had a hotplate for coffee set on top of his TV. One day he smelled burning but could find no cause for this. He even called one of the hotel staff to join his search. However, the clerk could smell nothing – even though Greenhouse still could. After opening all the doors to the empty rooms, he satisfied the guest that there were no fires, and the smell eventually disappeared. Reluctantly Greenhouse concluded he must have imagined it. A week later he took a trip to New York and returned to a scene of utter chaos. Firemen were carrying out the burnt remains of his TV set. He had left a saucepan on the hotplate, and it had eaten a hole right through after boiling dry. The result was a major fire, in which he lost a pile of valuable manuscripts.

H.B. Greenhouse is convinced that the phantom smell of seven days before had been a premonition of the disaster. He thought he had 'imagined' the smell. In truth he had probably 'imaged' it inside his mind, a rather different thing.[7]

There was no smell in that room, as the experience of the

hotel clerk shows. The case supports an associative explanation. The mind of H.B. Greenhouse had somehow picked up the danger of fire as information from the future. Such future instincts or intuitions usually come through as either hunches or motor actions (remember Vaunda Johnson getting out of bed for no reason). In this case the motif 'Fire' was all that came through. The most vivid association with this in Greenhouse's 'mind store' was a memory of a burning smell. So his mind replayed that one simple image, generating an illusory sense perception inside his head. Sadly it did not make much difference in the end.

The smell itself was a hallucination. It came from not the future but the past. Strange as it may seem, premonitions are action replays and not foresight. What *did* come from the future was the intuitive knowledge, in the form of an emotion, that was symbolized by replaying a smell from the 'mind store'. We may wonder if, had the psi-event been more specific than just a vague sense of smell, H.B. Greenhouse could have prevented the disaster? If so, how could he have picked up knowledge of its happening? For it would *not* have happened, unless the emotions that come through are only *possibilities*, not yet hardened into solid events.

There are bound to be many who prefer a simpler explanation. In the case of the lily of the valley smell, this might be that Linda Pezze detected the presence of a ghost – a ghost being, presumably, some form of discarnate yet living entity. But is such a solution truly more simple? It requires the acceptance of many things that are far from proven, not least that there *can* be discarnate entities. Is it not just as easy to view the experience as a *replay* (of the perfume smell and the gas-rings vision), which are inevitably coded in the woman's 'mind store', within a filing category we might call 'things associated with my dead mother'?

An interesting result of this choice is that those who wish to deny the existence of mind (and along with it that image bank or 'mind store') might be forced to plump for the ghost – a consequence I dare say they will not be too keen to think about.

What this seems to be driving us towards is the proposition that we do not need a 'sixth' sense to explain the psi-events we have met so far. But we *do* need the concept of a dynamic mind. We also have to face the fact that this is far less restricted by time (if it is restricted at all). Information from the 'past' or the 'future' (as we perceive such things in normal thought) is as easy to tap as sensory information from the present. The mind would appear to be timeless.

There is no psychic sense of smell, just the ordinary sense which is recorded in the 'mind store'. For some reason, and on certain occasions, this is triggered into an action replay which manifests as a convincing hallucination. To test the water of this disturbing idea, let us try it out another psi-event and see how it fares.

Young Catherine Logan was eight months pregnant on 19 November 1971. She was happily married, living in an upstairs flat in a north-eastern town and looking forward to the birth of her first child. But at 3 a.m. on that day a noise awoke her. The front door bell had sounded. She and husband Rod got up to investigate, but nobody was there. They dismissed it as someone playing an unfortunate joke.

Almost twenty-four hours later Catherine's uncle, Neil – who, only two years older than she, was more like a brother than an uncle – was returning from a concert with his band. He smelled burning in the van but could see no obvious source for it. Nevertheless, he was worried sufficiently to awaken Catherine's father, who lived opposite him, and they both gave the van a thorough checking over. Nothing was amiss and at 2.45 a.m. they gave up and retired to their beds, convinced that Neil must have imagined the smell.

Meanwhile, back at the flat, Catherine and Rod were deep asleep. They had been working late decorating the nursery ready for the imminent arrival of the new family member. However, despite the depth of her slumber, Catherine was awoken by a commanding voice which told her to get up because there was a fire. It was 3 a.m., the same time as the doorbell from the night before. But there was no sign of any danger in the room.

Sitting up, Catherine realized there was a faint smell of burning. Shortly an orange glow began to shimmer on the wall. 'The house is on fire!' she cried out loudly, and indeed it was. Forty-foot flames were leaping from the lounge next door to the bedroom, and the inferno was spreading fast. Down below in the streets there were people gathering, asking how they could get the couple out. One of the onlookers went to ring the doorbell.

Now fully to her senses Catherine had the feeling that Rod wanted to go into the room and try to put out the fire. He did not wish to see their hard work destroyed. Neither of them knew just how serious the fire was. That was obvious only from the road beneath. Had Rod attempted this move, it would quite possibly have killed him. 'Get the fire brigade!' Catherine kept on shouting and virtually dragged her husband down the stairs. Moments later their house was ablaze. Minutes later it was in ruins.

At 4 a.m. her father walked across the road to wake up Neil so they could go to comfort Catherine and Rod. Neil, still remembering the smell of burning, was half expecting to be told that his van had burst into flames. He was not expecting to learn of a fire some way across town.

Later that night Catherine's father reminded her of a dream. She had forgotten it. Several years earlier, when she was just a girl and living at home, she had woken in the middle of the night and kept on repeating the cry 'Get the fire brigade!' In the dream things had worked out very differently. Her home had been gutted, as in real life, but in the fire she had lost her husband and baby, even though the young girl had not then met her future husband. Catherine believes that her subconscious foreknowledge allowed her to prevent Rod's racing to his death. As for the baby, it would have died if the fire had been a couple of weeks later, for the nursery was completely wrecked. Even so, there was a fight for the child's survival. The drama nearly provoked a miscarriage, and the baby was born eleven days later by Caesarian operation.

This fascinating tale was reported to ASSAP eleven years after the event, but the witnesses moved before a full investigation could be undertaken. There seems little reason to doubt from Catherine's detailed account that the story is genuine, and it is of such potential value to psychic research that cases such as this cry out for study.

What can we make of it? Apparently the trauma of the fire was sufficiently powerful for its emotions to be detected by Catherine's sleeping mind years ahead of time. Why was this? Had she been dreaming about marriage, as many young girls do, and did this catastrophe from the future associate itself with that theme? What would have come through was no vision of the fire itself but the emotions and terrors of the incident. Key words like 'house fire', 'nursery' and 'baby in danger' would have been used to form the basis for her dream. The imagery in the dream would consist of appropriate replays from her 'mind store', with the result that the dream was close to being accurate but not entirely so. It was a *possibility* formed in her mind by working round the major emotional elements from the future.

Was the doorbell sounding an auditory hallucination? It seems likely that an event as dramatic as this, powerful enough to cross years of time, might also make its mark closer to the final unfolding. As Neil was emotionally close to her, did he detect things from the sleeping Catherine's mind and, using this, produce a smell-sense hallucination in *his* mind? Remember, there was no burning smell in the van. Just as with Greenhouse's hotel clerk, Catherine's father smelled nothing. Many psychologists, be they believers in psi or not, will accept that people who are emotionally close can share experiences. The phenomenon of phantom pregnancy, where the husband lives through symptoms of his wife's confinement, is just one example.

What then of Catherine's commanding voice? Was this a guardian angel or just her subconscious mind aware that the time had come? It may even have detected the *real* smell of the fire and used the vivid image of a voice to make sure that she woke up. Just having a dream about the smell of burning may not have been enough. Something had to kick her into motion. This may have been the best way her subconscious mind could come up with.

It is interesting that fires are the most common type of precognition, especially when the sense of smell is involved. You will realize that from the cases in this chapter. As a danger smell there is probably nothing more emotive. And emotion is what counts when a warning message is coming through.

The theory holds firm so far. We do not need to lose the excitement which psi-events bring. But nor do we require the invention of a sixth sense. The five that we have seem more than enough.

5. Touch: A Finger-tip Guide to Pain-Control and Crime-Busting

> 'I can, for example, take an object in my hand and receive from it certain "vibrations" which tell me where it came from ... I am inclined to believe that this is simply a highly developed sensitivity.'
> Bob Cracknell, psychic, describing his alleged ability to perform psychometry

Some years ago there was a stage magician who professed amazing powers as part of his act. He knew that psychics sometimes claim to 'see' without the use of their eyes, so he set out to duplicate this feat in the full glare of media publicity, doubtless expecting rich rewards.

According to psychics, this 'blind sight' is channelled through the sense of touch. Those possessed of the power, either physically blind or with some temporary blinker to prevent their seeing, can feel their way from place to place. Science, naturally, scoffs at this idea.

The experiment organized, newspaper men waiting eagerly and fame and fortune literally round the corner of his planned route, the intrepid magician seated himself in a car and was thoroughly blindfolded. Once it was proved that he could not see by any normal means, he began to edge rather cautiously forward, aiming to drive across an English town centre in this precarious condition. Incredible, the crowd whispered. Unbelievable, the journalists sighed. And unfortunately they were right. This would-be psychic negotiated his car just a few short yards – straight into the rear of a patrol vehicle used by the police to supervise the experiment!

It was not exactly the psychic performance of the century, but it does show that it is far from easy to reproduce mysterious phenomena using tricks or deception. Those who had said they could really perform such acts, and who had previously driven cars without using their eyes, still have a case which must be answered.

Of course, scientists do not attempt to answer it. According to the official interpretation of things, our sense of touch in no way includes an ability to 'feel' what a colour is like, or 'see' through one's fingertips. Yet there are psychics who do say this is possible.

One view is right and the other is wrong. Which is which?

What does logic tell us about the sense of touch? For a start: we know how something 'feels' when it brushes against our skin, if it is rough or if it is smooth. Silk is soft and rich, sandpaper rough and gritty. The stove is hot, the freezer cold. But the weather – what is that?

Here we begin to discover that it is not quite so straightforward as it first appeared.

Today, for instance, is a mild day. My mother comes in from a heavy afternoon's shopping and says, 'My – isn't it warm!' but I reply, 'No – actually I am cold.' And indeed I do feel chilled. How can we have such radically different opinions of the same day (which the weathermen and their objective instruments assert has an air temperature of 17°C, or 63°F, undoubtedly mild for the time of year)?

How we interpret a temperature – i.e. how we 'feel' it – has much to do with the interaction between our body temperature and the air itself. Since the air is at the same temperature for everyone in the same place, the difference must arise from the varying body temperatures of my mother and myself. She had been burning up energy walking about and lifting up parcels, so the average between her body temperature and the air was quite high. I was several days into a fairly strict diet and had been seated at my desk in front of an east-facing window for much of the day. Both of these things combined to lower my body temperature, and the average it formed with the outside air was therefore less than my mother's. In consequence we experienced the same day in totally different ways.

The generality of the human sense of touch is illustrated by the popular parlour game 'Murder', which a sadistic aunt loved to inflict on me during childhood visits. It also demonstrates an important influence on the way we experience things, which you ought to remember from Chapter 1.

The idea is that you sit around a darkened table with the lights completely off, creating an appropriately spooky atmosphere. The narrator has prepared the way and is the only one not taking part. They begin to relate a tale of murder filled with blood and gore. The manner of telling, thus enhancing the mood, is very important. Having reached the point in the saga where some notorious mass murderer has scythed down his latest victim, the story-teller explains how the hideously mutilated body has turned up in their kitchen – and here it is! This, for example, is one of the poor man's fingers, at which point there will be passed among you what feels for all the world like a finger covered in sticky blood. If you are not suitably impressed, there are more goodies in store, as one by one the victim's organs are passed around for your inspection.

Of course there has been no murder, but by the end of this game you will be hard pressed to believe that. Once the lights go up, the truth is revealed. The finger is a carrot covered in jam, the head a hollowed-out pumpkin, and so on. Working without visual clues, and on the sole basis of touch, we have interpreted the objects in line with what we were led to expect. The build-up of suggestion by a skilled narrator turns an egg yoke on a saucer into the dead man's eye.

You can learn more about the sense of touch by playing this game than in a whole course of lectures.

How we feel depends upon the strength of our other senses at any particular time, just as much as it depends upon the sense of touch. But how does any of this work?

We feel through the skin, with some areas more sensitive than others. In other words, there is no 'touch' organ in the same way as the nose or tongue relates to smell and taste. There are wide human variations too, both medical and sexual. Women, for instance, are genuinely more sensitive than men (if by this we mean responsive to touch).

Some parts of our body are more important than others – for instance, the hands and finger-tips. The skin contains 'receptors', which are cells of at least five different kinds. Some respond to heat, others to cold, others to pressure. The combinations lead some scientists to argue that there are really four senses, *plus* the many senses of touch – which cannot honestly be regarded as a single sense. However, these receptors do have a common operating function and link to the nerve cells (neurons) in the brain. The receptor cells feed into the neuron network in the same way as wires at the back of a hi-fi (an analogy to which we seem to keep returning). The links from the speakers, or the audio unit, or the record-player, all find their way into one final plug socket. Similarly, each neuron receives input from an assortment of receptor cells.

This might seem needlessly complicated, but nature never does complicated things when simple ones will do. If each neuron had only 'hot' receptor input or was fed merely by 'pressure' cells, our sense of touch would be as crude as (if not cruder than) smell or taste. Fortunately it is not. We not only distinguish between hot and cold but detect relative heat levels as well. 'Cool', 'tepid', 'warm', 'scalding' are all words that cover some of the many variations we are capable of feeling. Similarly, if we run our fingers over a polished surface with a defect in it, we can immediately sense the difference. Our pressure receptors can also record a range of sensations.

There are just 200,000 cells covering cold and heat, 500,000 for pressure sensations and a staggering 2.8 million reserved for something we might not regard as a sense, but which is seen to be extremely important. This is pain. All take different routes to the cerebrum of the brain, and some (especially pressure sensations of one sort or another) also route into the cerebellum.[1]

Pain is a blanket term we use to cover a range of sensations from the receptor cocktail. Whilst it has its own receptors, it also involves the triggering of others. For instance, from ordinary sunlight striking the arm we might infer that the day is warm. The neurons that fire in response convey a sensation of warmth and the message which says something like, 'This sensation is pleasant.' But expose your arm to more magnified heat and the situation changes. More and more 'hot' receptors fire, and also some 'pain' cells. Eventually the sensations brim over a threshold, and the pleasant feeling turns most definitely into pain.

Pain can come from other things too. Cold is just as effective as heat, and pressure is no different. Even itching or excessive tickling can do it.

That threshold above which the brain makes the choice between pleasant, bearable and painful sensations does not appear to be precise. It differs according to several factors, and we each have a unique 'pain threshold'. When our skin is damaged (e.g. by a rash), the threshold may be temporarily altered so that we hurt more quickly. Also, with practice, we can adjust the tolerance level and learn to put up with more pain than normal. Artificial chemicals can do this whilst remaining in the body; they range from localized anaesthetics which 'freeze' the nerve cells (e.g. novocaine injections at the dentist) right up to analgesics (so called pain-killers). The local anaesthetics block the transmission not only of pain signals from receptors to neurons but of any signals, so the area goes totally numb. Analgesics merely adapt the pain threshold, or the brain interpretation of the input, and let us accept sensations that were formerly regarded as painful.

There are added complications to the story, e.g. how pain can be 'dulled' or 'delayed' if rerouted a longer distance around the neuron network. But all we need to bear in mind is a simplified picture of receptors on the skin feeding into the neuron network a cocktail of sensations, which through chemical changes in adjacent neurons lead to the transmission of the signal to the processing centres in the cerebrum.

But there are alternative methods of pain-control. My mother recently joined the long queue of people dissatisfied with Western medicine. It could do nothing for her swelling feet, despite much effort. But an acupuncturist told her he could, so she let him stick needles into her ears and leave them there, explaining that if she felt any pain she should twiddle them a bit and it would stop. Gradually, and ridiculous as it must seem, the method worked its magic. Unfortunately my mother had to stop the experiment soon after, because the needles brought other symptoms (e.g. vertigo) that were worse than the problems they set out to cure!

Nevertheless, there is little question that in many cases this apparently daft idea (strategically sticking sharp objects into one's body) does seem able to remove, or at least reduce, medical problems that ought not to be affected. Eastern medicine has accepted this for centuries. Slowly we are catching up. In February 1986 a grant-supported acupuncture clinic to cure drug addicts was opened in Liverpool.

Paranormal researchers spout a lot of mumbo-jumbo (for which they have scant evidence) that this is all to do with 'energy centres' in the invisible 'spirit body'. In truth it is more likely to connect with biting your lip.[2]

A few years ago I had severe dental problems but was too scared to go to the dentist (a silly legacy of a nightmare experience as a child). Being a would-be scientist, I love to experiment with ways round those matters I would rather avoid. Eventually I discovered that I could significantly reduce the constant throbbing pain in my teeth simply by gnawing away at my lip. When I did this, I was naturally in some pain, but it quickly subsided, to be replaced by little more than a vaguely sore sensation. Along with it, at least for a time, went the considerably less bearable pain in my teeth. I do not recommend this practice, I hasten to add. It did little for my dental care and nothing for my lips. Ultimately, of course, the only answer was to overcome my phobia and seek a sensible solution. But it seems to show how acupuncture might work.

We know that pain impulses from one source arriving in the brain can effectively block those arriving from another. What happens is that the brain receives input from a new part of the neuron network which it decides to be more urgent or acute. The constant pain signals continue to come in. We are just not taking notice any more. The brain has been tricked, in a way similar to that with analgesics. Eventually the part of the brain which makes decisions realizes that it has been conned, particularly when the acute pain from the new source diminishes (as all receptor inputs do if they continue at the same strength for any period of time). It then switches back to interpreting the original source as long term and important and flashes its warnings to conscious awareness. Toothache happens *because* it is a warning. Otherwise we would go on ignoring our rotting teeth until they crumbled to pieces and fell out of our mouths!

Acupuncture would not be much use if it needed one pain to remove another. Of course, there has to be some sensation or the whole thing would flop, but acupuncturists seem to have learned the right places to stick their needles to cause minimum pain whilst still allowing distractions in the brain. If they chose to call these places 'energy centres' – *Chakras* to give them their full title – that is up to them.

This con-trick by the brain is not a cure for what ails you in the first place. Personally, I doubt that acupuncture works such miracles. What probably happens next is that, with the mind free to forget the pain or discomfort of the original problem, it speeds up the natural process of healing. Remember the old adage 'A watched pot never boils'. There is truth in that. By distracting the mind from watching the pot, it lets the body carry on with its ordinary (but no less magical) ability to heal itself.

We may now be on our way to understanding 'blind sight', the mystery with which we began this chapter.

There are receptors all over the body, as I said. Even when no light signals enter through the eyes, there can be rudimentary sensitivity to light through other skin cells. Obviously this is nothing like as sophisticated as real vision, or else all blind people would continue to see. But it is a genuine detection system and gives each of us some ability to see without eyes.

You will recall how different people have different pain thresholds. In *all* distribution curves there are extremes. The average curve for human heights may be $5\frac{1}{2}$ feet, but there are still some eight-foot giants and a few four-foot pygmies. One woman, for example, had great problems because her pain threshold was at the extreme end of the distribution curve. She noticed a problem only when she rested her hand against something scalding, *not* because of the pain (which never seemed to worry her) but thanks to the nauseating smell of roasting skin! In leprosy there is a similar danger. Sufferers from this dreadful disease may almost hack off a finger and not realize they have done so without looking to see. There is just no sensation transmitted to the neurons.

In the same way some psychics probably have extreme sensitivity levels from the cocktail of inputs they receive. Their ability to detect information from the environment without using their eyes may not be paranormal, just better than average.

The Soviets have been at it again in this area of paranormal study. There is no problem for their scientists to obtain grant funding. Psi-events are regarded as important starting-points for serious research.

Exploration of vision through the skin began there in 1962, and they call it bio-introscopy. Experiments commenced with one woman, Rosa Kuleschova, from Nizhniy Tagil in the Ural Mountains. Rosa used to help the blind and partially blind in her home town through local drama groups. By doing this, although fully sighted herself, she noticed a capacity for seeing images through her fingers. Her sense of touch was clearly remarkable. Training herself, she became quite an adept and was excited by the prospect of using her skills to help her blind friends see again. So she agreed to submit to extensive scientific tests which cost her dearly in terms of her own health. You see, Rosa was a sufferer from epilepsy – a potentially most significant piece of information (see page 43). At first she worked with her own doctor, then at a local laboratory, under the supervision of psychologist Dr Abram Novomeisky, and finally she moved on to the Academy of Sciences in Moscow.

This work demonstrated beyond much question that Rosa was not faking. She could tell the difference between various colours projected onto her skin even though she could not possibly see them. Ultimately her skills became even better, and not only colours but forms and shapes (sometimes even words) came within her grasp (quite literally).

What is significant about this is that psychologists believe there to be a relationship between primary colour perception and emotion. And we have already been discovering how emotion is the first thing to get across the barriers when a psi-event is generated.[3]

Subsequent experiments found that one in six of a sample of art students (whom you would expect to be more colour-appreciative than most) already possessed an innate ability to differentiate between simple colours using touch. Training could improve this. Eventually some blind people were taught to use this in a very limited way, but training programmes had to be intense and the final results, whilst challenging in terms of scientific understanding, remain impractical for everyday advantage. Nobody could read the text of *Pravda*, not even Rosa Kuleschova, although a few did occasionally get the *meaning* of the piece, as we might expect if it was emotion getting through.

There was a degree of consistency about how the subjects

said they could 'feel' colours. Light blue was invariably smooth, whilst red was coarse and sticky. This is what psychologists would predict from their study of the emotional perception of colours. The Russian scientists finally concluded that distinguishing between a red and blue piece of otherwise identical paper was the easiest first step towards proficiency at 'blind sight'.

How all this works remains open to debate, but they showed that it had nothing to do with radiation or wavelengths of light, by cooling and heating the colours randomly to mess up completely perception by this method. Of course, colours are visually unique because they are radiation at slightly different wavelengths. Red *is* fundamentally distinguishable from blue on this electro-magnetic scale. Doctor Novomeisky (by now an expert in the field) believes that the answer lies somewhere in this fact.[4]

The truth may well be a combination of several factors. There could be an influence from real differences transmitted through the skin in varying ways. The neurons operate on an electro-chemical basis remember. But the psychological effects of colours must also be important. That colours precipitate known emotions and relate to images in our 'mind store' (the sky is blue *and* tranquil, blood is red *and* sticky etc) cannot be irrelevant. That colour perception is the first thing that works through bio-introscopy suggests that it is using psi and the emotional messages connected with it.

Those gifted people who can drive cars blindfolded may be a little psychic in one sense; more probably they are freaks on the distribution curve of touch sensitivity or have trained themselves to greater ability, something we may all potentially do.

As with all our senses, it must never be forgotten that touch is *created* in our brains, sorted primarily at the thalamus and passed on to the cerebrum. If mind is superior to brain, this requires pain to be 'in the mind', as the saying goes. Presumably consciousness can effect it, which explains the current fad for bio-feedback and meditation, supposed methods to change your state of consciousness and take control over things such as pain.

Another method is to use hypnosis. Experiments to control pain through this have proved quite successful. Some people can be put into a sufficiently altered state of consciousness (the hypnotic trance) to allow minor surgery to be performed without anaesthesia. They can chat away to the doctor or dentist, feeling nothing whilst he removes an ingrowing toe-nail or a few rotten teeth. Medicine is interested in this phenomenon, especially if it can be reliable for more severe operations, because chemical anaesthetics always carry some slight risk to life, even with the healthiest of individuals. Whilst the risk is acceptably small, it would be extremely useful to get rid of it altogether.

At the moment, most surgeons remain scared of the rather different risks brought by our lack of understanding about hypnosis. Indeed, the only thing they seem to know for sure is that somehow it works!

Stage hypnotists (and those using it for more serious experiments) have long known that the mind can be told to feel either no pain when it ought to or some pain when no stimulus is present. Under hypnosis a chair may feel hot, because the hypnotist says it is, and the victim will jump up in apparent agony. Or a needle might be stuck into his hand and out the other side, with not a flinch as it happens. How can this be? What is most interesting for present discussions are those experiments where a hypnotized person is subjected to pain (e.g. by a needle in the hand) and, whilst saying he feels nothing, is then ordered to write the truth. His free hand will then pen something like, 'Ouch! You're hurting me!'[5]

In other words, there is again a con-trick. The effect occurs inside the brain, at the point of decoding input from the receptor cells. Yet the subconscious mind (which is reached through hypnosis) knows exactly what is going on. There is an uncanny similarity with the split-brain results, where the conscious and subconscious minds (or right brain/left brain) seem to know different things.

Frankly, this seems another case where the dualist alternative (brain and mind *are* separate) is the only one that really fits. Somehow we possess an ability to change the way the brain decodes its signals from the sense of touch. There is an automatic override by the mind, rather like the pilot who can switch off the computers and land the jumbo jet by himself if he so desires.

Hypnosis is not necessary (at least hypnosis *induced* by somebody else). A suitable person, either because of inherent abilities or because a personal crisis forces the circumstances, appears to be able to do this by himself. My grandfather told me how he lost a finger in the horrors of World War I, but he was in such a heightened state of mind that he scarcely noticed the pain until he was out of danger. The mind took over, changing the way the brain decoded input, and he just got on with the job. This is by no means an unusual tale in battlefield situations.

In 1984 a British farm-worker lost an arm in a terrible machine accident, but he was somehow able to find the state of mind that enabled him to suppress the pain (or rather con the thalamus into a false decoding process). He promptly picked up the severed arm, walked to get help and explained to a doctor what had happened.

That delightful Aladdin's cave of true but strange stories *Fortean Times* often has similar things in its pages. The artist Henry Benvenuti, upset at being refused an audience with a New York art editor, took out an axe and chopped off two of his own fingers in protest. Receptionist Donna Frost said in astonishment, 'He didn't make a sound.' Instead, hardly even bleeding, he walked out of the door to get a taxi, leaving this unusual calling-card behind. Money can be an even greater incentive than pique. Robert Yarrington was charged with fraud in September 1982, having received over $200,000 compensation after losing a foot in a motor 'accident' two years earlier. But the court found that he had set up the crash and chopped off his own foot on purpose![6]

But it must take a lot to top the twenty-two-year-old student reported by Ned Kalin of the University of Wisconsin.[7] He suffered excessive sexual urges and was afraid of what he might do. Failing to persuade the hospital to castrate him, he summoned up an altered state of consciousness and did it by himself! However, the success was limited, so he read a few more textbooks and decided that a dig around inside, severing the nerves to his adrenal glands, might be the next step. This drastic surgery was conducted in his bedroom using strategically placed mirrors. Things went well until, after pushing the liver aside, he ruptured his kidney. Calmly he phoned the police and handed an explanatory note to the stupefied doctors when he reached the local hospital. According to the report, he was last seen recovering on the wards, reading yet more textbooks and planning what to do for an encore!

This weird ability to withstand enormous pain seems

paranormal. African natives stick sharp bones through their lips and noses, and tread barefoot across white hot coals. An Indian fakir lies on a bed of sharp nails without bleeding. These things seem impossible, but clearly they are not.

There are ways to explain some of them. In fact, scientists in California became so convinced that anyone can walk across a bed of coals that it is now the rage at some nutty parties. The claim is that a layer of moisture which surrounds our feet vaporizes as soon as it touches the coals and sheaths the feet for a few precious seconds. Provided you run across the coals or skip very lightly, it is all very well. But there have been a few nasty accidents already, and this is one experiment I shall not be trying![8] However, it seems logical that, if the mind can overrule the normal decoding processes, it may be possible to prevent pain registering even in very extreme cases such as this.[9]

These third-world rituals and miracles often involve drugs, incense smells, rhythmic music and other paraphernalia which seem designed to create an altered state of consciousness, a sort of auto-hypnosis. Yet it remains amazing that the human race has learned these inner secrets despite the opposition of some pretty unimaginative scientists.

It is all very well to block out awareness of pain, but what stops the feet from turning into charcoal? Why do those self-mutilators never bleed to death?

Presumably we must accept that the mind can also control the automatic body functions which direct such processes. That is not wild speculation. The mind/body symbiosis goes on all the time. Indeed, we bleed when we need to and breathe when we should, entirely through such automatic actions. Breathing is such a frighteningly complex affair that, if we had to think about it in order for it to happen, few of us would last five minutes. And we would all stop breathing when we fell asleep – which would not be conducive to good health. Doctors researching the very sad 'cot death' syndrome are looking into the possibility that some young babies literally do just stop breathing when they fall asleep, because of a defect in this control process.

Returning to hypnosis, we find that it has been used to train the mind to remove warts or skin blemishes (presumably by the same mental over-ride taking on natural automatic processes). In the opposite fashion the mind can create marks on the body which have no physical cause. They appear as if the skin has been touched, but if so, it has been touched by the mind.

One patient of psychiatrist Dr R.L. Moody was asked to relive scenes of being whipped during childhood and developed the lash marks there and then on her back! These were severe enough to bleed mildly and require dressing, even though no whipping had physically occurred for twenty-two years.[10]

That it is not just hypnosis which causes these phenomena can be seen by studying something called 'stigmata'. These are marks, often of the crucifixion, which appear on the bodies of religious enthusiasts. There is no question that these do happen. They have been photographed many times.[11]

These marks are very important to the theorizer, because they prove that they result from the *mind* acting on the *body*. They reflect the popular (Church-inspired) image of a Crucified Christ, with holes in the centre of palms where he was nailed to the cross. In fact, the paintings and popular images have it wrong. The weight of the body would tear through the palms, which could not act as supports. So clearly these marks are produced on the body by the mind, based on the images in the 'mind store'.

It happens in other phenomena we loosely term paranormal. Poltergeist attacks sometimes leave marks on the victim's skin. This does not mean there must have been a real physical attack. The demons of the mind are just as dangerous.

A typical case was reported to me by a woman from Scotland. On a caravan holiday in Ireland in 1978, she claims that one night she woke up screaming. Her husband was used to this rude awakening as his wife had a very vivid dream life. On this occasion, in her dream, she had been approached by a man in a grey suit who had attacked her and smashed his hand into her mouth. She felt the pain and tasted the blood, all still in her dream. Waking up, she saw that, dream or not, the physical effects were very real. Several teeth had been knocked back, and one required emergency care. Her husband showed no signs that he might have struck her in his sleep. If so, her 'coincidental' dream is fascinating on its own. Nor was there any sign of blood around the caravan, which they both checked to see if she might have sleepwalked into a door or something. Somehow the vivid dream had translated into reality.[12]

In a previous book I included a photograph of most unusual stigmata, allegedly induced whilst the sleeping witness underwent a dream UFO encounter.[13] Other UFO 'burn' marks or peculiar body symptoms might also emerge through a combination of expectation, belief in the reality of the experience, and an application of mental control over automatic body functions.

In some situations the consequences are dire. On 4 January 1986 in the USA fifteen-year-old Felipe Garza died from a brain haemorrhage. His family said he was in excellent health, but a few weeks before his untimely end he had learnt that his fourteen-year-old girlfriend, Donna Ashlock, had a degenerative heart condition and would die unless a heart transplant could be performed. The chances of a suitable donor seemed slim. But, according to Felipe's brother, the boy had told him, 'I am going to die so I can give my heart to Donna.' For weeks he repeated this pronouncement, until brain death struck him out of nowhere. The day afterwards, 5 January, Donna received a new heart, care of the boyfriend who had somehow contrived to give his life for love.[14]

Hypnosis is just a good way of creating mental images powerful enough to help the mind change the operating principles of the body. Perhaps one day this will provide cures the medical world can only dream of. If it is possible for a young lover to commit suicide this way, who is to say what are the limits of possibility?

We have come a long way in understanding certain psi-events simply on the basis of already accepted knowledge. It is really quite disturbing that more scientists (outside the Eastern Bloc) feel inclined to dismiss what we call the paranormal on somewhat doubtful grounds, especially when the phenomena they ignore are of such potential value.

However, probably the strangest anomaly of the sense of touch is psychometry. The quotation at the head of this chapter describes how psychic Bob Cracknell regards what he does. He seems to be happy living without a sixth sense. I have watched Cracknell in public demonstrations, where he performs like a medium. Most clairvoyants tend to flop about like a fish out of water searching for a single, elusive genuine message amid wave after wave of conflicting images.

During December 1985 I was invited to teach at a weekend seminar organized by Manchester University. 'Science and ESP' was the impressive-sounding title, and I felt rather awed as the only non-academic among a gaggle of erudite professors. Part of the course involved a demonstration of psychometry by Dr John Dale, a psychiatrist by profession and psychic by preference.

Seventeen subjects took part in a three-hour experiment. We each secretly put one item into an envelope marked with a unique number. All the identical envelopes reached Dr Dale via an intermediary (a university psychology lecturer), so the psychiatrist had no way of knowing whose envelope bore whichever number he selected. Simply by touching the envelope, he believed he could tell us many secrets about our lives. Dr Dale 'homed in' first on the one he felt the most attracted to, but went on to cover almost all of them. No. 14 was his immediate choice, and as he spoke a flood of images entered his mind which he translated into words. 'This is the hardest part,' he told me later. 'What I see in my head is visual and loses a lot in the translation into words. When errors are made this is how they tend to originate.'

I recorded full notes at the time, and these show thirty-three separate statements offered for this envelope. They varied from vague comments such as, 'Matters have not turned out right lately' to quite specific facts, e.g. 'I see the number 32.' Later I spoke with the man who had provided envelope 14, although *no* identities were revealed during the experiment. He accepted that only four of the statements were obviously correct. These included the one about the figure 32 (on a computer floppy disc he had just bought) and something about a raffle ticket and a big prize he had nearly won. But what about the rest (including pictures of crumbling front doors, names like Betty, and so on)? None of these made any sense to the man.

John Dale alleged that details often seemed inaccurate at first but would later check out. 'Sometimes the images refer to the future, or the past – when the subject has no conscious recollection of them.'

However, what is interesting is that four of the statements offered to this man were remarkably appropriate to me! John Dale had given the name 'Jinny' and then referred to a black cat, a feeling of being very upset, and the date 23 November. The date certainly was on my mind as I had just returned from an emotionally exciting trip to the Canary Islands (commenced on that day) which had involved a very successful psi experiment (pp.155-7). I was also still very upset about the death of my black cat a few weeks before.

Now you may think it possible that any member of the group might have found four relevant statements. I am not sure about that. These do seem closer than the successes the real owner of the envelope claimed, and I could find nobody else who thought these John Dale's offerings appropriate for them.

However, there is a fascinating twist to this story. I had picked at random envelope number 11. The object I chose to put inside was a plastic Manx cat which I always carry in my bag. It is jet black. As soon as I put this into the envelope, I was reminded of the death of my real cat and for some reason changed my mind and tore open the paper. Taking a new blank envelope I had to write the number on myself, and to avoid duplicating another number I deliberately put 11A. The last 'l' and the 'A' were rather squeezed together. Inside the new envelope went my engagement ring. It is certainly possible to see that my 11A and the number 14 could be open to confusion if you are picking up mental images, especially as John Dale had no reason to expect that any of the envelopes (which he had not seen at this point) would bear a letter suffix.

The experiment continued with other envelopes. Many people were reluctant to discuss with me how accurate the often specific statements were. But I got the impression from my straw poll round the bar that night that no more than ten per cent had matched up. There were one or two claims of spot-on hits, and many obviously puzzled faces when meaningless things were said.

When the psychiatrist finally got to envelope 11A, my own experience was, I think, quite typical.

I recorded forty-two statements offered to me, and generally they were miles from the truth. Names Jessica and Rudolph meant nothing (and still don't), although another name (Granville) I did later discover to be that of a now dead uncle I had known simply as 'Uncle Gran'. But there was a recurrent theme in the reading and that was connected with writing. 'Get my pen out to write', 'Ink pots', 'I see several books' and other phrases all fitted in with this, and I can hardly deny the aptness of these. In *none* of the readings offered anybody else were books mentioned. But John Dale was absolutely correct in only two instances. He mentioned a giant plant with huge green leaves which dominated the room I work in. And the specific name 'Blackwell' popped out, being the publishers of a then current book (although they have published only one of my nine works to date).

Overall I could say that I was intrigued but generally disappointed. Certainly psychometry seems rather stuttering, if this performance is to be taken as an example. Yet weak overall results are balanced by the striking successes of one-off cases.

Dr Lawrence Le Shan first became interested in the paranormal when a doctor he knew disappeared. Weeks later he took a scrap off the shirt worn by the man the day before he vanished and gave it to a psychic, Eileen Garrett. She touched it, altered the state of her consciousness and offered a psychometry reading. She explained that the man was in La Jolla, California, and was there because of an emotional upset when his father had left him at the age of fourteen. The man's wife later confirmed this to Le Shan, and when the man was found he admitted that, incredibly, he had been in La Jolla on the date in question.[15]

Even more dramatic are cases where psychometrists assist the police. On 2 February 1982 two men disappeared at Lake George, New York, after they had gone to pick up some milk. Police searched for weeks but found nothing. As the men were not local but travellers from Canada, nobody knew for sure whether they had simply drifted back over the border – until the police sent for Ted Kaufmann.

Kaufmann is the type of psychometrist better known as a dowser. He uses a pendulum (not a hazel twig) dangling it over a map. By noting the way the bob rotates, he believes he can find a person or place. 'The pendulum becomes a tool enabling the psychic to concentrate his or her ESP,' Kaufmann claims. In other words, it is a device to transform subconscious images into external events, magnifying his sense of touch.

By this process the dowser became convinced that the men had driven over the lake and crashed through the ice, pointing out a part where the cover was thickest. The police were very sceptical, reasonably arguing that, if Kaufmann *were* right, they would surely have gone through the ice nearer the edges, where it was much thinner. But then on 29 March the body of one of the men turned up – exactly where the psychic had directed. Frogmen later found the other one, along with the truck and the milk. Faults in the lake bed had allowed warm spring water through, and it had unexpectedly thinned the ice at this spot. Of course, there was no way the dowser could have known that – at least, no normal way.[16]

The police chief, Ed Litwa, admitted that, 'This was one of the most remarkable experiences I have ever had during my twenty years on the Lake George police force.' But Ted Kaufmann was far less exuberant, saying, 'I never profess any kind of supernatural powers ... anybody can pick up a signal with the power of his mind.'

Bob Cracknell helps the police too, as we have already seen. One case he reports involved a man murdered in Leicester, a friend of my colleague, ASSAP researcher Kevin McClure. Bob's first impression in this instance was that the man had been homosexual. Kevin flatly denied this but after checking found to his complete surprise that it was true. Bob's further thoughts on the matter now had to be taken seriously. These included a street scene and a park. This information was conveyed to the police, and a couple of days later an arrest was made. The details matched what Cracknell had offered, with one exception – the image of the park. However, the name of the road where the arrest was made turned out to be 'Overpark'.

We see here the same problem of translation described by John Dale. The message is detected subconsciously and is predominantly emotional. This is turned into an *image* by the mind of the psychometrist. The 'park' symbol seems a good way to pictorialize that message, but by taking it literally as a park, the error was created.

The same pattern emerges in our dreams, which love puns, according to the psychologists who study them.[17] One I particularly recall involved the need for a boat to escape a flood. In the end I jumped onto a passing piano and floated to safety. A typically crazy-dream? Yes, but only when I followed the psychologist's rules for dream-interpretation did it occur to me that the shipping company which most readily springs to my mind is 'P & O' ('Pacific & Orient'). Imagine your mind receiving the input 'P & O' and having to come up with a quick visual image to illustrate it!

The more we look into the anomalies of touch, the more we are drawn yet again to the mind. There is no trace of a sixth sense. Sometimes sensitivity is enhanced. At other times what seems like a mystery of touch is in truth a mystery of mind.

The psychometrist *uses* an object as a focus to his mind. It can be a map, a piece of clothing, an envelope, a pendulum or a twig. In the end it makes no difference. Information flows in subconsciously and the source is neither the object nor the psychometrist's fingers. These are only tools that objectify the intangibles of consciousness. And consciousness seems to be unshackled by the boundaries of time and space.

The same process, in a different guise, seems to account for stigmata and miracle healing. They look paranormal only so long as we *want* them to. If instead we prefer answers, they are there to be found.

It is our mind which works the miracles.

6. Hearing – Ghostly Echoes from Past and Future

'Beneath the surface we are in constant telepathic contact with one another.'
Rosalind Heywood, clairvoyant

When the great inventor Thomas Edison was just twelve years old, he became deaf. As we have seen, the brain can compensate for such unfortunate deficiencies, particularly when they happen during childhood. It simply enhances other abilities to make up for the loss.

An example is the well-studied case of Nadia, an autistic child who made light of this infirmity by developing incredible drawing ability. Between the ages of three and eight it was rated at the level of genius, such was her brain's ability to compensate.[1]

Returning to Edison: he also discovered something which helped replace the loss of hearing. He began to have many experiences of what we might call telepathy – the hearing of a message *inside* the mind, with no real words spoken – ability to know what someone else is thinking.[2]

This is possibly the most widely discussed form of psi-event. It has been tested extensively in laboratories. Many of us have gone through one-off experiences of knowing who it was at the other end of a ringing telephone, or pre-empting what someone was about to say. In her anthem of the paranormal Kate Bush even sings about it: 'You hear your sister calling, but you don't know where from. You know there's something wrong, but you don't want to believe in a premonition.'[3] As Kate Bush shows, the borderline between telepathy and premonition is often far from clear. If you pick up a message in your mind, it may not be easy to determine if this is a telepathic communication at the moment of an incident, or a precognition of your later discovery that the incident has happened. Think back to Lucia Randles and that 'phone call' on a phantom telephone at the time of her husband's death (page 19). Which was that?

As Rosalind Heywood reminds us above, we are all in constant telepathic contact. We usually just don't realize it. 'Even when they do not know it, men and women are reacting all the time to elements not perceptible via the known senses,' she says [4] – which rather implies she is in favour of a sixth sense. So in telepathy have we found one at last?

Rosalind Heywood was a young nurse on duty at the Milbank Military Hospital when the First World War was at its bloody height. Amidst the death and mayhem she learnt how to *think* troubled patients to sleep. She never spoke of this strange ability but used it often. Once a soldier in delirium sat upright and said, 'It's no use trying to think me to sleep again.' He then began to mumble the name of a relative who was dead, cried out 'Oh the light!' and passed away.[5] Here she is demonstrating an interesting principle. Telepathy is an unconscious phenomenon, rooted in the mind. Just as neuron transmission, electro-chemical impulses and raw sensory input are the basis of the brain, so telepathy may be the messenger of the mind. It is a way of conveying information, using the now familiar method of images, symbols and emotions. It does not use factual data. In this way brain and mind are polar opposites.

There seems no point in our seeking out 'telepathy waves' emanating from the brain as some new kind of energy. They do not exist.

Recent research at the University of Iowa throws some light on this. Dr Antonio Damasio, a neurologist studying a brain disorder known as prosopanosia, worked with two women suffering from this condition. They were shown pictures of faces, some of whom were people known to them (e.g. family members) and others total strangers. Because of their illness they stated an inability to recognize any of the faces, yet records of the electrical activity in their brains proved that substantially more went on when a recognizable picture was presented to them. Their conscious mind was no wiser, but some element below the surface was able to tell the difference.[6]

The similarity with the split-brain results should again be obvious. All it really tells us is that vast amounts of data are processed subconsciously, but it is quite consistent with the prospect of telepathy.

Many psychiatrists have noticed apparent telepathic data coming out during experiments *not* designed for such a purpose. Professor Alvin Lawson and Doctor William McCall, trying to get hypnotized people to *imagine* UFO abductions, were puzzled when they found them using images related to material in the mind of the experimenters.[7] In a 'live' UFO situation I have come across the same situation, where a hypnotized witness appeared to use words taken from the mind of one of the interviewers.[8]

Similarly, Dr Berthold Schwarz tells of a patient, a businessman, who at a party went straight up to a woman and said (off the top of his head) 'Those who read *Reader's Digest* are idiots.'

The man felt a fool for uttering these strange words and rationalized later that he was just making 'small talk'. However, the lady was none too impressed by his line in chat. She worked for *Reader's Digest*! Struggling to mask his embarrassment, the man added, 'Well − I hope you are not in the editorial department.' She was.[9]

You might think this was just tough luck, but Schwarz suggests a radical view, that the man had picked up clues about the woman through telepathy. Then came the problem of translation. The image of *Reader's Digest* and 'editorial department' got through clear enough, but when he came to turn the pictures into words, he put quite the wrong emphasis onto them. Or it may be possible that his subconscious mind *wanted* him to mess up this would-be friendship. It is capable of such devious tactics, and what we believe to be good for us consciously may not look that way to our subconscious mind. This is the very essence of the so-called 'Freudian slip', where we think one thing and say something embarrassingly different. The words are expressing what we *really* felt inside.

On 19 October 1982 I walked into the living-room with my mind wandering. I was vaguely aware that the 10 p.m. TV news was just starting, but I was not listening. I had been locked in my room all day writing and had heard no bulletins that day. Suddenly came the lead-in announcement that they were going to discuss a record loss by British Airways and the suggestion it be sold to private owners. Completely on impulse and for no reason I can see, I blurted out, 'Yes – the Arabs are going to buy it and rename it ELAL.' ELAL, as I knew, is the Israeli state airline.

My mother, who was watching the news, turned immediately to me and said, 'Was that a joke?'

Still in this peculiar state of mind I said, 'Yes. But I wouldn't bank on it.'

These ridiculous exchanges would be utterly meaningless, but for what happened next. Within five seconds of my ending the sentence the story on British Airways concluded and, in a related item, the ELAL airline logo flashed up on the screen! A *bank* had that day put them into liquidation. Nobody was more astonished than I was.

What seems to have happened here is that information I received through hearing subconsciously was turned into a joke by those incredibly swift mental processes which we possess.

Sometimes the results are far less trivial than this, when a 'little voice' (as we call it) warns you what action to take. We have already met it once with Catherine Logan and the house fire (page 76).

I have a friend who was driving with his wife along the M62 motorway, when he swung the car on a crazy dive into the fast lane. He did not look and, as his wife said later, 'I was furious because he might have killed us.' But her anger was only fractions of a second long. Suddenly the truck in the lane that was directly ahead shed its load in an unexpected accident, tipping it right onto the spot where they would have been had he not made this 'insane' swerve.

Whilst cases like this are the most eye-catching, more often it seems ridiculously irrelevant whether we undergo the psi-event or not. Just what was the point of my ELAL 'joke'? And what is the meaning of this next experience?

On 24 May 1983 I was proof-reading, a dreadfully monotonous job that all authors face. Poring over the computer-set manuscript, seeking out every minor error and spelling mistake, I was tired but had found very few. Towards the end of the book one suddenly appeared. Instead of 'Doctor Malcolm Scott' the word 'Stott' had been printed. I saw this immediately but was tempted to ignore it. 'It's close enough,' I muttered to myself. I must have failed to change it, because the book appeared complete with the mistake.

Later that day I was doing my weekly radio spot with the local station in Liverpool and, as I often did, went down from the office to the studio some time before I was due to appear. DJ Brian Ford was on air in the same room, performing a regular feature in which he played very old records. Live across the airwaves he told listeners, 'The band-leader on that last record was Wally Scott. I don't know if it's our Wally. I'll ask him.' As I, and most of those tuning in, knew very well, Wally Scott produced Brian's show, and this was a jibe about his age that was an accepted joke. Brian plopped on another record and, now off air, turned to me and said, 'The name is Wally Stott actually, but it's close enough.'

Somehow my thoughts and Brian's had blended together that day. The Scott/Stott confusion and the same words, 'It's close enough', linked us in the space of just a couple of hours. Coincidence is no explanation for something like that. Much better is the suggestion that, with the situation in my mind, and as the two of us were harmonized thanks to our joint weekly radio show, I somehow made Brian read 'Stott' as 'Scott' and crack a joke he might never have thought of otherwise.

It is a case of directing attention selectively. We look out for things we would otherwise miss. Once at Radio City there were rumours that Brian Ford was to leave the company, and he did in fact leave some months later to join the BBC. In confidence, and because I was affected by any move Brian might make, I asked producer Wally Scott if the rumours were true. He denied it, and at that moment the denial was probably accurate. But after leaving the studios I bumped straight into a newspaper placard for the evening paper announcing, in bold letters, 'Ford's boss denies rumours'!

The Press item was not about the minor goings-on at an IBA radio station! It was, of course, to do with an industrial dispute at the Ford Motor Company. Obviously I did not engineer the wording on the billboard. Nine times out of ten I would never have noticed them, let alone practically fall over the placard. My mind, subconsciously detecting the relevance, must have made very sure that I saw it. But why? Was it trying to tell me that, despite the denial, Brian *would* leave and I would also lose my Radio City contract? My 'little voice', aware of the relevance, spoke to me and made quite sure that I listened.

In most of these cases there was nothing obvious to hear, even if we allow for the sense of hearing to be extended beyond its normal range. At other times (e.g. with the ELAL story) we might wonder if I had heard the news subliminally, without realizing that I had done so.

There certainly is evidence that we can respond to cues spoken so softly that we fail to hear them with our conscious mind, but we must hear them somewhere because we make choices based on the information. Picking up our own name is especially common. Psychologists recognize something called 'the Cocktail Party Effect', which makes it possible for us to hear our own name amid a babble of distracting conversation (e.g. at a cocktail party). They test this by feeding so much sound into the ears that little can be understood from the jumble.

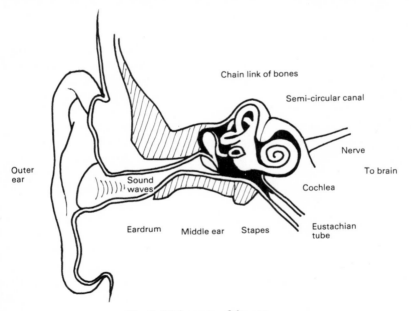

Fig. 9: Main parts of the ear.

But it is quite easy to pick out your name.[10]

Yet how would we account for the phenomenal abilities of Paul Whittaker, organist and choirmaster at St Cuthbert's Church, Huddersfield, Yorkshire? He is one of the youngest musicians to aspire to such heights and has been totally deaf from birth. He claims to 'feel' the notes inside him and constructs the sound of them in his mind – notes he has never 'really' heard. His mother said, 'I don't know how he does it.' Members of the choir are amazed. 'It must be instinct,' one of them suggests. Or telepathy perhaps?

Now seems the right moment to look at how the sense of hearing operates. The ear is the most complex of the sense organs, an indication of the relative importance of this sense above the three described so far. Only vision is probably more necessary to us (See Figure 9.)

The receptical which forms the outer ear garners sound in pressure waves. Sounds are air molecules squeezed together and apart to create waves, rather like waves in water. These vibrations impinge on the timpanic membrane, better known as the 'eardrum', which does indeed behave just like a drum. It resonates with the vibrations and transforms the air waves into physical vibrations in the ear itself.

These vibrations then pass through a series of small bones (called ossicles) which are attached to the eardrum. This reduces the impact of the energy, whilst retaining the essential relative differences. The individual vibrations thus remain in proportion but cannot cause damage unless the sound energy is considerable. All in all a range of over one billion times (from softest to loudest sound) is possible.

The spiral-like cochlea is a housing for fluid which completes the energy transformation. This fluid contacts the auditory nerves and terminates the production of electro-chemical signals which can be passed by the nerve to the brain.

Each of the auditory nerves covers a range of frequencies, so that in combination the thousands upon thousands of nerves allow a broad range of sounds to be heard. The normal frequency range for humans is between about 20 and 20,000 hertz (where one hertz is the name for one vibration per second). This standard deteriorates with age, and we lose a few hertz from the upper range each year after our teens. We are all slowly going deaf.[11]

The stereo effect of having two ears helps us to locate a particular sound. There is a slight difference in the time when a sound will arrive at each ear, because sound waves move at a fairly sedate speed. The brain works like a super-fast calculator using this difference to place the sound.

Again you will notice it is the brain which does all the interpretation. The ears are merely instruments that gather sounds, and even if we cut them off, a crude sense of hearing would continue through the auditory nerves. It is the decoding of the electrical impulses that manufactures our hearing. Whilst the sound of a bee buzzing is real in a definite way (as a sequence of fast vibrations in the air), the 'buzz' that we hear is the result of a series of energy transformations. It is no more the *real* buzz than electricity from our sockets *is* the sunlight. Clearly they are *not* the same. The sunlight is changed from one kind of energy into another. But then so is the vibration of a buzzing bee.

We should always remember that we understand little of the final stage of this transformation process, the one that takes place inside the brain. If something internal causes the same last stage, a 'hallucinated' sound of buzzing will occur, even with no real bees to set the chain into motion. It will seem to be identical to a real bee buzzing.

The same result can have very different starting-points, as we saw from the many buzzing sounds generated by psi-events. They are not responses to a flotilla of bees invisibly flying about. They are the same internal brain reaction to something very different in the first place.

All this makes our sense of hearing seem impressive. The fact that sound decoding occurs in the newer parts of the brain (the cerebrum) emphasizes the importance of the sense. Yet still our hearing is worse than that of almost every other mammal!

Bats have incredible sonar ability and use their ears to see, emitting sounds, bouncing them back, matching them up with a radar map inside their brains and locating an object with pinpoint accuracy. Their hearing range goes up to 115,000 hertz (six times man's upper limit), yet their brain size is minute compared with ours. Even dogs double our upper hearing limit (to 44,000 hertz), as shown by the 'silent' dog whistle. It may be silent to our paltry senses but is perfectly audible to many animals.

The fact that we cannot 'hear' a sound at very high frequency does not necessarily mean it has no effect on us. Research into the possible consequence of such high-range vibrations has produced some quite disturbing results. In the years before World War II the radio genius Marconi is said to have worked on a device that focused sound waves and could stall electrical equipment or even kill human beings. Indeed, the development of radar began in this strange way, although British researchers found that 'death rays' required too much energy to be practical.

Nowadays we have microwave energy and can cook foods without a heat source to prove the point. Although we cannot 'hear' microwave ovens, there have to be stringent precautions to prevent their leaking, as they can be extremely dangerous if faulty.

There is also little doubt that the secret services in both the USSR and the USA have been working on offensive weapons using sound energy. When, in one Soviet experiment into behaviour control, an 18,000-hertz signal was fed into subjects' brains, they immediately reported strange, mystical feelings. Clearly *something* was triggering the neurons in the brain to generate a pseudo-sensory impression, an impression just as real as any other in its effects on the witness.

Is it possible that some of us can hear vibrations at a level beyond the norm? It certainly is. The range is known to be quite variable, and even ordinary people can sometimes detect sounds outside the standard 20–20,000 hertz range, if the intensity is great enough.

A young woman called Frances from Tyne and Wear described to me her frightening night-time encounter which began in January 1978. 'I was awoken by a very high-pitched buzzing noise. This noise seemed to be coming from inside my head, and the effect was very unpleasant – something akin to having an electric shock.'[12] Ironically she ascribed this experience to 'nerves' (which in a much more literal sense it probably was!). However, it continued to happen as she lay in bed during the early morning hours, and later she went on to experience visual phenomena. A strange figure appeared in her room and took her hand. Her bones seemed to light up as if she was looking at an X-ray photograph. Eventually she had to drag her arm away. 'The sound would build up to such a pitch that my head felt like it would burst,' she added. Whilst the sound worried her deeply, the visual aftermath was quite different. It was as if she were in a trance, which probably means some altered state of consciousness. 'There was a dream-like quality to the experience,' she explained. But it was not a dream.

I can sympathize with Frances, because these nocturnal buzzings are just what I went through as a child (see Chapter 1). I distinctly recall the electrical coursings that ripped through my body – not physically painful but mental torture, as if my whole being were vibrating. I shiver even now as I recall them.

The humming/buzzing sound is a prominent feature of UFO encounters and closely relates to what I call the Oz Factor. I believe the symptoms (which also include unusual calmness, disappearance of external sounds, and a sense of oneness with the experience) are markers pointing to an induction of sensory deprivation. This strange discovery is crucial to our understanding of what is going on, so I will describe in some detail the case which first alerted me to the matter. It was reported to me in 1978, when I was working with the magazine *Flying Saucer Review*.

The witness requested anonymity, so I will call him Roy. He lived in Colchester, Essex, and has undergone many strange experiences, far more psi-events than chance should predict. We call such a subject a 'repeater'; in other situations he might be called a 'medium'. It may only be a matter of words.

Roy feels in tune with his environment. 'I have had vibrations, good and bad, from places I have visited,' he told me. But his first really specific experience came when he was seventeen. He was walking down a narrow alley when a glow in front of him caught his attention. He could hear footsteps walking towards him, but nothing visible was causing them. The alley was too narrow for anyone to have passed by unnoticed, so he quickly realized that something very strange was happening. The next thing he knew there had been a 'time lapse' and he was now at the far end of the alley, soaking wet. He had no idea how he had got there or why he was no longer dry. It was not raining.

On 10 November 1971 Roy saw a UFO. It was crystal clear; dome-shaped with a window on either side. The object hovered over a café and changed colour from green to red to yellow to white and was tilted slightly from the horizontal. Some years had elapsed since his experience in the alleyway, but as he watched this unusual 'craft' for about five minutes, time became distorted. After a period of uncertainty the UFO just 'blinked out'. Roy believes he was the only witness, which he finds exceptionally odd because the area is normally busy. This is a very typical Oz Factor symptom. As he put it, 'The only way I can describe this is that it felt like opening a door to a party ... as I turned the corner people were walking about, cars, noise etc. Everything normal ... This part of the phenomenon is stranger than actually seeing the UFO.'

It is also weirdly similar to the 'reality blink' which Mrs Sage faced nine years afterwards. That too was in an alleyway, possibly a relevant fact. Some doctors who study epilepsy think that visions are more likely if the field of view of the subject is suddenly lowered. Looking through a window would create this 'tunnel' effect. So might the confines of an alley. The 'aura' which many epileptics feel before an attack, a strange sensation that warns of its imminence, is similar to the Oz Factor in some regards – none of which means that the psi-event and time-lapse *are* epileptic attacks, but it does point us towards a mental event or a disfunction of consciousness as the common origin for both.

A few weeks after Roy's encounter, on 25 January 1972, he had a second experience at almost the same location. Again he suffered sensory isolation. But he noticed something additional on this ocasion. The white ball of light that he observed seemed to make 'the air and ground become alive with vibrations'. It was 'the feeling when you get an electric shock'.[13]

Another consistent clue emerges: the electrical vibrational effect, which seems to tie in with the electro-chemical disruptions in the brain. It is fascinating to speculate what would have happened fifty years ago if Roy had seen his 'ball of light'. Would it have 'appeared' as a UFO? Or would the images in his 'mind store' have moulded a quite different interpretation onto it? A ghost? A religious vision? It hardly matters. What does is the internal sensation *felt* in all these cases. The Oz Factor, now we have distilled it out from all the weird visual trappings may show us the way towards an answer.

I have come across many 'repeaters' since Roy. Another is Keith, from Birkenhead, Merseyside. Aged thirty-two in 1985, he has been plagued by psi-events since childhood. There are so many of them they would fill a book on their own, and the one I quote must not be seen out of context. He has met ghosts and UFOs and had timeslips and premonitions. He is a walking dictionary of the paranormal.

As a child he once experienced 'an incredible fog, the thickest I have ever known'. He set off to walk through it just a few hundred yards to where a friend lived. But then, 'Something inexplicable occurred.' He heard a strange rushing sound above his head. It felt like a pressure wave swamping over him. 'I dived to the ground and covered my ears,' he says. But this did *not* prevent the sound. 'It was just as vivid, almost as if [it] was in my head.' When he stood up, the noise had ended, so he scrambled into his friend's house to tell the tale – assuming it must have been a crashing plane. All he received was an incredulous stare. There had been no noise. 'Show me the fog!' he was asked. Only seconds had gone by but the day was bright and clear. There was not a hint of mist.[14]

We pass up great opportunities by ignoring cases like these. It is clear from Keith's actions that the sound was *inside* his mind. Just as with the buzzing 'heard' by Frances, or myself, the noises are not external. A tape recorder would not pick them up. Perhaps they are by-products of the Oz Factor. This, as I said, is a sort of induced sensory deprivation. The mind deliberately 'tunes down' the constant rumble of sensory input from the outside world, and this manifests as loss of ambient sounds that should be there, or curious visual disappearances (e.g. of traffic or people). It must do this for a reason, and the only one that seems apparent is to facilitate the 'tuning-up' of information that arrives internally, messages from the inner-self, with a marked lack of restriction from time and space.

At the start of the chapter I likened the neuron impulses to electro-chemical transmitters of information, and said that telepathy might be their inner world equivalent: messengers of the mind. Perhaps these hummings and buzzings sometimes occur when we pick up the content of those messages and hear the whistling of the messenger delivering his goods.

Let us develop these ideas with a further psi-event, reported by Mrs Jepson from Kent. In February 1982 she was up late reading when, 'Suddenly I became aware of hearing marching feet.' She put down her book to listen. It sounded like an entire regiment tramping along. After a time, the noise faded away. She never located a *real* source for these sounds but does explain that in the eighteenth century there was a military camp at Coxheath where she lived. Had she detected an echo from the past, she wonders.[15]

This idea has been suggested many times before, because there does seem to be a connection with emotional traumas from the past. I visited the scene of a harrowing encounter in the ancient Roman city of Chester, which demonstrates this point.

Paul Whetnall was a jeweller, working in a basement shop beside the ancient Northgate of the city. He and a colleague heard footsteps echo down the old stone stairway and went to the door, presuming it to be their boss. Nobody was there. They could hear the steps and were even able to follow the path of the invisible walker as he reached the bottom and turned away. This was not a freak reflection from a nearby building. The footsteps had been heard before, and all the workers who visited the cellar knew of the ghost they called 'George'. The building was on the site of a former jailhouse where condemned prisoners were kept before hanging. Intense emotions may still cling to it.

One argument is that emotions can be trapped on some invisible tape, exactly like sounds on a cassette recorder. When conditions are right, the system switches to replay. Certain kinds of building or stone are said to act like the stylus on a record-player, translating the 'electrical' signals into acoustic sounds.

Whilst we might see the merit for this, problems occur when the true nature of mind is understood. Consciousness might be the equivalent of an electro-magnetic field, but it is not a *physical* field in the same way. The 'replay', if it happens, must take place inside the mind, not the room. Mrs Jepson and these jewellers might have picked up a message from the past (reverberations of a long-gone emotional upheaval), but the message is on an emotional level and is translated into images or other sensory experiences by fishing from the 'mind store' a representative image. The sounds of the footsteps *were* replays, but of *real* steps once heard and stored in the minds of the witnesses. They may have been triggered into replay mode by a subconscious message from the distant past, but there is no need to assume a physical signal that we could trap in a cassette recorder. The idea of hearing the Sermon on the Mount (recorded 'live' by this method) will, I fear, remain a dream.

A case which helps to put this into perspective involves a family from Northamptonshire, who in 1973 owned a large modern house on formerly open land. Soon after moving in, the husband began to hear children's voices. They seemed very excited and appeared to be upstairs. If he went to investigate, they always ceased, but then when he came back down into the lounge he often heard them again. After a long time he shared his experience with other members of the family. Nobody else ever heard the voices. Eventually the husband awoke from sleep to see an apparition of a child in a long nightgown, holding a candle. Thinking it was his own son, the man called 'What's the matter?' But the figure promptly walked right through the door!

We might think this is another example of a record from the past, with the phantom being the visual phase of an audio-visual replay. But there is no evidence that any other building had stood on the site or that a traumatic event had occurred there. So maybe we should pause in our quest for paranormal solutions and wonder if, sometimes, there may not be normal ones.

The vision might have been a dream, precipitated by the hearing of the voices.

Sometimes when I am writing, I also hear the sound of children. It depends on how quiet the house is and the way the wind blows. Every so often they waft my way from a school almost a mile away and seem to be just outside my door.

Years ago, in the Lancashire Pennines where I was born, I loved to play on 'Echo Hill', an eerie spot near Waterfoot. If you stood in exactly the right place, you could hear your own voice echoed back several miles across the intervening valley, delayed by a couple of seconds because of the distance. The geographical and atmospheric conditions were in alignment, producing a freak of hearing. It can happen on a smaller scale in many other circumstances.

Perhaps the ghost voices in Northamptonshire were *real* children many miles away. It is interesting that the effect seems to have been confined to one location and vanished if you moved from that spot. Maybe the husband's hearing was abnormally acute. There may be no cause to invoke the supernatural at all. However, this clearly does not work all the time, and I am satisfied that real phenomena which we call telepathy or time-recordings *do* exist.

The manner in which we explained how the ghost army and the spectre in the Chester basement 'materialized' in the minds of the witnesses was rather like that employed for premonitions. A message (from past or future – since they seem equally available to the mind) is decoded by consciousness and translated into sensory images fished from the 'mind store'.

But if a ghost from the past can be created this way, surely there can also be ghosts from the future, echoes of a time not yet come, that are clothed by the mind in some appropriate way? It may be hard to prove or disprove, but there could be a phenomenon which fits. Strange technologies or advanced human beings manifesting in thin air: that description would fit the flying saucer.

7. Vision: Out of Your Body or Out of Your Mind?

'I asked these spirit figures if I was seeing them, or
if I was seeing what was in my brain. They
answered "Both".'
                    Eileen Garrett, medium, addressing the
                    Parapsychology Foundation in 1967

In a fascinating study of blind people, Frank Musgrove reports
on a fifty-nine-year-old man who lost his sight twenty-one years
before. He had been a tailor but had been forced to leave that
profession. When he compensated by turning inwards to become
a creative writer, the substitute enriched his life.

Whilst in his fifties the man suffered a stroke and spent
several weeks in deep coma, 'sort of in another world –
conscious, but I was not there'. Quite unable to know what was
happening, a relative who had been away for years came to visit
him, bringing a son along. Sadly they had to go before there
was any improvement in his condition, but when he awoke he
knew they had been there. He explained his knowledge by
saying, 'I had a very vivid dream.' In this 'dream' the comatose
patient (far from being out cold as one might expect) had a
perplexing experience. 'I am looking down,' he remembered
'And then ... I seemed to be on a different plane, looking at
them looking at me.' But he was blind, do not forget. Even had
he been conscious, he could not have looked at anyone!

Frank Musgrove is not a paranormal researcher, and his
report makes no mention of the correlations. But we can easily
recognize the man's experience: like the young boy looking
down at the operation as doctors insert a new valve, or the
patient passively watching his rescue from a heart attack. This

blind man simply had an OOBE. His eyes may not have been
able to see, but his mind could.[1]

Perhaps you will seek a way out of this dilemma. Could it be
that the man was not really blind? Experiments on animals have
removed all visual links to their brain, yet rudimentary sight
remains. It is doubtless very crude, but it is something.

One man lost connections to the left visual field. His
description of what happened is interesting, and predictable. He
was able to see but did not consciously believe that he was
seeing. As with split-brain patients, there was subconscious
understanding only.[2]

However, we have no medical grounds for presuming that
anybody in a coma can see. And even if they could, we do not
have an answer to the OOBE. Why was this man's account so
remarkably like all the thousands of others?

How does human sight function? It is of great survival value
to us. The processing-centres in the cerebrum are parts of the
newly evolved brain. The eye is a complex organ, and we take

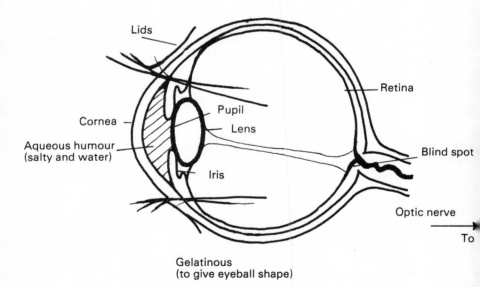

Fig. 10: Main parts of the eye.

more care of it than any other. We have eye-doctors (opticians) and fit spectacles or contact lenses whereas defects of the other senses (except for hearing) tend to get ignored.

Figure 10 shows a cross-section through the eye. Its purpose is to collect the rays of light that are bounced off objects in the universe around us. These light rays are electro-magnetic energy waves at varying frequencies, similar in many respects to sound. It is the frequency (the number of vibrations per second) which dictates the colour of light. This is the essence of a rainbow or spectrum since red light is of lower frequency than blue and is less bent by passage through a medium. When this is all smeared out at the other side, we have the colourful patterns we see in our skies or at the far end of a prism.

The adjustable lens of the eye, just like the lens of a camera, focuses the light rays into a sharp picture, which is then projected onto the retina at the back. Unlike most cameras, the lens shape can be altered by muscles at either side, allowing it to capture light rays from different sizes and distances. Defects of our eyesight usually involve problems with the lens and its muscles, and artificial lenses (glasses) simply make up the difference.

The retina comprises millions of receptor cells, as does the skin, but these are much more complicated and sensitive, as befits the importance of sight. They are photo-sensitive, like chemicals on a film, and react photo-chemically when light shines on them. The nature of this light is related to the precise changes that occur.

Two main types of cell are found. They are called rods and cones, thanks to their shape under giant microscopes. The rods are about 0.05 millimetres long and 0.002 millimetres wide. They are most sensitive in dim lighting and respond to neutral colours (e.g. various shades of grey). Cones tend to be bigger, varying from 0.03 to 0.09 millimetres long, and 0.003 to 0.008 millimetres wide. The distribution of the cells across the retina is well organized (there being no rods in the centre, for example) and there are twenty times more rods (125 million) than there are cones (just 6.5 million). This deficit in cone number is made up for by their diversity. Three main sub-types react to red, green and blue wavelengths of light. These are the same colours used in a TV set to provide all the subtle tones you see on the screen. When mixed together in assorted combinations, every colour imaginable can result.

A light ray will be quite a mixed bag of frequencies and wavelengths, and different rods and cones will trigger in appropriate ratios to generate characteristic chemical reactions. The optic nerve from the back of the retina completes the energy transformation and carries the electro-chemical impulses into the brain.

However, this is only the very basic background to vision. On its own it would leave you seeing shapeless, colourless blobs. You can stimulate the effect by closing your eyes and gently massaging the eyelids, as you do when you are tired. Phantom spots and colours appear on your retina. But note that you are unlikely to ascribe a false position out in the 'real world'. They seem to be *inside* your eyes, which is where they are. But, as *all* visual signals are patterns on the retina, what makes us see the world as if it existed beyond? In order to detect this, and shapes or orientation, the receptor cells are also grouped into kinds that react to various options. Some will trigger only if a line is vertical, others if it is horizontal. Some react only in darkness, others to light densities.

However, we remain baffled by a great deal of what happens after this. There are theories and a few stray facts, but not a lot of understanding.

Visual perception in the mind is a result of a lengthy procedure during which errors are more than possible. To come up with the perception of a letter such as 'A', the light ray is split into its component parts, cells are triggered according to colour, density, angles, shapes etc, the chemical reactions become electrical impulses, the various split reactions are then merged together, and a *seemingly* appropriate image is selected from whatever already exists in the 'mind store'. If we observe anything that is not in the store, it will be misperceived, and we will match it up with something that *is* in the store, something that may be similar, but also wrong.

That is why we have a tendency to interpret all strange things in acceptable terms. There is no way we could perceive them otherwise. This is of major importance when we are discussing the paranormal, for we constantly encounter unknown things which will not be in the 'mind store'. The chances are we shall misperceive, either by matching up with a familiar object that *is* there or by adapting our perception so that it changes to look like something familiar (even if that something comes from a science-fiction film).

Those sceptics who denounce a witness to a psi-event by suggesting that they imagined what they saw, based on watching too much *Star Trek* may be right for all the wrong reasons. It is possible the perception *has* originated from this source, but what counts is the *reason* for the perception in the first place.

Remember Professor Gregory wondering what would happen if we met an alien life-form? We can make a reasonable guess. Perception *would* occur, by selecting something out of our 'mind store' that seemed to be a close match. It could *not* be the real thing, because we will never have experienced that. The closest match might be a human being, or an animal, or a robot seen in a film. Precisely what it is matters less than the fact that something 'alien' has been seen.

The 'mind store' is crucial for determining the *format* of what we see (be it something quite mundane or totally alien), but it does not make the thing exist in the first place. Only a trigger signal in the brain or mind can provoke a selection from the store, and something must have set that procedure into motion. It might be a real, external perception or it might be information at a consciousness level. We think of the former as objective and the latter subjective, substituting real and unreal into this sentence. But a consciousness event is as real to the brain as a sensory experience from the external world, just a different kind of reality.

Richard Gregory said another wise thing: 'All perceiving requires some guessing.' He shows this by asking you to think of two tins of equal weight but different sizes. The bigger of the two *feels* lighter than the smaller. This seems contrary to expectations but is due to the content of our 'mind store'. The past experience in here teaches us to expect the bigger tin to weigh more, so we set our muscles in anticipation of this. The process is subconscious, but when we pick it up, we have over-reacted and the tin feels surprisingly light. Knowing the 'truth' about the weights of the can will make no difference. In our mind we accept the reality, but our brain is tied down by programmed reactions it cannot escape. We have to live in schizophrenia, with two realities: the reality of mind, which knows the truth intuitively, and the reality of the brain, which *is* the illusion.[3]

When a scientist tells you that something is not real and is only in your mind, remember this example. Reality can be in the mind, whilst the 'truth' is an illusion.

An *illusion* occurs when the perception is distorted on the way to the brain, or a mismatch follows in the 'mind store'. A *hallucination* is quite different. Here there is no external object to provoke a sensory response. There is instead an internal message from consciousness which reaches the 'mind store' and is clothed in symbols, translating the message into sensory images. The word 'internal' is the key. In all other respects both processes are the same. (See Figure 11.)

'Hallucination and illusion can seem equally true, because reality is what the brain creates within itself,' said brain-researcher Anthony Smith in 1984. Less recently the philosopher Bertrand Russell made a similar point when he

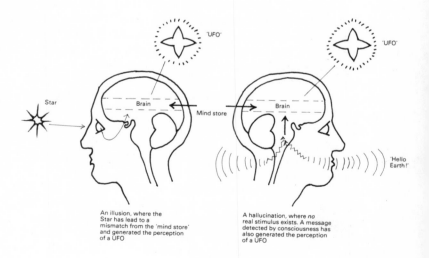

An illusion, where the Star has lead to a mismatch from the 'mind store' and generated the perception of a UFO

A hallucination, where *no* real stimulus exists. A message detected by consciousness has also generated the perception of a UFO

Fig. 11: The difference between illusion and hallucination.

argued that real objects 'must be an inference' because we only ever see perceptions in our brain.

Naturally, this does not mean that we should invest every hallucination with reality. The wanderings of a mind sodden with LSD or a mentally disturbed patient who sees snakes beneath his bed are clearly very different from what we are discussing. In some cases there may be a physical malfunction in the brain which makes it trigger neurons without external cause. Chemicals can do the same. However, even in these cases the hallucinations will be chosen from the 'mind store' to represent a message within the subconscious. The meaning of the message may be personal and obscure, but the process is the same with hallucinations generated during psi-events, the difference being that in these cases *meaningful* information is transmitted. The message was purposeful, the translation into images from the 'mind store' was at least partially successful.

The gap between the ramblings of a hallucinating schizophrenic and the claims of a witness to a psi-event is not that great. They work in identical ways, but even though the effects may be similar, the reason why they happen is quite different. This reason may be the only way to distinguish what is meaningless and what is meaningful hallucination.

It is hard for the person who faces a psi-event to accept that its existence was in the form of a hallucination. Our language is so constructed that uttering such a statement makes it appear that we are doubting their sanity. The same difficulty dominates this book explaining why these things are hard to write about and may not be easy for you to follow. We paint the world in black and white, insisting on fixed divisions between what is real and imaginary, but there are no fixed divisions, and if we have to make a choice it must be that imagination is superior to reality. Imagination creates reality. There is no way to escape that. Until we learn to give the hallucination its due, we shall continue to misunderstand something terribly important about the universe. Some mediums can live with this knowledge, although many cannot and insist that their 'spirit guides' *must* be real. Clearly they are not, or you and I would see them. They *are* hallucinations, but they may be more than *meaningless* hallucinations.

Eileen Garrett received a very perceptive answer when she put this big question to her guides. (See quote at chapter head.) Rosalind Heywood, another medium we have met before, knew the truth as well. She tells how in 1918 she was on a visit to the Aegean whilst the love of her life remained in Paris. Yet one night she 'saw' him in her tent, and at the same moment (they later discovered) he 'saw' her in his Paris rooms. Neither of them perceived the other as a 'ghost', but then ghosts are never transparent, as they are in cheap movies. They look like ordinary people, because they are hallucinated perceptions of ordinary people.

Rosalind Heywood made some honest remarks about her 'vision'. 'There is no evidence, of course, that I was there. A more plausible explanation is that both his hallucination and mine were self-created. But why did we create them? Was it merely frustration, or was this the only way that our conscious minds could be told of subconscious telepathic interaction between us?'[4]

As you might expect, I endorse every word of that. Both 'ghosts' were products of the two people's 'mind stores', responding to a message which their minds shared at the level of consciousness. The message was simply a desire to be together, and this was achieved by pulling out the partners' visual image from the store and projecting it as a hallucination onto their view of the world. It is no coincidence that this 'shared hallucination' occurred at night when there was little sensory input coming into the brain. The mind had less trouble inducing the Oz Factor than it would if either partner had been standing in the middle of Piccadilly Circus at Rush Hour – which is why psi-events tend not to happen in situations like that but *do* often strike suddenly in bed during the 'wee small hours'.

Dr Vernon Harrison, a noted psychic researcher and professional photographic expert, has bemoaned the lack of photos of ghosts. He and I studied the meagre collection which ASSAP have been sent during their work investigating psi-events. There are shots of ectoplasm which turns out to be a camera strap caught in the field of view, cowled monks that are damp on the wall, eerie spectres that are real people reflected in plate-glass windows, and phantoms built by chance coincidence from light and shade or dust and grime in all sorts of situations. We have yet to find a single one that stands up.[5]

UFO researchers tell the same sad story. There are a few interesting pictures of blobs of light that may be anomalous atmospheric phenomena, but there are no aliens posing for inter-galactic tourist albums, and no shots of strange craft sitting on the ground. There are also many hundreds of stars, weather balloons, specks of dirt in the camera lens, and film or developing faults that look suspiciously like a UFO after the event (although, of course, nothing was seen when the photograph was taken).[6]

The dismal lack of both these things is serious indeed, if you are a believer in the absolute reality of spaceships or spooks. But it is not important (indeed it is predictable) if one accepts, as I must, that these things are *not* objective phenomena. They are psi-events in the guise of hallucinations, and you cannot film hallucinations.

There are cases of mistaken identity, where the reported psi-event turns out to be an illusion. The ghost that is a result of random patches of light through the trees is one example. The spacecraft that is a re-entering Russian booster rocket is another.[7] These are a different kettle of fish from the true psi-event, when there is *nothing* external present. Psi-events are produced *in* the mind (as all things are) but catalysed *by* the mind (as 'real' things are not). But to claim that something is not 'real' and so cannot exist, fails as a valid argument.

We all have regular experiences of realistic hallucinations, which are powerful enough to make us believe they are true. For a few hours every night we live in a world invented by our minds. In fact, we spend so long in this land of illusion that it is hard to explain why we call it 'unreal' but have no doubts about the status of other places.

It comes as a shock to learn that most of us spend seven or eight times as long being residents of the dream academy than we spend in every classroom of every school or college we ever attend. Yet we grow up to believe that what teacher tells us must be important to our whole well-being, whereas the content of our dreams is all stuff and nonsense.

As it happens, there is no evidence that nature would arrange to give so much time to hallucinations unless they were equally important. Indeed, they might well be far more important than 'real' life.

I am no longer shocked by how the world works, but sometimes demonstrations can be numbing. The very day I had begun this section of the book, circumstances conspired to give me a chilling illustration of that point. You may find what follows extremely 'convenient' – that is your privilege – but I promise that I tell only what happened.

On 28 November 1983 I stood awestruck at Cape Canaveral, Florida, as the US Space Shuttle *Columbia* rode into the sky atop a trail of orange flame. This was the fulfilment of an ambition for me, not only to visit the Cape but to see a real launch close at hand. I had been even more fortunate, because earlier a colleague and friend, space scientist Dr J. Allen Hynek, had arranged for us to dine with one of the astronauts from the NASA team. He was not aboard the mission which flew successfully into orbit that mild winter day, but we had talked of his future voyages and listened to some of the plans NASA had for putting a civilian into space. Delays forced the programme back, but when these plans were later made public, I remembered my promise to try to get back for the launch.

I had been in the USA researching a book on UFOs, with a colleague who was a co-author.[8] Eleven months after my return to Britain, the book appeared and did in fact briefly mention this meeting, in the context of NASA involvement with the UFO case. The adjacent chapter in which I developed the theme had the ironic title (which I chose) 'Houston – we have a problem!' On 23 October 1984, two days before the book was published, I travelled by train to Wolverhampton to do a promotional interview with Beacon Radio. I was in a deeply depressed mood because of a terrible dream I had suffered the night before. It was one of my worst nightmares and was notable because of its intense emotions of terror and sadness. Even when I was wide awake, the aftertaste clung to me.

I know it was a dream, but it was one of those power-soaked visions we get from time to time that can destroy you until you force yourself to believe it was *just* a dream. It had been about the space shuttle, something I had no obvious reason to be thinking about at the time. I saw it rise from its tower in a perfect launch, just as I had really seen the year before. Then it exploded into a massive ball of fire. The picture which remained vivid afterwards was a weirdly frozen tableau as the cloud of burning debris spread out from the disaster.

My thoughts in the dream had been of the astronaut I had met the previous year. When I awoke, I had the dreadful feeling that I had just seen his death in a mission yet to come. I do not remember if I told anybody about the experience – possibly not, as I left so early that day, but I did write the dream into my diary, something I now have the habit of doing when a dream is particularly unusual. The words give some evidence that I am not making this up. They say starkly, 'Dream about shuttle exploding on take off. Feelings of absolute terror. Saw tank rupture and blow apart. Felt horrible.' It does little justice to the force of the nightmare, but the third sentence is especially interesting.

Some hours later I had pushed this memory aside and was approaching Wolverhampton on the train, planning what to say in the interview. Suddenly ahead was a pall of smoke rising into the air from an apparent explosion. I looked in bafflement and then concern as the train slowed to a halt. It was some time before we moved again, to inch past a scene of devastation. Right beside the track there had been an explosion and fire in a chemical tank at some large plant. Fire-engines, police vehicles and pandemonium were still in evidence as we went by. It was only when I got to the radio station that I learned the situation. On-the-spot reports were being given from the plant, describing the tank which had ruptured and then blow up.

Of course, it did occur to me that this was the fulfilment of my dream. Indeed, 'What about dream?' I asked (a bit enigmatically) in my diary the next day. I have had a few dream premonitions before (including one of an air crash twenty years ago), but this dream had been unusually vivid and full of emotion. Whilst it came close, it was not a particularly good premonition. (My aircrash dream had been far better, set in Stockport where I have never lived, and preceding by just a few days the only time an aircraft has ever crashed onto that town.)

My best guess was that my sleeping mind had picked up a message about the plant explosion. It was obviously important because I have never before come that close to such a major disaster. Since the message had to be illustrated in some way, perhaps the Shuttle take-off was used to illustrate a huge tank filled with chemicals which could explode when ruptured. This *is* what the Shuttle is when it lifts off. Since I was travelling to an interview about a book which mentioned Shuttle flights (and the book was what I was thinking about at the time of the real explosion), it was easy to see how the images might have got confused.

This is the kind of dream interpretation that psychologists like Jung might appreciate. But it remains vaguely dissatisfying, which may be why I never made a fuss over it, even though I have sometimes written magazine articles about previous dream premonitions.

Fifteen months later, on 28 January 1986, I was locked in my room deeply engrossed in this chapter and about to set off discussing dreams and premonitions. I know it must sound ridiculously melodramatic to say I had just written the words that appear immediately before 'I am no longer shocked ...', but I had. Not a single addition was made to this chapter.

Into my room burst my mother saying, 'The Shuttle has exploded on take-off!' I stopped work immediately to watch the horror unfold live before the TV cameras. Like everyone else I sat feeling helpless as the film was repeated on the screen again and again. I needed to see it less than most. It was too much like my dream from October 1984.

Just as in my dream, my sole concern for the next few hours was the safety of 'my' astronaut. I knew he had a mission scheduled, but with all the changes to flight timings I had lost track of when he was to soar into space again. Shuttle journeys were now so routine that no newspaper that morning had carried the names of the seven crew. It was some while before I learned to my relief that he had not been aboard. He was safe.

My dream had not been an accurate foresight of the explosion as it happened. It had closely prescribed the emotions I shared after the event and my fears for the safety of the astronaut I knew. The scene in my dream (of a fuel tank rupturing and exploding into an expanding mass of flames) *was* exactly what occurred, but the picture I have etched in my mind differs from the TV images which are now also etched. They are horribly similar, but not identical. Presumably my dream was a *personal* drama using things from my 'mind store', expressing the 'message' about the shuttle explosion.

Why did I have this dream? The answer to that question is

something we would all like to know, because premonitions are such an emotive subject. It may be relevant that the flight of *Challenger* on 28 January 1986 *was* the first to carry a civilian (teacher Christa McAuliffe), just as I had discussed in the preview with the NASA astronaut.

Why did I have the dream fifteen months early? I can only think that the coincidental chemical plant explosion was the trigger. Maybe the two events got mixed up in my mind. Perhaps the dream was an attempt to warn me about both coming disasters. Who can say? But I will never forget this terrible experience.

If my idea makes sense, dream and hallucination will be almost identical. Dreams are, if you like, hallucinations that occur when you happen to be asleep. Both make movies by shuffling images from the 'mind store', with the script originating in a message detected subconsciously. Sometimes the message is about the day just gone, internal psychological problems working out. However, there is plenty of evidence that messages can also come from far away in time and space. This may mean Cape Canaveral, or both the future and the distant past. When they are mixed together, using appropriate images from the 'mind store', the result is a seemingly confusing vision, but cut through the candy floss that surrounds the dream and you may find within it something extraordinary.

The content of a vision (be it dream or hallucination) is built out of replays of things already in the 'mind store'. All have been placed there by the five ordinary senses. The devastating sorrows are *real* feelings we have once felt. The visual pictures are *real* sights we once have seen. And so on. It matters not whether the dream is about something inconsequential or vitally important, the future or the past. We never *view* the future, only a probability of that future constructed out of images from our past.

These ideas are totally consistent with scientific thinking about the brain and the mind. Indeed, most dream-researchers use a similar hypothesis to describe what goes on inside our head. There is only one major difference: my willingness to accept the mind's ability to travel in time. This is outlawed by science.

There *are* scientific arguments about the possibility, which I will mention later, but often it takes personal experience of a dream premonition to persuade yourself. A lot of people have had such proof. An awful lot more have forgotten they have had it. But once you go through several precognitive dreams, doubts about what is possible no longer seem relevant. There can be no meaningful objections to mental time-travel, whatever clever theories scientists come up with, and no objections, because the mind *must* time-travel. Psi-events do it, and psi-events are formed in the mind.[9]

If you need a bit of help over this crucial difficulty, consider a few words from two people who have already supported my thesis. The physicist Albert Einstein said, 'The distinction between past, present and future is an illusion; although a rather persistent one.' And another great scientist, Ernest Schroedinger, added, 'The barrier between them [past, present and future] cannot be said to have broken down; this barrier does not exist.' These are not carefully selected examples. Scientists live in two universes: one where they *know* the truth about time, and another (which they call the 'real' world) where they pretend that they do not.[10] So pardon me if I continue looking at what happens to people in this 'real' world, without worrying too much about scientists who tell me these things cannot happen.

F.H. Whiting of Avon described an experience in a letter. Several months after his wife died (September 1981) he was sitting looking at the floor 'daydreaming' when he realized that somebody was standing in front of him. 'I looked up,' he says. 'It was my wife, absolutely perfect ... she walked round to the left of me and placed her hand on my shoulder, which I felt. She then kissed me on the forehead, which I also felt.' She had been wearing 'one of her wigs' and a black skirt and blouse. An after-life that requires one to wear a wig seems odd to me; much easier to accept is the thought that Mr Whiting produced the psi-vision of his wife from images in his 'mind store'. But why was it re-created? Was some aspect of his wife's consciousness communicating with his mind? That is the only real survival option left.

The 'ghost' in this case disappeared quite unusually. It went 'into one big matrix made up of pieces which were oscillating. There seemed to be three sizes, the small ones gradually faded away, then the larger ones and finally the very big ones. This was not hurried ...'[11]

In this case there is little doubt that the image of his wife was in the *mind* of the witness. The only question left is *why* it happened. Psychologists would prefer a human reason (Mr Whiting was missing his wife, and so on). However, rarely is there much evidence for such a view. But does that mean that we should accept a disembodied mind communicating months after death? It is an exciting concept, and there are few who would not yearn to believe in it, but whilst it *might* be true, the thought is so extraordinary (even in terms of psi-events) that we must require extraordinary evidence to prove it. This case and most like it are tantalizing but not proof.

A girl from Hereford remembers a time when she was waiting for her mother in a country village. In her letter she describes the strange clothes of an elderly lady watering a line of geraniums on a wall. She wore an old-fashioned crinoline skirt and had a bonnet on her head. A fancy dress costume? We might think that if it happened to us, and give it little more than mild interest. But next day, at the same spot, there was not only no woman but no geraniums. The scene was quite different. It is as if not just the old lady but the background scenery as well had been snatched right out of the past.

Post-mortem lives for geraniums and bricks make even less sense than spectral wigs. Again we suspect a psi-vision in the mind of the girl. She was waiting for her mother and idling time away, just as Mr Whiting was daydreaming: this seems to be a clue, not unlike the Oz Factor (which is an *imposed* sensory deprivation). In these cases the witnesses were paying little attention to the world 'outside' and so (perhaps unknowingly) were open to receive messages from the world within. When we are asleep and dreaming, we have reached the ultimate of this inward tuning, which is why dreams are important to any seeker after psi-events.

Why did this girl in Hereford have the experience when thousands of other residents did not? Presumably she was in the right place at the right time and in the right state of consciousness. It is also worth noting that children seem more prone to psi-events than adults. Often we wave them away as 'imagination' – that marvellous word we can use to sneak out the back door and avoid explanations. There are scientists concerned about such matters. They feel that we *force* our world-view onto young children, insisting that the universe is divided into things that are real and things that are not. If that world-view should be wrong, as there are at least major grounds for suggesting, our whole education system and our entire culture are founded on a mistake.

Dr Fritjof Capra is one such scientist, a brave physicist who published an extraordinary book in 1975 and generated a tidal wave of unease amongst his peers. He argued that science as it stands in the last third of this century has grown ever closer to mysticism and religion. The Earth is not a clockwork toy with our mechanical brains its cogs and wheels. It is far more like a living, inter-dependent organism. We cannot separate man from mind, one mind from another, or the human race from the consciousness of Earth. Fantastic as such claims may sound, Capra has prompted a sea-change in society. Swept along by new-age beliefs (some silly, others profound), there is a movement to revolutionize the world.[12] Let us hope that the revolution is not too late.

In the last couple of psi-events the message that generated visual hallucinations seems to have come from the place where the witness was located. But mind is unfettered by space. Remember Rosalind Heywood and her lover, separated by hundreds of miles but joined by consciousness. It is necessary to adopt this view in cases like the one reported to me by Stella Bennett from West Kirby, Merseyside.

It was June 1965 and she was busying herself in the kitchen. Her husband had gone to work, by way of the Mersey Tunnel linking Birkenhead with Liverpool. Suddenly through the window and out in the garden (the trigger of 'tunnel vision' again involved), Stella saw a scene as if projected into her shrubbery. In the vision were her husband and his car, which had broken down. It was being towed from out of the tunnel, and he was facing a hefty fine for causing such a hindrance. She had no doubt this was something happening *right then*, several miles away from where she stood.

That evening Mr Bennett came home and said nothing. He was keeping the news of this minor upset from Stella. So *she* told *him* all about it! At first he assumed that she had followed him in another car, but this was only one of several psi-visions that his wife has experienced, so in time it became a part of family folklore.[13]

We might guess that the man's decision not to tell his wife had not been shared by his subconscious mind. It had overcome the situation by using Stella's visionary abilities and the state of consciousness she was in at the time. The message had got through and was dramatized from her 'mind store'. It ended up 'in the garden', simply because that was where she was looking at the time.

We have used the term 'psi-vision' over the last few pages to describe a particular sensory anomaly. There is now a clear pattern that we can develop from sense to sense, giving a classification scheme for psi-events.

All psi-events are sensory hallucinations generated as responses to a message by the mind. The simplest way this message might come through would be at the *emotional* level. Emotion seems to dominate everything. The information content of the message would then combine with emotions selected from the 'mind store' to create a feeling that something is wrong, a sense of dis-ease or a gut reaction. We might call this first type the psi-emotion.

Of course, there are a few anomalies of the sense of touch, taste and smell. These can be the essence of a psi-event. But instead of losing ourselves among too many names, only two other psi-events are of major importance. The next stage up would be the replay of sounds, or the simulation of the 'warning voice'. Again these are produced just like the psi-emotion but are more immediately captivating. We can call these things psi-audios.

In the case of the Mersey tunnel, a psi-emotion would have involved Mrs Bennett's *feeling* that something had gone wrong. If she had heard her husband's voice, it would have been a psi-audio, but the experience as reported was the ultimate sensory anomaly, a psi-vision.

These three things seem very different at first sight: a bad vibe, the warning voice and a fully fledged apparition. I do not think they are different at all, just varying degrees of the same process involving our senses.

Already it can be seen that space is no obstacle to these psi-events. Let us look again at the question of time.

In July 1980 Charlotte Richards was in the kitchen of her Tacoma, Washington, home. She was at the sink washing dishes, with her thoughts wandering. Immediately we see two very consistent clues: the internal focusing of the witness's mind, and the window above the sink creating a 'tunnel' effect.

Beyond this frosted window was the garden. It was a warm evening and she could hear the sounds of her husband mowing the lawn. Suddenly this typical suburban scene changed. A mood of depression swept across Charlotte, although she did not know why. She was experiencing a psi-emotion. Such was the intensity that she closed her eyes for a moment. During this time she 'saw' masses of blood and a hospital room. Of course, she was hallucinating this. The images were being taken from her 'mind store'. But she did not know this at the time. Nor did she realize that the act of closing her eyes had allowed the psi-event to step up a gear and turn from a psi-emotion into a psi-vision.

Nevertheless, in the quick-fire way our brain can process data, she soon *knew* that these experiences were a premonition. On the surface she had the rational thought that her husband was about to have a disaster with the mower, and her instinct was to shout out a warning. However, she felt this consciously. Subconsciously, her right cerebral hemisphere (which dictates these things) had a very different plan in mind.

Just like my friend on the motorway, swerving suicidally out of lane, Charlotte did *not* yell a warning. Instead she actually jumped back *away* from the window, entirely the opposite reaction to what she would have done had the conscious self been in control. It was fortunate that rationality was not in command. Seconds later, by a million-to-one fluke, the mower blade caught a rock and threw it into the air. It crashed through the kitchen window, sending splinters of sharp glass cascading over the sink. Had Charlotte remained where she was standing, these visions of blood would have become horribly real.[14]

This simple case is rich with material for us to work on. We see how the primary event was emotional. This got through quickly and easily, and even afterwards the psi-emotion was the thing best remembered by Charlotte Richards, just as we best remember the emotions of a nightmare. However, the feeling of depression was not enough to act as a warning. Possibly, in the seconds that followed, a psi-audio ('warning voice') might have got through. As it happened, the brief closing of her eyes (possibly a motion triggered by her subconscious) allowed a psi-vision to impress itself upon her. The pictures of blood and gore were *not* premonitions. They were graphic symbols plucked from her 'mind store' to sum up the essence of the message. This did the trick and made her step back. Thus the psi-event succeeded. But it may have been a close-run thing. If it had failed and Charlotte had been injured, do you think she would later recall her feelings before the accident? The terror of the moment would provide too many conflicting emotional memories to make it likely.

You can perhaps see why the Oz Factor is sometimes essential. It is a kind of last resort by the mind, forcing the person to pay attention to the message. It does this by switching off sensory input from the world outside, so (for the duration of the psi-event) he has no choice but to see the dramatized consequence of the incoming message.

One of the first researchers into premonitions, J.W. Dunne, found from experiments with dreams that we all have psi-visions from time to time. He also concluded that the vision is concerned with our personal reaction to the event when it happens, rather than with the event itself. An example he gives concerns a volcanic eruption. He had a dream which foresaw this but in his dream a wrong figure was given for the number of deaths. When the incident actually happened and he read the Press reports, he made the genuine mistake of seeing the death toll as the number in his dream. In other words, his dream was a foresight of *his* involvement in the discovery of the tragedy, not a premonition of the disaster itself.

A lady from Portmadoc who wrote to me with her own premonitions had a similar experience. In a dream she saw a hearse pull up outside an aunt's house. She asked who had died and was told 'Mrs Jones, 5 Heoly Parc'. This was odd because her aunt lived at number 3, which she knew perfectly well. The dream was precognitive. Although my correspondent did not know it at the time, her aunt was critically ill with cancer and died a couple of days later. But the dream paradox was resolved only by the newspaper obituary printing the wrong address: 5 instead of 3 Heoly Parc.

I think these psi-events leave no doubt that premonition concerns our own future states of mind. It is not a detection of actual events. This may explain why there are so many seemingly trivial precognitions. With all the turmoil in the world, you might expect there to be more than enough plane crashes and bomb explosions to make meaningless psi-events redundant. But there has to be some sort of connection, probably emotional, if only in the way we react to the event.

This is why the murder of President Kennedy produced so many premonitions, and the Aberfan coal-tip tragedy. They were exceptionally emotive disasters and effected millions of people who had no connection with them. Their chance of producing psi-events was considerably better than normal.

For this reason I would make a definite prediction that my dream of the Space Shuttle tragedy was by no means the only one. A survey of NASA astronauts and workers might prove very interesting. It is already known that some had warned of problems with the rocket tanks and that a number of key NASA people had migrated away from the company in the days before the disaster.[15]

The need for a personal connection might also explain why my Shuttle dream was interwoven with my own close encounter with the chemical-plant explosion. It provided the otherwise missing link.

You might argue that since millions of people dream every night, by simple statistics a few must match with real events. What about the countless dreams that do not? We hear only of the spectacular successes. There is indeed some validity in this claim. But it should be recognized that premonitions tend to be forgotten, or not seen for what they are, and are rarely ever spoken about. The true number of successful dreams is therefore quite unknown. Also future dreamers stress the emotional nature of their experience. It is this which makes it vivid, different and beyond the mundane levels of chance.

So convinced am I that psi-visions can act as premonitions of major disasters that there is a real prospect of a computer-based system that could record emotive dreams, sift through them for common elements and make percentage probabilities of things to come. It is certainly possible that disasters might be averted. Charlotte Richards proved that in her own small way.

This unique marriage between 1980s technology and human consciousness is exciting but would be remarkably easy and cheap to implement. When you think of the potential results, I believe we all might ask why the computer is not already programmed and running.

8. Emotion: The Sixth Sense?

'I see no apparitions, hear no voices, merely pick
up the feelings and emotions of people who have
died violently or are in some form of distress.'

Letter to me dated 6 February 1986, from
a lad in Hampshire

We have covered the five known senses in the last few chapters.
Now we confront what might seem an intrusion. Emotions and
feelings are not senses, yet we have constantly been drawn to
their importance. They are the basis of all psi-events.

In fact, we use the word 'sensation' quite happily to describe
an emotion. And what is a sensation but a product of the
senses? Whilst on a strict interpretation of the rules we could not
count emotion as a sense, I wonder how strict we should be. Of
course, there is no organ of the body which produces emotional
input. Feelings are something that happen in the mind. They are
a response to sense perceptions. But in other regards they are
the first stage of the psi-event (remember the sequence
psi-emotion, psi-audio and psi-vision).

If there is a sixth sense, emotion is it. Whether you choose to
call it that, remains up to you, but we canot deny the existence
of our feelings. Nor, after what we have found, can we possibly
deny their primary importance.

Wherever we have looked, we have been routed firmly in the
direction of emotion. Remember the psychometrists 'reading'
emotions from objects, and the precognitive experiences which
are always more emotional than ordinary dreams or
hallucinations. The raw emotion is the first thing that cracks the
barriers of our defence. As Henri Bergson, a philosopher, once
said, 'Perhaps our senses are intended to keep things out, rather
than to let them in.' Once through, it becomes a psi-emotion. But

to be transformed into a higher-grade experience there has to be a translation process. That is where mistakes are made. That is why psi-visions are rarely one hundred per cent accurate but are often close enough to be dramatic. This translation takes only micro-seconds as the brain forms pictures or words, but these will always be distortions of the truth. Only emotion knows that.

A Justin Hayward song I often quote summarizes this perfectly. He suggests that you 'trust your feelings, it's easy now. Understand the voice within and feel the changes already beginning'.[1]

We all know how hard it is to describe the way we feel inside. How do you put depression or elation into words? There are analogies that can be used. Depression is a deep well in which you sit, trapped forever on your own. Elation is like soaring high in some mystical flight way above the world, seeing all its glories. They are the best we can do, but you see their restrictions. They demonstrate the limits of our translation process.

Words are left-brain functions. Emotions belong to the psychic world of our right cerebral hemisphere.

With ghosts you can also notice the problem. There are sad ghosts, mournful ones, revengeful spirits, lovers who died in tragic circumstances. The common denominator is always emotion. Ghosts never seem to be ordinary people who died in ordinary ways. Have you ever wondered why? It is probably because the essence of all ghosts is a mood. They are an emotional message felt in our mind. Their 'real world' existence is just a hallucination, and all hallucinations stem from emotion.

Premonitions are no different. My own dream of the Space Shuttle catastrophe made me ill and withdrawn for a couple of days. When the dream became reality, the emotions were reproduced. We foresee death and disaster far better than success, because painful emotions seem to create the most powerful impact.

Even in paranormal phenomena where there is no expected emotional pattern, the rule does not break down. UFO witnesses frequently speak of being emotionally drained after an encounter – feeling 'sad' that their 'friends' have gone is one common way of phrasing it. Psychokinesis (PK) – where the mind seems able to move physical objects, is still debated and little understood, but one thing we do know is that it often occurs when witnesses have bottled-up emotions. The PK releases them as a sort of emotional tantrum.[2]

There are no reasonable grounds for doubt. Emotion is the missing link. All psi-events are just sensory translations of an emotional message picked up and decoded in the mind.

Latest research by brain physiologists seeking the home of memory suggests that we tag information with feelings as an aid to recovery. We first recall the feeling, then search for the memory which relates to that feeling. Gordon Rattray-Taylor provides an excellent summary of this work and points to a common experience that illustrates it. We have all known that frustrating feeling of being aware there is something to be remembered, although we do not remember precisely what. The emotional tag of the memory is the first thing through the barriers.[3]

Nostalgia is a curious thing too. Science takes little notice because it is 'just' an emotion, but we all regularly feel it. It seems to be a kind of distillation of all the tagging emotions associated with a past time or place. We use the term 'bitter-sweet' to describe nostalgia, and that is appropriate. We do not recall more than a fraction of the experiences, or attendant emotions, which constitute our sum perception of the past. There are good ones and there are bad ones. The end result in essence is a blended mixture, which is just another example of the primary significance of feeling.

As the lady from Hampshire (quoted on page 134) serves to show us, the psi-emotion is very common. If we all trusted our feelings, there would be benefits. Psi-audio and psi-vision are the events which bring media headlines and appear strange and paranormal, but they are second- and third-stage psi-events, less widespread than the psi-emotion which happens to all of us. We live in a world where we are taught to 'think straight'. Science argues we should make decisions on the basis of logic and deduction. There is no doubt of the value this can bring. But it is time we also learned to 'feel straight'. We are walking round with one eye closed, missing out on so much.

It can work. I proved it to myself. I had been out shopping and collected an official form to fill in. Living in Wallasey, as I had for more than two years, I knew the name of my current doctor and the one I had used before that. But the name of the one I needed for this form, who had been my GP five years previously, had gone right out of my head.

Then I told myself to trust my feelings. So I closed my eyes and walked across the road (a rather dangerous thing to do!). Fortunately I did not find myself underneath a truck but at the front door of the Poulton district library. I felt absolutely that this was the right thing to do and was determined not to question my moves. I had no books or tickets with me and no reason to be visiting the place, but I walked in and went up to the counter, with embarrassment not registering yet.

One book lay flat on the counter with the author's name prominently displayed. The name was 'Pattinson', and instantly I remembered that my doctor's name was 'Pattiniot'. I left the library with a smile beaming all over my face. Who needs magic tricks when we have subconscious minds?

Of course you will tell me this was just a coincidence, but you did not share the feelings I had as this two-minute experiment was underway. I have never done anything like it before or since, but as it was happening I knew without a second's hesitation that the answer could be found if I followed my instincts.

Henri Bergson said that the senses are designed to keep things out. There is a truth in this which psychologists have come to realize. Remember cryptomnesia? There is no way we can consciously retain everything on display. But the subconscious seems to have conjuring tricks and magic spells that can invoke the memories of absolutely anything.

Dr Lyall Watson described a time when under hypnosis he was able to relive his childhood journey to school. So accurate was his action replay that he counted all the lamp-posts, then checked to find he was correct. He had never really counted all the posts on the way to school, but the information was in his mind, so he could do it years later.[4]

Nor do you need to induce hypnosis to prove the point. If I ask you how many windows there are in your house, the chances are you will have no idea. It is unlikely you have ever counted them. But most of us can find the answer without moving an inch. In our 'mind store' there are pictures of each room. All we need do is flip through them, as if browsing through a store catalogue, and count up the windows as we go. Aside from showing that questions can be answered more easily if we use mind instead of logic, this little exercise also proves that the 'mind store' is no invention. You must have one or you could not have done this test!

It does seem that there is a facet of our mind that determines which data to allow into consciousness and which to keep out of reach (unless you ever need it). Survival factors are probably what programme this behaviour, which might (or might not) be genetically encoded.

For example, it would doubtless be decreed important that your conscious self should be fully aware of the car careering down the road and heading straight towards you, but the registration number on the front is likely to be something excluded by this process. If you leap out of the way, the memory of the near-miss will be retained, but this will not include the details debarred from entry into awareness. However, either they have been recorded in some separate file, or the mind has an access route to find them later, because in circumstances just like this, when the police have successfully hypnotized witnesses, they *have* then come up with the registration number and other information they did not know they could recall.

Retaining, or accessing, literally everything seems like science-fantasy, but when you remember that the number of neuron connections outstrips the atoms in the universe, it begins to look somewhat less fantastic.

We need a name for this part of the mind which makes the decisions. Some researchers call it the censor. I prefer the term 'doorman' because censorship carries misleading connotations about sexual motives, and 'doorman' better describes the flexible approach this process seems to show. Things are turned away or let through according to its choice.

The doorman is not some alien life-form or spirit guide. It is a part of ourselves, a mental procedure. It may be a higher level of consciousness. We have a tendency to adopt an external origin for aspects of our mind that seem to be superior. This is why mediums believe that the messages they produce are really conversations with the dead. As Colin Wilson puts it, 'An experience that comes from a higher state of consciousness seems to come from outside rather than within.'[5]

This doorman effect is the filter which chooses the sensory information which requires priority tags and should be routed into conscious awareness. But it is also the process which filters the emotional messages from our 'sixth' sense, those which form the basis of all psi-events.

This question of priority tags is central to the issue. It does seem that for most of us much of the time the doorman considers sensory input from the world outside more important than emotional messages from our field of consciousness. The information offered by our eyes and ears and other senses is the raw data that we use to survive in this world. However, even amid all this some emotional messages are allowed in. When you look at a new-born baby, you do not only register the sight of it: you *feel* it too.

This situation, where sensory input dominates, is what I call 'normal reality mode'. Because we exist in the world of objects, its laws are what are important to us. Rationality and science have driven us increasingly into normal reality mode. It is now much harder for us to escape.

But at night we do escape. Now the senses are channelling very little input, and the doorman can afford to let through more of those messages from consciousness. We are in a world of subjective images where emotions are king. The laws are different here. Time and space seem to disappear. Things happen in a dream-like and coincidental way. This is what I call 'synchronistic reality mode'.

Two sides of a great divide: normal reality and synchronistic reality modes. We all spend part of our lives living in each, so it is foolish to regard one as real and the other imaginary, or one important and the other entertainment to while away the night.

Psi-events occur when emotional messages with a high enough priority tag reach the doorman. It will then allow these through into awareness, either as rudimentary psi-emotions or (when the 'mind store' is used to generate sounds and pictures) as much more dramatic psi-audios or psi-visions.

Of course, there has to be more to it than this or we would *always* get a warning of an imminent catastrophe, and this is clearly not the case. But it happens far more often than we realize. We just fail to recognize the psi-emotion for what it is.

William Cox proved this in a dramatic experiment some years

ago. He collated American passenger-train accidents for several years from 1950 onwards and compared the number who had travelled on trains which crashed with that of passengers on the six preceding days and also the four weeks before the accident. The results were clear-cut. Fewer people always travelled on trains that crashed, whatever the weather or the time of year.[6]

It would be fascinating to do this test again, perhaps with plane crashes. But it appears to be demonstrated that there *is* a tendency for people to stay away from danger situations, even if when asked few would believe they had premonitions. They might not *consciously* realize why they stayed away.[7]

We are rooted in normal reality mode. Feelings and hunches are easily dismissed as irrelevant, even if we act upon them unconsciously. We also listen very inattentively to that 'little voice' inside, which often leaves the doorman with no choice but to force a change of consciousness to ensure we get the message. So it will make use of sleep or other occasions when we are receiving less external sensory input. UFOs are seen by witnesses driving lonely routes through open countryside, not on busy motorways. Ghosts appear as we lie in our bedroom, not at the local discothèque. These things can hardly be yet more coincidences.

When there is no other way, the doorman can perform an emergency override and block out some of the sensory information coming from outside. This forces the individual to attend to the message and manifests in our experience as the Oz Factor.

Let us take a look at some examples in action, as the best way to show what I mean.

'The house worried me right from the beginning,' says Elizabeth Dempster of a very old building in Highgate, London. She entered it many years ago and felt sensitive to its atmosphere. After living there a while, she tried to combat its sombre mood by painting it in bright colours. 'I felt that was what the house wanted,' she explains, yet the house continued to ooze a 'horrible feeling'. One night she awoke to find a woman at the bottom of the bed. The woman wore her hair in a bun, and her expression was 'utterly sad, almost without hope'. The psi-vision vanished in the corner of the room, leaving her only concerned about how she might help.

Elizabeth Dempster reported this to a national newspaper as a ghost, still searching for solace. She explained that after the events she had learned the background to the house. It had been owned by an Italian literary lady and a man who died suddenly and left her in a terrible state. She spent weeks on end locked in the room in total despair until, not long after her husband's death, she too succumbed.

How do we interpret the incident? It seems that, as soon as she entered the house, Elizabeth's doorman became aware of the emotional message. There must be reasons why Elizabeth Dempster was so in tune with this long-dead woman who once owned the building. Perhaps they were kindred spirits. But it was a very low-level detection and never rose above the psi-emotion stage. Presumably the doorman considered that enough under the circumstances. However, possibly because the matter had begun to effect her life, the doorman ultimately took advantage of a time when the witness was awake, but *not* bombarded by sensory input, and upped the psi-emotion into a psi-vision. The ghost was created from her 'mind store', but the message was real. It explained the emotions to her conscious mind and somehow enabled her to cope with the sadness. This may *seem* meaningless but it served a real purpose deep down.[8]

On 8 February 1971 Jane O'Leary of Los Angeles was at a very low emotional ebb, ill with flu. In this state she had a psi-vision as little more than a flash. It was a newspaper headline reading, 'Los Angeles Hit By Devastating Earthquake'. She fell asleep after this, worried about the prospect of some heavy bookcases by the side of the bed collapsing on top of her. At 5.55 a.m. she awoke. Ordinarily she then listened to the six o'clock news on the radio, but for once she just got up without thinking. Moments later an earthquake *did* strike, and the bookcase *did* topple over onto the bed where she had been. Had she been listening to the news broadcast, she would have been badly hurt.

The earthquake, whilst not minor, was hardly 'devastating'. It was typical of the sort that residents of the San Andreas Fault zone know only too well. There were no Press headlines exactly like the one she saw, but there was Press stories, of course.[9]

We can ask many questions here. Did Jane's weakened state make it easier for the message to get past the doorman? The newspaper image was clearly symbolic, extracted from things in her 'mind store'. The earthquake was even beefed up in status to try to boost the warning – although, had she stayed in bed, it certainly would have been personally 'devastating'. However, she did not act upon the psi-vision, and so the (seemingly unusual) step was taken of following this with psi-emotions.

The first of these, the intuition about the bookcases, probably created the worry as she fell asleep. To make doubly sure, the doorman, using her half-awake state, precipitated a second intuition, making her get out of bed 'for no reason'. No consciously obvious reason, but reason there most definitely was.

Renie Wiley is now a dab hand at this sort of thing. As daughter of the first woman to graduate from the Florida police academy, she has become a detective – but a most unusual one: she calls herself an 'empath' and has developed a technique for feeling how others feel. She then translates the emotions into visual flash pictures and uses them to solve crimes. She reckons this is no big deal: 'It's awareness, something we all have to varying degrees.'[10]

Of the stories about murder and psychic detection with which I could close this part of the book, I find one most revealing. It came long ago when she was still at school but knew even then that she had these abilities. To her it was something to cultivate, not stifle – a lesson for us all.

She 'saw' that her teacher's car had a flat tyre and so thought it wise to pass on this psychic intuition. The car, outside the school, did indeed have a puncture. But the teacher was not one who tolerated psi-events in her classroom. She accused Renie of knowing because she had flattened it! Before the girl could argue, she was marched off towards the principal's office. In this schoolgirl's crisis the doorman engineered a way out. It picked up some emotions from the principal and allowed Renie to empathize with him. These translated into visual pictures and she proceeded to tell him what she saw. She described the lady he had escorted to dinner the night before, which rather impressed her headmaster. It earned the girl an instant reprieve, although nobody is saying how much this was due to the brilliance of her performance or to her threat to repeat the tale to the principal's wife!

9. Beyond the Five Senses: Scientific Experiments

'We divide reality, forget we have divided it, and then forget that we have forgotten it.'
Ken Wilber, theoretical psychologist

We have now looked at all five human senses and wondered if emotion might constitute a sixth. The point is arguable, but emotion is undoubtedly a key. Along the way to this understanding we have also found disturbing things, not least of them the idea that *all* perception is at heart an illusion, occurring in the brain but using images from a 'mind store'. In this regard hallucination may be all that there is − a prospect few will care to dwell on.

It must be clear from what I have said so far, and indeed from my own experiences, that I am quite willing to believe in psi-events. However, personal acceptance is very different from scientific proof. And scientists are rather shy of the paranormal. Often their reasons are debatable. Sometimes they are right to beware. There is a great deal of nonsense spoken on these subjects, and everyone who makes speculations about the strangers in our psychic world must be willing to make fools of themselves. I am not immune. Every scientist knows that you must offer theories carefully and expect them to be sunk by experiment. Progress never happens by sitting on a fence. You must risk making an ass of yourself, because, for every dozen wild ideas, one becomes the truth.

So I declare my vested interest, but I do regard the need to test the paranormal as ever more vital. I want to see careful and controlled experiments, yet brave and imaginative ones. I am

willing to be persuaded if some of these work out, even in ways I
do not expect. I am also quite prepared to recognize the facts
when these experiments fail. Any psi-researcher who does not
will indeed be a fool.

If a natural solution seems better than one which is
supernatural, it is our duty to say so. But either way we need to
know, and we shall never know by continuing this silent,
artificial war. One camp argues there is no need for exploration
of ESP, because it quite evidently happens and that is that. The
other insists there can be no justification for researching
something which is plainly not there!

Spontaneous experience with psi-events is all very well and
often exciting, but it is no substitute for objective experiment.
That is how mankind discovers answers.

However, there is a problem here. If what we have learnt in
previous chapters reflects an approximation of that truth,
objective science is ill equipped to handle psi-events. Science is a
left-brain function, using logic, rationality and normal reality
mode. ESP is intuitive. It seems to have more in common with
the right cerebral hemisphere and emotion, images or
synchronistic reality.

Early experiments to seek out ESP always beached
themselves on this difficulty. For years it was believed that the
way to prove a sixth sense was to isolate somebody in a lab, get
them to 'guess' which playing-card was coming next and
compare the results with chance. Provided you did this a few
million times, the answers ought to be significant.

Zener cards were specially designed for this purpose, and an
American professor, J.B. Rhine, became the world expert at
using them. The cards offered five choices (cross, square, circle,
star and wavy lines), meaning that each time you made a 'guess'
there was a one-in-five chance of being correct. If 10,000 trials
are conducted, the laws of chance say that everyone should get
2,000 guesses right. Psychic researchers would do this
(repeatedly) and get wildly excited if you could bump this score
up to 2,100. But nobody ever got 5,000, let alone every guess
right, which left the idea that 2,100 was an 'incredible' result,
facing hordes of scientists who scoffed at such a suggestion.[1]

A few measly cards better than chance is a million miles away
from psi-events that predict disasters or create apparitions or

give warning of things that are happening on the far side of the Earth. No statistics claiming odds of billions-to-one can ever bridge that disturbing gulf.

This kind of research is on the wane, but it still pervades the thinking of establishment parapsychology, entrenched in the principles of traditional science. One-off stories prove nothing. Boring lab experiments might. The opening to the 1984 hit movie *Ghostbusters* illustrates this well. A university psychic research lab is obsessed with such methods and gets absolutely nowhere, so it loses the tiny grant awarded. In response the scientists set up their own group and go out solving public psychic manifestations, like ultra-modern rat-catchers. This was satire, of course. But there are lessons to be learnt. Scientific psi-research is ridiculously irrelevant to most people who undergo a psi-event.

Where laboratory work often fails should be easy to see. Real psi-events thrive on emotion, and there is precious little of that in guessing a few thousand playing cards. In fact, the results showed this boredom factor rather well. Guessing fell back to chance level, rapidly and progressively as the series of guesses continued. Subjects got fed up with the robotic process of choosing yet another card. Earlier results were more spectacular, but the nature of the experiment prevented their being of help. A hundred guesses was far too few for statistically valid results. Even if somebody got seventy-five guesses correct, the odds of that occurring by fluke are not extraordinary.

Years have been spent in this scientific dead-end. It is time we recognized once and for all that psi-research has to duplicate psi-events as we find them in real life. An experiment that lacks emotional involvement will never be up to much.

It is also surprising what already goes on in psychological research, beneath the noses of students of psi. Two Canadians, for example, conducted a study into the relationship between an objective (real-world) event and an internal one. Using two dozen subjects in the period between 10 November and 10 December 1980, they attempted to find a link between weather and emotional mood. Detailed scale questionnaires were filled out every day and compared with the meteorological data provided by the airport at Edmonton, Alberta.

There were definite patterns. Optimism, for instance, was

positively correlated with the amount of sunshine. Scepticism went the other way but also showed a tie in with temperature. The higher this was, the more sceptical people tended to be. Whilst these results are not too surprising, and we all feel intuitively better on pleasant days, they are nonetheless important, because they show that the two types of reality (matter and mind) *can* inter-relate, and that scientific testing of both is very easy.[2]

It is a small step from weather/mood relationships to a study of weather and the incidence of psi-events. Yet one is scientifically credible, the other little more than a joke. The former earns a respectable place in scientific journals; the latter must be sought among the adverts for astrological dating agencies. In such a place (a respectable one in fact, but who explains *that* to most scientists?) you will find Dr Scott Rogo's paper on precisely this. A conference of parapsychologists *had* produced evidence that changes in brain chemistry, precipitated by the weather, were relevant to an increase or decrease in psi-events.[3] But how many scientists read *Fate* magazine?

Frank Musgrove's study of blind people is another case in point.[4] Performed entirely in a non-psi manner, it threw up fascinating material because it studied real, emotional experiences instead of abstracts. Yet while this is happening, the learned parapsychologists have moved from Zener cards to their latest toy, computers that make the statistics look even better. If anything, this is *less* related to real life than the cross, circle and wavy line!

Two of Musgrove's patients show the nuggets of value to be found there. One, a man named Clark who had been blind for twenty years, noted how his sensitivity had increased: '[I get] a certain intuition. I notice some things more than other people ... [but] ... there is something else [to it].' One day he felt his head being stroked and a cold sensation: he had no idea that his brother was dying at precisely that moment. No conscious idea. Subconsciously things were apparently quite different.

There is also an amazing chap called Mills who had been blind for years, was diabetic and had suffered strokes, hepatitis, meningitis and other illnesses. He dispelled all this misery by insisting, 'I think you possibly gain more than you lose.' Why so? Because he can 'tell when my wife's been to see her mother and if there's been an upset, even before she gets to the house'.

The loss of one sense (especially the most important one of sight) allows people access to that hidden sensitivity, touching emotions and knowing intuitively. Being blind is rather like having a partial Oz Factor permanently in force. The reduction of input from the world outside affords an increase in attention to the messages within.

One of the great parapsychologists of this century is Professor Arthur Ellison, twice President of the Society for Psychical Research and an electronic engineer with extraordinary dedication. I had the privilege of working with him whilst writing early drafts of this book. His thoughts about our research bear much contemplation.

'Science is a process of making mental models that represent our experience,' he explained. It is not concerned with accepting messages from spiritual mediums as proven fact. What you must do is observe the facts that are real, make sure they happen by replicating them, set up a model (or hypothesis) and then make predictions based on this model. There ought to be new things not seen but expected. Their observation will be the key. If you *do* observe them, you develop your model into a fully fledged theory of explanation. If you do not, you revise the model and try again, and keep on trying until you find one that works.

A more concise description of what we are about could not be asked for. This is all I am endeavouring to do: set up a model for anyone to test. A successful model will work in the real world, not just in a psychic laboratory.

Ellison reminds us that, 'Good scientists don't talk about things they cannot test.' However, concepts such as magnetic fields remain good science whilst being just as abstract as our hypothetical field of consciousness. 'There is nothing more metaphysical than a magnetic field. Nobody has ever smelled, touched or seen one. It is a mental model, but a jolly useful one.' The existence of such a magnetic field developed out of experience with observed facts – facts that were very unpalatable to nineteenth-century physicists, because they flew in the face of old beliefs that nothing could move without a visible cause for that movement. Yet to their credit the scientists fought on. The facts replicated and they had to postulate crazy models.

To me there seems little difference between what physicists and

electrical engineers got up to a century ago and what serious
psi-researchers are doing right now. Our task is much harder
because the mass media have glorified psi into something it is
probably not. But all we can do is battle onward, hoping that
our work will pave the way towards the future. Perhaps in 2087
there will be no occultism, for its true ideas will have become
normal science. Its superstitions will have died, no doubt to be
replaced by new ones.

Professor Ellison sees a major difficulty in the fact that
psychic phenomena overlap. There is a tendency to believe that
clairvoyance, telepathy, precognition and so on are all different
things. As Ken Wilber says, we *do* divide reality, placing all
things into neat little foxholes of our own making. I trust that
you will now be suspicious of that practice. By approaching the
paranormal through our five senses, we have seen that there is
just one principle (psi), which manifests in a range of ways. All
these manifestations interweave. There is no real difference
between telepathy and precognition.

Whilst this might simplify our thinking about the psychic
world, it introduces new factors into research. How can you
exclude one area from another? Indeed, is it even wise to do so?

Arthur Ellison gives some good examples. A famous
researcher from some years back, Dr Soal, was very impressed
by Mrs Blanche-Cooper, a popular trance medium of the day.
The messages she offered him were supposedly fed by Soal's
dead brother, and the scientist says that if he had left it at that he
would have been quite impressed by their evidential content. But
instead he decided to test the model he was developing, so he
invented a fictitious Scotsman called James Ferguson and went
back to the medium. She proceeded with more reliable messages
but professed that they came from a new 'Spirit Guide', a certain
Scotsman called James Ferguson!

Clearly the medium could not distinguish between a
clairvoyant message and telepathic information from the sitter
himself. Even the great Irish medium Geraldine Cummins faced
the same dilemma when giving a reading to the famous poet
W.B. Yeats, by way of automatic writing (where she simply
wrote out a stream of words dictated by her subconscious).
These words described an old castle and its inhabitants, and
Geraldine (unsure if this 'message from the dead' was of

relevance to the poet) asked if Yeats found it of interest. He did. The medium was telling him the outline of the 'plot' of his new novel – a novel that existed only in his mind.

It is a brave researcher who seeks to isolate different psi phenomena. There are few grounds for doing so. But if he must, there can be ways around the problem.

Ellison has one way. You build a box which produces random numbers. But these are visible only from around the back. The subject, seated at the front, has no access to them. Indeed, nobody sees the numbers appear. But the electronics in the box record the number and compare it with a guess that the subject inputs at the front. If he is correct, it adds one to the tally; if he is not, it simply records the number of attempts. The total number of trials and successes can be spewed out at any time. But as each individual guess is made, nobody will know if it is right or wrong. This device avoids telepathy, since nobody holds the information in their mind as to whether a guess is correct or not. It also avoids precognition, for the subject will *never* know the individual answers. The only seeming way to score consistently

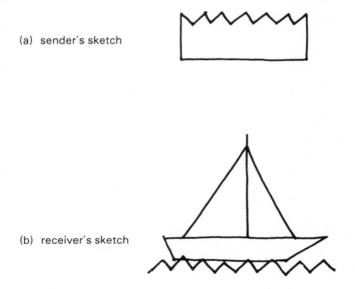

(a) sender's sketch

(b) receiver's sketch

Fig. 12: Results of a telepathy trial by Dr B.E. Schwarz

is to travel out of the body to the back of the machine and clairvoyantly 'read' the number.[5]

Results are inconclusive so far. Not that I am surprised by this. It has all the faults of the Zener card, ingenious as it is. There is absolutely no emotional incentive. Even if you *could* get the answer by way of psi, who on earth would want to, several thousand times? Besides which, deliberately to stifle the natural link between telepathy, precognition and the OOBE seems a destructive (not constructive) thing to do. It lessens the chance of a successful outcome. Surely the mind should be free to choose the method that comes best to the subject at the time.

Psychiatrist Berthold Schwarz has a much more realistic approach. He takes emotion into account. The many tests into telepathy which he conducts do not use the stupefyingly dull cards or computers. Instead the 'sender' is free to select a picture to draw, as Schwarz watches a 'receiver' in another room. Their task is to reproduce the same picture.

Obviously there are no clear rules here. Chance is far less easy to score against. But the results are much more interesting. For example, in one case the sender sketched out a light blue crown (Fig. 12a) and the receiver picked this up (Fig. 12b). The precise shape did not get through, but its feel did: the wave effect and the colour. Indeed, the receiver wrote 'light blue' beside the waves he drew.

Schwarz realizes that feel, colour and mood can be conveyed from sender to receiver, whilst the precise detail may not be. To send a crown and receive a sailboat floating on water would doubtless score a miss by the casual observer, but predictions based on our knowledge of the mind might allow this result to be anticipated. The miss is in fact a quite spectacular success.

One man sent the image of a mound or small hill this way. The receiver was sexually motivated and drew a breast in response! Schwarz claims that this shows how the basic message gets through but is tainted by an individual's psychopathic thinking. More simply, we might argue that the 'breast' was an appropriate image in the 'mind store' of the receiver which best expressed the overall feel of the message.

A marvellous illustration of just how fascinating this work can be comes from a time when the psychiatrist was himself the receiver. He drew a fireman's hat. Before his pictures could be checked against those of the sender, Schwarz clocked off for a while to go to the shops. Whilst out he bought a fire-extinguisher 'on the spur of the moment', thinking this would come in handy for his wife in the kitchen. Back at the office he found that the picture corresponding to his fireman's hat *was* a fire-extinguisher. The truth was seemingly in his subconscious mind all the time. His 'mind store' had merely used the wrong image.

However, this is not the end of the story. When he got home that evening to present the extinguisher to his wife, he discovered that she had called the fire brigade around the time of the experiment. A fryer had burst into flames in the kitchen and she had no extinguisher to put it out.

This is a beautiful example of how minds interact beneath the surface.[6]

Two other researchers, Patricia Hayes and Ann Phillips, had an even more novel way of testing psi-emotion – which in many respects is the equivalent of telepathy.

Thanks to the assistance of the University of Miami, they worked with three dolphins (Nat, Terce and Misty) between October and November 1977. Dolphins are the only animals on earth whose brain cortex/body size ratio is similar to man's. They are not fish but mammals who simply chose to remain in the sea. These gorgeous creatures have lived unchanged for millennia and fascinated us since the dawn of history. All indications are that they possess language, intelligence and a society. It is different from our own but probably no less 'advanced'. For all that they have built no technology, they also have no wars, starvation, self-made pollution or violent crime. It is a matter of debate who has the better deal! Countless people who have studied dolphins feel that man has already made contact with an alien life-form. If he would only open his eyes, or perhaps his mind.

The dolphins in the Miami experiment seemed instantly to detect the feelings of Patricia and Ann. Pat loves water, but her colleague is scared by it. The dolphins sensed this and took Pat for long rides into the deep on their backs. With Ann they never strayed out of the shallows. Eventually the team graduated to 'communication by images', provoking a response in the dolphins by transmitting a thought picture. They began with five-year old Misty and claim an eighty-per-cent success rate.

Teaching her a complex swimming movement through their minds, they asked her to pass this on to the others. 'We mentally taught Misty how to do it and again mentally asked her to teach Nat and Terce. Now all three do it.'

By the end of the experiment there was an intense rapport. In fact, their parting was so emotional that Pat cried all the way home. She felt that the dolphins *knew* that their friendship was over. Terce, who had been taught to overcome a fear of injections that were helping a back malformation, was asked how she felt about them now. Both girls claim a telepathic image along the lines, 'I hardly notice it.'

Bizarre as these stories might seem, the dolphins' permanent trainers were convinced. One said there had been no use of hand signs to 'talk' to the animals and that, 'A form of non-verbal communication did exist.'[7]

I have also spent some happy hours with dolphins in Florida, and there is no doubt in my mind that these gentle, wise creatures share something with us at the level of consciousness.

On a remote Australian beach called Monkey Mia, landowner Wilf Mason has even set up the first child/dolphin playschool! Every day the two species interact within the mild blue waters of the Indian Ocean. According to Mason, the dolphins love children, and the smaller they are the better. Could this be because young children have not yet learned to impose boundaries on reality, to believe that mind-to-mind communication is not possible – especially with an animal? Mason has no doubts. 'I am sure that dolphins can size up sorts of people. If you are angry or insincere, they won't come anywhere near you. They pick up the vibes.'[8]

I am quite certain they do. One of the paranormal dreams I will never forget occurred when my pet cat was trapped on the roof of a three-storey block of flats. It was early morning and I had no way of knowing this, but in a dream I saw my cat, on the roof, looking at me pleading for rescue. No sceptic with his logic can ever dispel the conviction such an experience brings. I felt sure that his cat consciousness and mine were joined.

It is a short step from communication between human and animal minds to inter-human communication across distances. There is no real reason why they should have different explanations. 'Remote Viewing', as it is called, is one of the most important developments of modern psi-research.

We met it in a way with Arthur Ellison's random numbers box. If the mind can use an OOBE to travel to the back of the machine, why not to the far side of the Earth? Indeed, theoretically, why not anywhere? At Stanford Research Institute (SRI), in Menlo Park, California, they have been testing this assumption for years. Russel Targ and Harold Puthoff are the two physicists who started it, joined by Blue Harary (an oddly named subject who became so involved that he qualified as a psychologist to work with them under his less exotic title, Keith).

Targ and Puthoff launched their institute with a look at Uri Geller in the early 1970s. Their results were published in *Nature* and were a prestigious breakthrough for psi-research. But there was uproar from the scientific community, and *Nature* soon backed off this tentative step towards the paranormal. Targ and Puthoff countered the charges of slipshod methods by progressing to test psi-capacity in *ordinary* people, using their technique of Remote Viewing.

Through a system of random selection from sixty possible sites, one is chosen and the first experimenter sets off to go there without anybody else knowing the destination. Meanwhile, the second experimenter stays in the lab with the subject, who attempts to 'view' this remote location by whatever psychic means he desires. This could be telepathy from the mind of the first experimenter, for instance, or it might be an OOBE to visit the site. Of course, the subject does not know what method is employed. The choice is made subconsciously.

After the impressions have been recorded by the second experimenter, the first returns and shows the subject six sites. One of these will be where he visited. The idea is that the subject then rates the sites according to how close they are to the images he detected. As a double-blind check, another researcher (who knows neither the subject nor the sites) matches up verbal descriptions and photographs of the sites with a transcription of the subject's impressions. This removes any cueing or bias that might lead the subject to select a site the experimenter wants him to.

Targ and Puthoff achieved phenomenal results with this work. They claim a sixty-seven per cent success rate. Of course, what they call a 'hit' is open to interpretation, but the results have shown fascinating trends. Whilst subjects often get the feel of the place correctly, they also put false interpretations onto it. Numbers and facts convey poorly. Emotive impressions get through much better.

This is precisely what our model would predict. And its similarity to the findings of psychometrists (who pick up feelings from objects and may then translate them badly) is really quite startling. Anybody can get psi-emotions. Turning these into accurate psi-audios or psi-visions is much harder.

The scientists also discovered that initial feelings bring the most spectacular results. The psi-emotion sneaks past the doorman, but then the conscious mind takes over and works on the message, fishing out images from the 'mind store'. The intrusion of rational thought tends to take these away from the essential truth. So Targ and Puthoff recommend that subjects take much more notice of the first few impressions (however silly) which enter their minds. Later ones are likely to be misleading.

Feedback is another important clue. If the subjects are *not* taken to the correct site after the experiment, the results are less spectacular than if they do go there. This result seems odd, but it is again consistent with our model. Precognition is a preview of our own future mental states. Presumably this personal observation of the site offers another channel for the psi message to use. Now telepathy and the OOBE are joined by premonition: information from the subject's future discovery of the true site. When this is not available, the mind has to make do with two out of three options, and so might be expected to succeed less often.[9]

Remote Viewing is a promising way to head towards the next generation of psi research. It retains the emotional element and the real-world relevance of the experiment. It takes account of the fundamental similarity between all psi-events. Its success undoubtedly comes from a closeness between the controlled situation and spontaneous experience of psi.

By 1984 SRI were claiming twenty-eight replications at other laboratories, over half of which had apparently been successful.

One of the most prolific experimenters is Robert Jahns, Dean of the School of Engineering at Princeton, New Jersey. Jahns devised a scoring system for Remote Viewing that leaves much less to subjective evaluation. His multiple-choice questions about the site (e.g. 'Is it hot or cold?') offer yes/no answers to be matched against the real location. Computers can then take over the role of scoremaster and remove all human bias.

Jahns has also varied the distances involved to see whether there are optimum or maximum values. Energy in the physical universe follows an inverse-square law, which simply means that the further you are from the origin of the field, the more the energy level reduces in a mathematically predictable way. Not so Remote Viewing. Increased distance has produced no notable difference. Even more controversially, neither has time. There are a few experiments (not enough so far) where the receiver views the target *before* the experimenter gets to it. Yet it still works!

Again this is all that we might expect. Mind does not appear bound by the laws of time and space. So if Remote Viewing functions through the medium of consciousness, it should not be effected by these variables.

I have begun to develop this kind of work in Britain. My November 1985 trip to Tenerife (see page 94) included a pilot project on Remote Viewing. Ten people in Britain attempted to view four sites which I visited on this island 2,000 miles away. I had never been there, so had no way of knowing what the sites would be like. The subjects had no idea where in the world I was.

This was not a controlled experiment, but it taught some useful things. There were several dramatic successes. One description of a harbour scene with whitewashed houses was particularly accurate, as I was on a hill overlooking the port of Puerto de la Cruz at the time. Another of the trials found me with a large white shoulder-bag, precisely described by one of the subjects. I had taken a blue one with me, but this had broken at the airport and I had unexpectedly purchased another. A further hit came from one woman who described 'voices talking French' and 'a Dutch girl' in the same phrase. That day I had flown to the island of Lanzarote and was up a mountain on a camel sitting next to a Dutch girl, talking French, as it was our only common language.

It should be stressed that only the times of the experiment were decided beforehand. I saw none of the responses until I arrived back in Britain, and nobody who participated even knew that I had left the country, let alone where I had gone. The overall success rate was about twenty-five per cent.

The most amazing result came from one man who got the dates of the trial wrong. He sent in his answers before I left and informed me I was standing by a waterfall when the first experiment began. Having decided to discard this result as invalid, and consciously determined that, wherever I ended up at that time, it would *not* be near a waterfall, I was astonished when fate decreed that I should be! I had no way of knowing that the bus I boarded would stop right in front of an artificial cataract as the test began.

My aim in conducting this dry run was to show the feasibility of a large-scale experiment. If the paranormal is a real force that we can all use, it should be possible to demonstrate this by using dozens of participants simultaneously. Then science must take note of the results, whatever they are!

In March 1986 the magazine *The Unknown* gave me an opportunity. This publication circulates in bookstores around Britain and assured a good base of would-be remote viewers. At two dates and times a random-number computer-programme directed me to a location, and readers attempted to describe it. Both verbal (on tape) and written accounts were accompanied with a Jahns-style computer score-sheet. Over sixty people responded fully to the time-consuming experiment, and the yes/no computer scores afforded hard statistics to support the more immediately arresting images drawn in words or pictures.

The overall success rate was not high. However, two questions were thrown in that give an instant guide. These asked the reader to say yes or no according to whether the site was above a thousand feet or near the sea. All possible sites were deliberately chosen so that both these questions were certain to give 'no' scores. But participants had no way of realizing that. Both questions did rate very low, with overwhelming 'no' bias on the score sheets. There were some notable descriptive hits too. The first site (which offered feedback – site two did not) was a lock on the Manchester Ship Canal. There were several river and canal images, some representative drawings and a quite remarkable 'dry dock' scene by Ken Phillips of London that was very close indeed.

The next step is to persuade a national media source to try this out with millions of potential remote-viewers. The results should be fascinating and might turn up dozens of unknown psychics – people who have no idea that they can do these things until they give them a try.

One of those people could well be you!

10. The ESP Myth: The Nature of Psi

'The world may be called physical or mental or
both or neither, as we please.'
Bertrand Russell, philosopher

Psi-events defy our rational thinking about the universe, which
says that time flows from past towards future. There is no way
to recapture moments gone, and no way to preview those left to
come. All we have are a succession of 'nows', dripping one by
one like water from a tap.

Yet, despite these 'impossibilities', precognition happens. And
so do ghostly apparitions. It is no use crying 'foul' and running
away. Jarring contradictions often mask the truth. It does no
justice to the victims of a strange anomaly. Nor does it do
justice to ourselves, for we surely have the capability to figure all
this out.

Rational science is not omnipotent. It faces similar threats all
the time. Part of its purpose is to find a way that incorporates
new facts into old theories, even when the new facts seem to
make no sense. Until the beginning of this century the universe
was viewed as a giant clockwork model, relying on laws that we
have taken for granted. Drop a ball and it falls to the ground, to
bounce in quite predictable fashion. Isaac Newton taught us
that. Put two chemicals together and they will always react in
the same sort of manner. The great chemists such as Lavoisier
and Mendeleyev taught us that. It was automatically assumed
that, as our microscopes grew bigger and we saw inside the
atom (the basic unit of all things as we had discovered), we
might find some interesting things, but these absolutely crucial
laws could be no different. We would still find matter behaving
quite predictably.

Instead we found a universe of phantoms.[1]

This field is now called Quantum Mechanics. It developed from Albert Einstein's theories of relativity, published between 1905 and 1920, which at heart are very simple. Matter and energy fields (radiation) are identical, just two disguises for the same thing. One can be changed into the other with dramatic results. Alchemy, the quest of man for centuries, almost became fact. You could turn one element into another, even invent new elements by stuffing in lots of radiation and turning it into matter. When you go the other way, staggering sums of energy are forced out. This could solve the world's energy crisis. But, as you know, we prefer to build bombs with it.

Yet even more destructive than an atomic explosion is the effect Quantum Mechanics has on the nature of reality.

Physicist Louis de Broglie said of it, 'In the history of the intellectual world there have been few upheavals comparable to this.' The only ones he might accept would be the discovery of fire, that the earth is not flat and that it goes around the sun (instead of the reverse). The revolution is that important.

Another famous physicist, Eddington, explained: 'Something unknown is doing we don't know what.' Which can be fairly translated as 'Help!'

Heisenberg's 'uncertainty principle' of 1931 was one of the first major revelations of the subject. In fact 'uncertainty' is a poor word in English that does not adequately explain what he meant. Although it is the word that has stuck, a much better translation would be 'the fuzziness principle'. It means that at these sub-atomic levels if you work out precisely where something is, the other properties of that something become fuzzy. Or if you calculate its exact speed, its location can never be specified. It becomes no more than a blur.

Since all our existence is built from sub-atomic matter, this means that the 'real world' is nothing but a blur. Everything solid is formed out of nothing. Probe into the hardest of steel, densely packed and virtually impenetrable, and all you see is 'empty space' filled with invisible fields of energy.

Physicists continue to wrestle with the implications of this theory. We can even see the results in our own lives. Everything has come down to fuzziness. Nothing precise can ever be stated, although we *can* offer probabilities. We know, on the basis of previous figures, that so many thousand will die on the roads of

Britain in 1987. Any such projection will be surprisingly accurate, although we cannot name a single one of these victims. So what *makes* the right number of people die? It is a question that still defies an answer.

There are three main attempts to resolve the problem. The one most favoured by science is to get round it by claiming that the question is invalid. Nothing *makes* people do anything. All we have are mathematics and basic facts about the way things are. We need no spurious motives to turn road-death statistics into actual deaths. Relatives of future victims might not be too convinced. And physicists themselves can show the unsatisfactory nature of this answer.

In the face of these dreadful consequences other schools of thought have gathered strength. One is called 'the many worlds hypothesis' and suggests that *all* the billions of possible outcomes do really happen. But we experience only one of them, being the one that we experience. Whilst this has interesting applications to psi-research (e.g. to precognition, where we might alter the fulfilment of a premonition by switching to a different 'world' outcome), it is widely considered circular logic. It explains what we observe by saying that we observe it! There are very few physicists behind its wild ideas.

The last major suggestion is 'the hidden variable' solution'. Einstein favoured that in the end. Many brilliant modern researchers, such as David Bohm at Birkbeck College, London, also support it. This argues that the actions of all things are directed by an unseen, or hidden, factor. One or two even propose that consciousness is that variable. That our *minds* determine the end result, telling the sub-atomic particles how to behave.[2]

This remains far from proven. The controversy rages on. But if it is the answer, psi-researchers are bound to be excited, because consciousness manipulating the sub-atomic building blocks of everything *is*, quite literally, mind over matter.

I am baffling you with these way-out theories because in modern science they are not way-out. They are the stuff that physicists dream by. As you can see, they are just as crazy as any of the ideas we have met concerning psi-events. And psi-events are a good deal easier to see in action than microscopic sub-atomic particles. On such a basis science appears to be denying the paranormal on pretty specious grounds.

Einstein was responsible for a famous thought experiment which seems to show that modern physics must be wrong. At least, this is the only alternative to its apparent outcome. If physics is right (as physicists obviously believe), it involves an almost telepathic contact between sub-atomic matter at speeds faster than light. In 1964 a scientist called Bell was able to perform the experiment and it worked. Quantum Mechanics was vindicated. But this left a paranormal phenomenon as its best theoretical explanation! Nobody will have learned that in school, because science seems afraid of the implications.[3]

All these things show the state of confusion in which science now finds itself. Clearly there will be answers. The truth will out. But we are a long way from beginning to understand them so far. Our fairly minor difficulties about consciousness fields independent of time and space are obviously neither new nor inconceivable. In fact, they are *consistent* with scientific thought.

Einstein and his colleague Lorentz are the subject of another popular myth: that nothing can travel at the speed of light. There are certainly problems with anything that exceeds C (the shorthand way of describing the speed of light). But all their equations state is that when travelling *at* C an object would contract to zero length. Because zero length is an impossibility, the argument goes that there can be no travel at the speed of light.

We do have problems conceiving a substance with zero length, but conceive it we must, for something *does* travel at the speed of light: light itself! In fact, all electromagnetic energy or radiation fields travel at C. Nor is this a trick of mathematics. The speed (about 186,000 miles per second) can be accurately measured.

This realization causes a jolt in our thinking. Quite incredible consequences appear. Light and radiation fields *must* have no length – indeed no size at all. And the Einstein/Lorentz equations offer another surprise, something called 'time dilation'.

Time dilation is another *real* property. It has been measured in laboratories. There is no doubt that it exists. What it means is that, when something approaches the speed of light, the subjective time decreases (or dilates). At C this time becomes zero. In other words, light, or any energy field, is both timeless and spaceless.

In our quest for the nature of psi, we uncovered evidence that mind is timeless and spaceless, not dependent on either. We also proposed that consciousness might be an energy field, in order to overcome the major problems of the brain-mind paradox. Now we have just seen that physics proves all energy fields to be timeless and spaceless. This result completes the circle, and the facts all fit together. It would seem to support the nature of our model too well for it to be coincidence.[4]

We can put this into graphic language. Journeys to the stars are highly unlikely in a physical spaceship confined to speeds less than C. Even the best rockets, of the most amazing designs we can imagine, will take millennia to get to the nearest stars. Yet nothing can attain the speed of light except energy fields (such as consciousness). In achieving C the field must be everywhere at the same time, because it has no space or time. Energy fields, such as mind, permeate the universe and reach the stars.

There will be no rockets to Alpha Centauri. But we can get there by way of our mind. To do this we need only stand still, because our mind is *already* there!

As I mentioned, David Bohm is one of a growing number of modern physicists who see potential in the study of the paranormal.[5] He uses many complex analogies to show how we might be constrained by thinking in three dimensions.

All our experience is set in terms of length, thickness and breadth. We can conceive of no fourth or fifth dimension. But science recognizes that to understand the universe many dimensions might be needed. Because we see only a few of them, our view is very blinkered and might even be illusionary.

Plato had a good way of showing this. He imagined a man seated in a cave, facing away from the entrance. On the wall at the back he could watch shadows cast from the world outside by the light that poured in. But the shadows were not true reflections of what went on out there, only representations that were often misleading. (Remember how as children we played with our hands to form animal shadows on the wall?) In order to see the truth, the man need only turn around and face the entrance to the cave. David Bohm suggests we may be in just this position.

All this may be beyond our ability to understand, but we do see the essential point. Bohm suggests that psi-events look impossible only because of the limits of our thinking. If we could find the missing variable, they would all make perfect sense.[6]

But can this missing variable be mind? Bohm is not sure. Others are already persuaded.

Imagine that you are desperately ill and the doctors advise of only one hope. They must amputate both your arms and legs to leave your head and a few other organs on life support. Your mind would survive, but there would not be much else of you. Our urge for self-preservation dictates the outcome. Few would not allow the doctors to get on with their job. But suppose you were told that the problem lay in your brain. In order to solve it, they would have to destroy most of your mind. Your body could remain physically normal and you would still exist, but it is very improbable you would know much about it. What then? The entire picture changes, and how many of us would consent to this operation without very serious thought?

What this shows is the fundamental value we place upon our minds, as opposed to any physical part of our body. Yet many

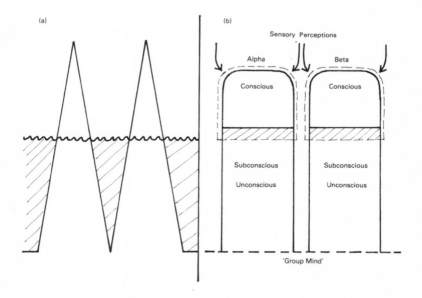

Fig.13: Working model of the human mind.

scientists still regard mind as nothing more than fairy tale. Our
sense of identity (the 'I' that we each feel inside) constantly
informs us that mind is no myth. It is very real, more real than
our arms, legs or brains. Most people could cope with losing half
their brain. And, as the evidence shows, it often makes little
difference to them, but we all dread losing even a tiny chink of
mind.

Physiologists have awarded names to various parts of the
brain, and we have met some, especially the major division into
cerebral hemispheres and the cerebellum. Psychologists have
tried to do the same thing with mind, but it is much more
difficult, because there is nothing there to cut to pieces and
inspect under a microscope. It is an abstract, invisible thing,
possibly a field of energy. However, some agreement is
beginning to emerge.

I was helped in establishing a working model by the
Manchester University psychologist Dr John Shaw. Figure 13
gives an outline of this, although I should stress that any errors
or assumptions are mine and not Dr Shaw's.

Figure 13a is an analogy of 13b to demonstrate the concept
from a familiar real-world example. It shows a series of linked
icebergs protruding above the surface of a sea but joined into a
common ice sheet below the waves. The icebergs may be
thought of as individual minds, and the ice sheet something
called the group-mind that will be important in the pages that
follow.

Figure 13b shows two individual minds, of fictitious persons I
have called 'Alpha' and 'Beta'. We may think of them as
husband and wife perhaps, or any people close to one another.
Complete strangers are also linked, but there is reason to
suppose that an emotional bond between people helps bring their
individual minds together.

Individual conscious minds, like the part of the iceberg that
floats on the surface, are what we use from day to day to relate
to the world. They take in sense perceptions and contain the
necessary thoughts, memories and behaviour traits of a person.
Clearly they differ from one another. This is why an individual *is*
an individual. The sense perceptions coming in must get through
the doorman, which is like a fine filter mesh that sheaths the part
labelled 'conscious'. Any perceptions that are allowed in become

a part of conscious awareness for the individual.

The shaded part of each conscious zone is the 'mind store' we have met so often. This is the personal stock of images we use to create mental pictures, experiences and action replays – everything (from imagination to our view of the 'real' world) that constitutes inner perception. It is a workshop that builds both dreams and psi-events.

The 'mind stores' of Alpha and Beta will have many things in common, because they will have shared many experiences. And remember that the content of these image banks is totally reliant on things that we *have* personally experienced. So everybody's 'mind store' will be broadly similar, thanks to the fact that most human experience is the same, whoever we are and wherever we go. Reality, if you like, *is* the content of the 'mind store'.

However, there will be differences to. Things that Alpha has perceived and Beta has not. For example, Alpha may have been to the moon. This would give him quite unique perceptions to enter into this store. The saying 'travel broadens the mind' is another folklore comment that reflects intuitive truth. It is fascinating to note that several of the astronauts who did visit the moon came back with a sense of having undergone a mystical experience. At least two of them went on to be virtual gurus of consciousness. Since so few humans have been to the moon, this can hardly be a coincidence.

Dotted lines are shown on my model separating the conscious zone from something labelled the subconscious and unconscious. These are like the parts of each iceberg out of sight beneath the water, yet still quite separate structures. The point of the dotted lines is to show that there is a kind of filter or permeability between these two areas of mind. Information is not permanently available but can filter through. The dotted line is an extension of the doorman, and so this is what determines if information makes it into consciousness or not.

We can see this process in operation when we 'retrieve' long-forgotten material that is not in the conscious mind but can be brought here from the subconscious or unconscious. (Don't worry about the meaning of these names awarded by psychologists, incidentally. It is their function that counts.) Special techniques seem able to speed this up. Hypnosis is one example. If it occurs when we are being coerced into remembering a 'past life' or a supposed kidnap by aliens (both real examples of commonly used approaches), it is very possible that information filtering up will get misinterpreted. Data from long-forgotten books or films and TV shows can be misperceived as genuine memories, if the influence of the researcher is strong enough to suggest this. And when he is looking for them to be just that, his influence usually is very strong.

We saw instances of this phenomenon when I rewrote the exact same notes about a dream years after I had done it the first time (page 48), and when Dr Lyall Watson was able to count the number of lamp-posts under hypnosis from his consciously forgotten route to school (page 137). It is this filter process that creates many pseudo-mysteries that look paranormal when they are really very normal.

One of the differences between these two major zones of the mind (conscious and subconscious/unconscious) is their time-appreciation. Conscious awareness is rooted in time, because it is in permanent contact with the outside world (where time and space dictate the laws of nature). We can order our experiences into past, present and future quite easily, but subconsciously or unconsciously it is much more difficult, which is why we often misinterpret material that filters up from here, giving it a false location in time. Time may even be a creation of conscious experience, with no existence anywhere else.

Funnily enough, the analogy with the icebergs holds good again. Above the surface they are in contact with the rhythms of night and day. Beneath the waves they are surrounded by water that virtually never changes. It is at a constant temperature and a constant level of darkness. Time would mean nothing there.

Finally we see on our model another dotted line that separates the individual subconscious and unconscious zones from something called the group mind. It also has the less obvious name of the 'collective unconscious', coined by psychologists and psychiatrists such as Carl Jung – who believed in its importance. This is like the ice sheet which joins all icebergs and from which all originate. It is something common to every individual mind: a group mind that consists of emotions and consciousness experiences on a racial level.

The group mind appears to be completely timeless and

spaceless. It is the essence of consciousness, the field of energy we postulated before. Because it has no time and no space, it must be everywhere at once. All minds are part of one mind. All times are part of one time.

It is not very easy to discuss such concepts without making them sound religious, for the group mind has many similarities with our conception of God. These are tricky waters, best steered clear of. So I intend simply to leave that thought with you.

Group mind information potentially includes all things that have happened, or will happen, anywhere. Since psi-events show access to such things, it must be from here that they stem. Jung was interested in the myths which mankind shared, irrespective of culture. All races have them, of 'little people' and of 'gods'. He regarded these, any many others, as merely different attempts by conscious minds to express things that we all share at the level of the group mind: fundamental truths about the universe, clothed in 'mind store' images that are relevant to the society in question but obviously about the same thing when you strip them of their fancy dress. Jung was fascinated by the 'modern myth' of the flying saucer (to use his term), because he saw it as an update on the 'little men' (three-foot-tall aliens) and 'gods' (always superior to us) which have pervaded history. To him this showed that UFO's came from within and expressed a truth that was basic to the group mind, although what this truth was he never succeeded in discerning.[7]

We can now begin to understand why psi-events are difficult things to materialize in the real world. Emotions which express basic messages at this group mind level must filter up into the personal unconscious and be anchored by time and space. This distorts their meaning a bit. They may then stay here, as nothing more than feelings, moods or cultural beliefs without any conscious application or explanation. The belief that man survives death is a good example. There is no conscious evidence of a persuasive nature, yet almost every society on earth (from primitive bushmen to modern Western Christians) implicitly accepts that it is so. It could be one of the group-mind messages about fundamental truth that is powerful enough to enter most of our unconscious minds and effect us this way.

In order for any message to manifest openly in the 'real'

world, it has to get through the second filter and pass the doorman, thus entering conscious awareness. This may be only as a psi-emotion or it may use images from the 'mind store' to become a psi-vision. But in making this transition it becomes firmly rooted in time and space, and many errors of translation are possible in the process. We saw this expressed most clearly with psychometrists, but it was true of almost every psi-event. They are never reproductions of the truth, only distorted images that reflect it.

I would not blame you if these seem wild speculations that would be impossible to prove, but one brave young plant-biologist has staked his reputation on proving them. Dr Rupert Sheldrake, from Nottinghamshire, made a stunning impression on his fellows with the publication of his version of a group-mind theory in 1981. The prestigious journal *Nature* hailed the book as a candidate for burning! Meanwhile its rival, *New Scientist*, and the BBC television science programme *Tomorrow's World* were both sufficiently intrigued to agree to a test of the hypothesis.[8]

Sheldrake's arguments about the group mind (which he refers to as a 'species field') is built on the idea that all forms of structure and behaviour within one species are governed not only by genetic codes. There is also a 'morphogenetic field' which is invisible and independent of time and space. It dictates the working of evolution, thus explaining why a rabbit always grows up to look like a rabbit, and why inbred behavioural abilities and phobias can be passed across generations. In order to test this bold suggestion, Sheldrake proposed that any change which is made at the level of the group mind should transmit itself throughout the species. If the species used in the experiment is man, the results should materialize as adaptations in behaviour. He calls his theory 'formative causation', and it is as revolutionary and controversial as Charles Darwin's first proposition. Like Darwin, Sheldrake knows he must fight to gain acceptance. But fighting through experiment is exactly what he intends to do. By challenging scientists to prove him wrong, and openly calling for do-or-die tests, he has earned the respect of many who disagree with his ideas.

Two major trials of the concept have already been conducted. In October 1982 *New Scientist* ran a competition for the outline of a test that could prove or disprove the theory. The Nottingham University scientist Dr Richard Gentle came up with the one the magazine considered easiest to implement. This proposed the use of nursery rhymes, as powerful influences at a group-mind level. So many children learn and re-learn these that they become part of our collective consciousness. According to Sheldrake, any established rhyme would be much easier to learn than one newly created, for which there was no pre-set learning pattern in the group mind. To demonstrate this the idea was conceived whereby a foreign nursery rhyme could be learnt by British schoolchildren with no proficiency in that tongue. At the same time two alternative rhymes in the same language would also be attempted, one that was newly written by a native poet and the other which had the same structure and rhythm but consisted of jumbled words strung together. To an English child all three would sound similar, but if Sheldrake was correct, the traditional nursery rhyme ought to be easier to learn.

The trial was carried out using three Japanese rhymes, and it worked. However, Sheldrake is less happy with the experiment than *New Scientist* staff evidently were. He accepts the feeling that the established rhyme might have become established *because* it was easy to learn for obscure linguistic reasons. Even so, the results matched the theory and can be fairly called encouraging.

The second experiment relied on television to involve thousands of people at once. It has been conducted twice (on a local TV show and on the BBC national transmission of *Tomorrow's World*). Although the basic idea was the same on both occasions, different content made these two trials quite independent. They used hidden pictures, similar to the one depicted on page 43 of my book *UFO Reality*. As blobs of light and shade they look meaningless when first glanced at. In fact, they are real drawings with a lot of the detail obscured by this blocking process. If you stare at them for a time, knowing that a picture is contained in them, a reasonable percentage of people will be able to recognize it. Others never will, until it is pointed out. This is partly a psychological phenomenon and also connected with the visual experience of any subject and the images in his 'mind store' that allow identification.

In the first trial (transmitted on 31 August 1983) two pictures were developed. One thousand people were tested with them before the show, and 9.2 per cent got picture A without prompting whilst 3.9 per cent identified the more difficult picture B. A random selection just before air-time flashed picture B onto the screen for several seconds.

A different set of 847 people were then tested *afterwards*. These came from fourteen cities (half in Britain and the rest in several other countries, including South Africa and the USA). Most of these could not possibly have seen the TV show, which had a region-only audience of two million. The number able to identify picture A remained almost identical to that before transmission. However, those now able to spot the transmitted picture (B) almost doubled, to 6.4 per cent. Maybe you are still uncertain about people having somehow watched the TV show: when British subjects were entirely removed from the sample, the increase in scoring was even higher!

A second trial with the eight million BBC audience took place in November 1984. The results were similar, although American subjects scored far less significantly than Europeans. This has led some benevolent sceptics, such as parapsychologist Dr Sue Blackmore from Bristol University, to question if other factors might be responsible.[9]

Obviously more work has to be done before we know the truth. But Sheldrake has challenged his critics, and in five years all tests conducted have either vindicated him or produced no clear result. None has gone against the hypothesis of the group mind. That does appear to be significant.

There are many exciting avenues of exploration Sheldrake has opened up for psychic research, and he is well aware of them, assisting both the Society for Psychical Research and ASSAP.[10] Has metal-bending spread as a craze around the world because of Uri Geller's television appearances? Their effect on the group mind might have made this an accepted behaviour pattern. Perhaps some other form of psi-event can be made to spread like a contagion through public demonstration. If a telepathy experiment were performed on television before millions of viewers, would it later work better when carried out in a different country? There are endless possibilities.

Whatever the outcome, Sheldrake's lead deserves to be followed. Mass experimentation of these ideas can be conducted.

If we are to learn the truth, it may be the only way.

Let us try to piece together a working model. It should use all the things that we have discovered throughout the book and take account of what we know about the mind.

We have suggested that there is a two-mode pattern for reality: Normal reality (of the brain and its electro-chemical impulses, constrained by the laws of time and space, and working in terms of facts, figures and objective sense perceptions) and synchronistic reality (of the mind and its consciousness field, unrestricted by time or space and working in terms of symbols and emotions and subjective 'mind-store' images).

I have had to warn several times not to treat the world as black and white, fact or fiction, truth or hallucination. These twin reality modes are not set in concrete as all there is. They form opposite ends of a spectrum with many shades of experience in between – like a colour spectrum with violet at one end and red at the other, but blue, green, yellow etc somewhere in the middle.

Our spectrum of reality is shown in Figure 14. Normal reality is at the left end, Synchronistic reality to the right. This matches the left-brain/right-brain representation within the cerebrum. The dotted vertical line through the middle is a half-way house that is half of one reality and half of the other. You will notice two sliding scales, one above the horizontal line and one below it. The upper one is labelled 'objectivity content' and the one below 'hallucination content'. The first goes from zero to one hundred per cent right to left, and the latter is the reverse of this. In other words Normal reality is a hundred per cent objectivity with zero hallucination content; synchronistic reality is a hundred per cent hallucination content with zero objectivity. Working with this model, we can now rate any experience according to a percentage of objectivity and hallucination content. This will give it a unique location on the spectrum. Because of the sliding scales a sum of both contents for any position will always equal one hundred.

Normal reality (a hundred per cent objectivity, nought per cent hallucination) relates to our experience in the 'real' world, when we are wide awake and the doorman is only letting through sense perceptions from outside. Messages from the deeper levels of consciousness (i.e. 'within') are not allowed. The

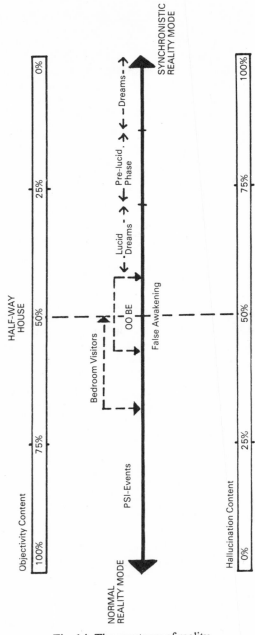

Fig. 14: The spectrum of reality

far extreme of synchronistic reality (a hundred per cent hallucination, nought per cent objectivity) is more difficult to describe. Deep dream sleep *might* represent it, with the doorman only letting through messages from within and no sense perceptions from the world outside. However, most sleep states *do* include some sense perceptions. Otherwise we would sleep through any life-threatening situation. Normal sleep is probably not quite at this right-hand end of the spectrum. So what is? I am sure some mystics might try to persuade me that the answer is death.

Let us now try to position more difficult states of consciousness onto the spectrum, using these same rules. For example, a typical dream. This has a high hallucination content and relatively little objectivity. But usually some. There is a joke about the man who dreamt that he was eating a huge pile of marshmallows and woke with indigestion, to find the remains of his pillow scattered across the bed! There is substance to this humour, as psychologists and dream analysts know. The doorman does allow sense perceptions through to enter the scenery of our dream. And so most dreams will locate *towards* the right-hand end of the spectrum, and we can ascribe a reasonable rating to one typical (perhaps eighty per cent hallucination, twenty per cent objectivity.) (Note, as I said, the sum is always a hundred per cent.)

If we move left from here, we come to a position on the spectrum marked as the lucid dream. This is a very special type of dream which needs some discussion. One in ten people have them regularly, although many more than this have very occasional experience of them. I have had several myself and, as any reader who has shared one will know, they are breathtaking.

A lucid dream is characterized by the person *knowing* that he is dreaming whilst the dream goes on. At the borders between an ordinary dream and the lucid dream (known as the *pre-lucid* phase), this knowledge is no more than a fleeting impression with no influence on the dream. It is a near-miss. In a lucid dream proper it is possible to control the scenery within the dreamscape. It is rather like watching a Hollywood movie at the cinema and then suddenly finding yourself inside the film. The scenes you have been viewing, with a detached interest and which seem quite flat, are now vivid, three-dimensional and spread out all around you. The film set is there for you to use, and you can either follow the plot or ad-lib and rewrite the script.

One of my most spectacularly lucid dreams saw me inside a house. I suddenly thought 'I am dreaming this' and passed the pre-lucid phase to gain control. Before me was a door and I wondered what lay outside. However, I decided that there was power at my disposal and I ought to use it. So instead of opening the door, I levitated myself and dematerialized right through it. Now outside I stood marvelling at the street scene. A bright sun was shining down on an urban location I did not recognize. There were houses, people, little dot cars crossing an intersection hundreds of yards ahead of me. Everyone was going about an ordinary day, totally oblivious of me, the dreamer, who had created them all. All I could think was, 'this is just amazing. How did I conjure so much detail inside my head?'

The feeling of realism is incredible. The lucid dream *is* real, far more real than a pale, shadowy, normal dream, but not more or less different than life in a genuine street – just a different kind of real. Words are very inadequate to express such a thing, but the over-used adjective 'magical' is certainly appropriate.

I stress lucid dreams because I believe they are important. They are the only location on the spectrum of reality (apart from normal dreams) which every one of us can experience without special method. The effort is very worthwhile. A recent BBC television programme focused on the subject. That it was in a religious series adequately shows the impact they create. One contributor described the feeling, 'The dream takes on a three-dimensional vividness. It becomes more *real* than before.'[11]

On this programme a girl described a lucid dream she could still recall even now she is an adult. It was of the special kind known as the 'false awakening'. She dreamed that she had got up and gone to school. It was so realistic that she believed she *had* woken up and the experience was real. The truth came to her only when a loud noise on the school bus sent her back to her bed. Here she woke up and went to school, only to be hit by a book thrown at her, to find herself back in bed! This happened three times and that night, after a normal school day, all she could think of was, 'Am I going to wake up again and find out this is *still* a dream?'

That example is rather extreme. False awakenings tend to be quite brief, although they are not uncommon. They would appear to locate even further left on the spectrum than the lucid dream. The reason we suggest this position is that, whilst both lucid dream and false awakening are 'real' in feeling, the former is known to be a dream and the latter is often mistaken for real life.

The most detailed research into this phenomenon has been carried out at Oxford by Celia Green, whom we met in connection with apparitions.[12] More recently Dr Morton Schatzman (who worked with the hallucinator Ruth), Dr Peter Fenwick (of St Thomas's Hospital, London) and Dr Keith Hearne (a noted British specialist on dreams) have combined to devise a method that allows those who have regular lucid dreams to signal the outside world whilst they are happening. With electrodes coupled to his eyes, the dreamer is able to manipulate the current by a flick of his eyelids. If his dream becomes lucid, he can manoeuvre himself into the laboratory where the experiment is underway. Once here, he can imagine himself performing a task he was set before he went to sleep. Of course, he remains fast asleep on the bed, but in his dream he is hallucinating the task. The electrodes record the movements he is making, and later his dream description can be compared with the real-world evidence of the electrical record.

This research is considered of great significance. Dr Hearne said of the first successful trial in April 1975, 'It was like receiving a message from another galaxy.'

How should we slot the lucid dream onto the spectrum? Firstly, as these last few pages show, we must consider the pre-lucid dream, lucid dream and false awakening as three different (but interconnected) things. They blend into one another, and the pre-lucid phase blends into the ordinary dream at the right end of the spectrum. We might give it a rating of seventy-five per cent hallucination, twenty-five per cent objectivity – a bit more 'real' than the dream, but still very dreamlike.

The lucid dream itself must be more real still, because the dreamer's conscious awareness takes control. So we should locate this further left on the spectrum. Its hallucination count is less, but still dominant. The objectivity content increases. We might rate it as sixty per cent hallucination, forty per cent objectivity.

Because the balance of a lucid dream favours the hallucination content, the dreamscape remains essentially that of a dream. The person recognizes he is conscious, but the entire scenario comes from within. In fact, any experience to the right of the half-way house will have a dominance from hallucination content. It will be predominantly dream-like.

With the false awakening the dreamer makes the error of believing this to be real. The landscape also loses its dreaminess (the bedroom, school bus and so on – all the kinds of things that the senses would be bringing into waking consciousness). Whilst it evidently blends into the lucid dream, this can only mean that the false awakening lies even further left on the spectrum. Indeed, this very confusion over whether it is real or dream-like shows us that it must locate at about the half-way house.

I suspect that there are many similarities between the false awakening and the OOBE, and that both straddle this mid-position on the spectrum. In this regard it is interesting that lucid dreams often describe an ability to fly. Indeed, dreams of flying are remarkably common, which begs the question of where the 'mind store' gets the image from. None of us has had real experience of flying. Or are OOBEs so common that we have *all* experienced them? OOBEs, like false awakenings, occur in the real environment where the person is at the time – usually the bedroom. This is another demonstration of their close similarity.

If a false awakening or OOBE is just to the *right* of the half-way house (perhaps fifty-five per cent hallucination, forty-five per cent objectivity), the result will be a background that is dream-like but with a high content of sensory impressions from the external world. It might be a grossly distorted version of the house you are sleeping in. It may be hard to judge if this is dream or not. It will seem quite real but also very dream-like. Since the balance favours hallucination content, the correct decision will probably be taken.

On the other hand, if the false awakening or OOBE is just to the *left* of the half-way house (e.g. forty-five per cent hallucination, fifty-five per cent objectivity), the environment will depend more on real sensory input than on dreamscape distortions. The person will *be* in the bedroom. But the high hallucination content will allow all kinds of strange things to happen. He may drift up out of his body, or see an apparition. Many 'bedroom visitor' psi-events lie here on the spectrum. Because the balance favours objectivity, instead of hallucination content, these experiences may well be considered real (although feeling dream-like.) Indeed, anything to the left of the half-way house, by definition *is* real, even if it involves a monster in your bedroom!

We have now slotted most strange experiences into the spectrum, but there is a yawning gap to the left of the half-way house. Nature prefers balance, and so we might expect that some state of consciousness does locate itself here. Let us try to predict its character by using the rules employed for dreams, lucid dreams, false awakenings, OOBEs and bedroom visitors. Again there may be several types of experience blending into each other, because there are no sharp divisions on a spectrum. However, let us select a typical location, with twenty-five per cent hallucination, seventy-five per cent objectivity rating. You may notice how this is the mirror image of the pre-lucid phase (between dream and lucid dream).

One thing we can immediately say about this state of consciousness: it is well to the left of the half-way house. Its objectivity percentage outweighs the hallucination content three to one. So it will *feel* real. Any person in this state will certainly decide that he is awake, fully conscious and living in the 'real' world. By definition he will be correct, but there will be a definite dream-like aura surrounding the experience, because twenty-five per cent hallucination content is not insignificant.

In a lucid dream your conscious mind invades the hallucinatory world of dream images, moulding and reshaping them. In this mirror-image state we now define, the opposite occurs. Emotional and hallucinatory input from within will invade the 'real world', moulding and reshaping that. This strange new state of quasi-consciousness is, if you like, a waking lucid dream, but it is also precisely what we have studied throughout this book: it is the psi-event.

Imagine that you are standing at a bus stop in normal reality mode. Suddenly the doorman detects a message from within that is considered important. A temporary block on the input from the senses comes into effect. This is the Oz Factor and is experienced by you as sounds disappearing from the environment and so forth. Your perception of time alters too, because you are being hauled away from the left end of the spectrum where your mind is time-rooted. You have now been shifted to a new state of consciousness, between the left edge and the half-way house, the zone where psi-events occur. The background remains the real world, exactly as it was before your shift in consciousness, so you still perceive yourself as standing at the bus stop. You also regard yourself as wide awake, although you may notice the slightly dreamy aura which indicates that this is not normal reality mode.

Now the message uses things from your 'mind store' to create hallucinations. These will intrude upon the real-world environment. Perhaps a flying saucer will suddenly appear in the sky above the road. Indeed, the mind could well use an ordinary perception that is there, distorting it to create the right effect. An aircraft flying over might be the basis out of which the hallucination is developed. When the mind is satisfied it has got the message over, you switch back to normal reality mode. The UFO disappears. Time regains its grip. You begin to wonder what has happened to you but remain certain it was a 'real' event. However, when you ask other people at the bus stop, they look at you as if you are mad. Flying saucer? What flying saucer? Nobody saw any such thing. You will leave, shaking your head in absolute bemusement, perhaps to report what you saw. Or perhaps not. You might decide that the safest thing to do is forget it ever happened.

That could well be a mistake. Unless you are psychologically ill, and most people who undergo psi-events are *definitely* not, there must have been a reason why the doorman let the message through. You probably owe it yourself to try to figure out the meaning.

This is only one example. The circumstances could have been different. The message might have dramatized as many other things, e.g. a ghost or premonition. You could have stepped into the psi-event from the real world (normal reality mode) or from sleep (synchronistic reality mode). When the experience ends, you might return to full consciousness or to sleep. All these options are possible. They create the apparent differences in the paranormal experience.

The concept of ESP as we tend to understand it seems to be a myth. Psi-events are sensory, not extra-sensory. Beyond that we may have to face a quite surprising discovery. Researchers into psychic phenomena should not be seeking objective proof. If they hunt for this, and it does not exist, only disappointment can follow. They should also not be seeking to dismiss psi-events from someone's life. The exorcist or ghost-buster may be doing a dis-service.

Instead the future may require a whole new breed of investigator – in a sense like psychologists, but also different: a unique minister to humankind, who will analyse the psi-event and seek out its meaning, not a searcher after facts to trap ghosts on his camera, not an explorer out to discover alien civilizations. Someone who will look behind the myth of ESP and, as a doctor finds the reason for the symptom, works out its meaning and importance.

11. An A to Z of Strange Phenomena

'I don't believe in ghosts, but I believe my friend
who says she saw one.'
                    Conversation between two girls on a train,
                    overheard by the author, December 1985

Now that we have surveyed the claims and counterclaims and
proposed a general model to explain these things, it is time to
look at the range of psi-events and see how close we are to
understanding them.

These phenomena are scientific mavericks, outcast by their
own peculiarities. They refuse to come to heel and submit. Yet
neither do they go away. We may chose to disbelieve them but,
as the two girls on the train show, when they happen to
ourselves (or someone close to us), everything changes. There is
nowhere left to run. No matter what the sceptics say, that
particular psi-event was real and it demands some sort of
answer.

In the pages that follow I will briefly recount fourteen types of
psi-event. Most we have met before, in one form or another, but
I will add a new example and offer a simple suggestion of how
our model might resolve it.

Of course, all this *is* just a model in the manner Arthur
Ellison advises. I am not proclaiming that I have solved the
riddle of the paranormal. All that I provide is a plan to help us
move forward, a scaffold round which to build a better
hypothesis. We need more data from brave witnesses (which
tomorrow might well mean you!). We require bold, decisive
experiments.

If psi is a real force, it is open to us all. This is not the ground
for mystical acolytes or cult-ridden misfits. By using my model
and the range of psi-events, it should be possible to devise

experiments that work for anyone. If they fail, my views must be wrong and someone else will have to find out where I erred. But if the experiments succeed, we are on the way to truth. Who knows what we can then do with the power at our disposal?

Clairvoyance

This is the reception of a message within the mind which appears to come from some source beyond oneself. The term is generally used to presume an origin as the conscious mind of a person who no longer lives, but it is important to remember that this might be a restricted view of a much broader ability (and indeed might be a false interpretation of the source of any message).

The story I recount comes from an American, Elaine Polin, and is similar to hundreds of other cases 'proving' that we survive death. Whether it does so remains largely a matter of personal choice.

Both her grandparents died before she bore her first child, a cause of sadness as they had longed for great-grandchildren. Very soon after their deaths Elaine did become pregnant, and one month after her daughter was born she had a vision of both grandparents standing by the crib.

Three years later, in July 1969, men first landed on the moon. It had been a sort of family joke that her grandparents wanted to go there one day, and that celebratory night a second contact occurred. This time it was a psi-audio and they talked to Elaine.

So far we have nothing too extraordinary. Clearly both events (the childbirth and moon-landing) were important psychological triggers that could have led the woman's mind to remember her grandparents and imagine the rest. However, the now three-year-old daughter overheard the discussions and announced, 'I talk to grandma too'. Naturally it was assumed that she meant her own grandmother (Elaine's mother), but the child insisted that two unknown grandparents often came to her room late at night. Some weeks later the girl was fishing through a box, as children often do, when she found some photographs. 'I told you so,' she cried with delight, handing one picture to her mother. It showed Elaine's grandparents on their fiftieth wedding anniversary and was, supposedly, the strangers who came to pay nocturnal visits.[1]

It may be possible that Elaine's wishes transmitted themselves to her daughter (who was sleeping and so in a particularly receptive state). Young children also seem more likely than adults to experience a psi-event, because they have not yet learned the need to divide up the spectrum as rigidly as adults. But why was the form of the 'ghosts' that of very old people, just like their granddaughter's final memory? Where did the young child's 'mind store' get such an image from? She says she had never seen them in a photograph, and of course she had not seen them in real life, but had she seen pictures and forgotten this consciously?

If the mind *is* timeless and spaceless, perhaps the grandparents' desires could have projected into their future (which would be the present for the little girl). Or, if there truly is survival, maybe they did travel in an out-of-body way and pop up to see their great granddaughter now and then.

Energy cannot be destroyed. It can change in form (even into matter), but it never disappears. When our bodies die, the chemicals return to the earth from whence they came. We see this when a corpse decomposes. But where does the energy field of mind and emotion go? So far as we know, it does not go anywhere, so it presumably must still be somewhere. And since energy fields are timeless and spaceless in any case, mind presumably has to be everywhere, even after that thing we call death.

Human survival remains possible. But we do not know which option explains a particular clairvoyant experience such as this. Remember Arthur Ellison's tales of mediums who detected imaginary information from the minds of their sitters and then assumed it came from a land beyond death. In those cases it certainly did not. But does it ever do so?

All we know for sure is that the mind of the little girl, in a particularly receptive situation, picked up a message and translated it into regular psi-visions. That message, wherever it came from, was the emotional desire of two people to see their great-grandchild.

Coincidences

Undoubtedly there are pure coincidences, things that happen simply by chance. But we have seen how probability lies at the centre of all modern physics. The universe owes its existence to it.

Remember the 'hidden variable' argument that mind could select the outcome (from millions of possibilities), thus engineering what might seem to be random. Perhaps this process explains synchronicity. A message slumbering deep in the subconscious or unconscious mind might struggle to materialize as a full blown psi-event. The easiest route could be through re-ordering circumstance to create serendipity.

In June 1983 my regular series of weekly programmes on paranormal topics was in full flow. Radio City had asked me to do an extra show that week as there was a general election. My normal feature, two days before, had been about objects that fall mysteriously from clear blue skies (usually fish or frogs).[2] Now I was doing a special about predictions and psychic phenomena associated with politics.

After the election spot was concluded, I went up to the office to deal with matters arising from my normal show and to open my mail. One letter came from a young man on the Wirral who asked to be remembered to rock music DJ Phil Easton, with the enigmatic words, 'Tell him I'm on the Kipper Express.' This meant absolutely nothing to me, and there was no obvious way to fulfil this strange request. I worked in the morning and left by early afternoon. Phil had a late-evening programme and we simply never met. However, I took the letter over to Marc Jones, another City DJ, intending to ask him to pass the message on. Just as I did so, Phil Easton walked through the door. He was doing an election results show that night and had popped in on the spur of the moment to do some preparation. I showed him the letter (from someone who had signed himself 'Skidrack'). I discovered that 'Kipper Express' meant a boat trip to the Isle of Man to watch the TT races. Although I did not know the term, my husband was also on the island for the same reason, leaving me alone that week – one reason I had been glad to do the two spots.

We discussed these things very briefly, and Marc introduced the topic of falls from the sky, the subject of my earlier presentation. He is noted for his madcap humour, and he began to crack jokes about kippers falling out of the sky.

Against this background I went to a cinema where a long double bill was showing. Only the circumstances of the week allowed this, and nobody knew that I had gone. When I emerged, after four hours in the dark, the sky was broiling with a fierce storm that blew in from the sea. I hate lightning and had no desire to get soaked, so I ran flat out (like an express) to the nearest bus stop. I went a few yards and was passing an ordinary block of houses when I skidded and fell backwards on a slippery, wet kipper on the pavement. Picking myself up, feeling dumb (and amazed), I went home. There were no fishmongers close by. Never before, or since, have I seen a kipper in such an unlikely spot. It is an incredible coincidence. Or is it?

It seems that our discussions about the 'kipper express' (maybe even the name 'Skidrack') had translated into real events, presumably concocted by my mind. But was the kipper 'really' there? Perhaps it was a hallucination, and I tripped up to enhance the effect of the psi-event. If so, a message must underlie the experience. Unfortunately, Carl Jung is not around to tell me what it was.

Ghosts

We have already met quite a few ghost stories. Their traditional interpretation is that a spirit of some dead person has returned to earth, but plenty of reasons have been advanced to doubt this view. The ghost is clearly an hallucinated psi-event, located towards the middle of the left side of our spectrum of reality.

A very helpful case comes from psychometrist Bob Cracknell, who needs no persuasion about the existence of strange phenomena. He lives with psi-events almost every day. But his ghost-sighting convinced him that there could be an explanation different from the one that is generally applied.

His youngest child, Nathan, had been involved in a serious accident. A concrete bunker had collapsed on top of him, causing major head injuries. Cracknell rushed the boy to hospital and was carrying him along a corridor when he saw the vision of a nun standing nearby. She said, 'I will take care of him. He will be all right.' So convincing was this that the psychic turned to hand the boy over. But there was nobody there.

Bob Cracknell's interpretation of an experience like this is interesting. 'My psychic self was feeling and reacting to the vibrations, and my conscious mind had translated it into something tangible.' The nun was an image of calmness and reassurance selected out of his 'mind store' to represent those emotions and the intuitive knowledge that all would be well. As indeed, despite the poor diagnosis, it was.[3]

I think this is probably the correct way to evaluate ghost experiences. They *are* representative hallucinations, projected onto the real world environment to describe feelings and emotions picked up at deeper levels of the mind. Their exact shape is not what matters, because its form depends on a selection from the 'mind store'. It is what this shape reflects that counts.

Sometimes the messages are personal (as Bob Cracknell believes it was). Other times they do seem to refer to genuine information about real people who may indeed be dead. (Elaine Polin's clairvoyance case is relevant here.) The main question is where the message originates, because there are often several options, of which the surviving consciousness of the dead person is only one, and not necessarily the best one.

Because of this there seems little reason to assume that ghosts have any bearing, one way or the other, on the question of whether we survive death. That is a highly controversial statement, which I am sure many people will challenge, but all that we have discovered in this book seems to bear me out.

Hauntings

These are different from apparitions or ghosts, although that might not seem obvious at first. They involve persistent phenomena, which may last for weeks or months and centre on one house or building. At least that is how they seem to be. Closer inspection reveals that they more likely grow around a single person.

The haunt I wish to discuss involves a lady called Mrs G, who wrote to me from Essex and whose anonymity I preserve. Her story is unusual but, so far as I can tell, quite sincere.

In 1968 her husband died, aged just thirty-seven. This left her with a young family to raise. He was cremated and for the entire period when his ashes remained in the house, she believes that his spirit continued to haunt the building.

Many strange things are described by Mrs G, beginning on the night of the funeral. Furniture moved about on its own. She awoke in the early hours to see the vision of a bird flying over her head. And a white glowing mass appeared in front of her before dawn arrived. Later instances included the lifting into the air of the bed by some mysterious force, and her daughters witnessed some of the noises and disturbances that followed. The only cure came when she had her husband's ashes buried, an obviously symbolic act which realistically should have no effect on the proceedings (unless it is thought that ghosts dwell in urns like genies in a bottle!). The only reason I can see why it had any effect is because Mrs G *believed* it would, and she was responsible for the events in the first place.

Mrs G was always present during them. She explained how she often got 'feelings' that something was about to happen, a clue that she is good at switching reality modes. Most, if not all, the haunting phenomena occurred late at night, many in the bedroom. She had a belief in spirits returning from the dead, quickly decided her husband was responsible and linked these things to the presence of his ashes. She also spoke of the need for an exorcism. All of this helps us understand the dynamics of Mrs G and how she provoked the phenomena.

What is the meaning of the events? It is *possible* that her husband was communicating after death, but if this is the solution, or through her own belief, either way a message was filtering up from her unconscious mind and manifesting as psi-events surprisingly often. The fact that so many attempts were made to express the message (psi-visions, psi-audios, poltergeist effects etc) *implies* that something urgent was involved. It is hard to conceive of anything within herself persisting that long. The idea of her dead husband communicating his survival by *using* her innate abilities seems to fit as well as anything.

However, all this is secondary to the effect the whole affair had on Mrs G. It radically altered her life. With her husband's ashes safely buried and the house now quiet, five years passed and she continued to live in the same home. Then she contemplated a second marriage, and soon after her wedding the bed once more began to move up and down in the night. Her startled partner asked what was going on. 'It's my late husband,' Mrs G informed him. 'He doesn't seem too happy.'

Later that day Mrs G returned home to find that her new spouse had left her. He never returned, apparently driven from her life by the jealous ghost of a former husband.

Healing

Bob Cracknell, in his 1981 autobiography, explained: 'I will make a prediction for Uri Geller. We will not hear of him for a few years, and during that time he will become more aware of himself and his ability. ... I predict that he will then learn to channel this energy and power and become one of the world's greatest healers.'

It is certainly the case that, after the metal-bending craze died in the mid seventies, Geller disappeared from recognition. Psychic researchers (if not the public) know that he has lived in London for a couple of years and, since 1981, *has* begun to do healing. I am aware of one case, whose details I am unfortunately not at liberty to discuss, where the Israeli was barred from a London hospital following his attempts to cure the teenaged son of a friend of mine.

Perhaps Cracknell's prediction will prove correct. If so, Geller will not be the first psychic who has grown tired of flaunting himself before laboratory scientists with limited imagination and moved on to healing, where he believes he can do something useful.

Researcher Lawrence Le Shan is not one of these unimaginative scientists, whose experimental thoughts seem tied up in knots. He has taken a special interest in healing and trained himself and several students to perform it. He accepts that a shift in the state of consciousness is the first step towards achievement in this field. Once in the psi-event zone of the spectrum, he believes he can even heal at a distance. How far does not matter. And since mind is a field and unaffected by time or space, this makes good sense to us.

He describes a case where a fifteen-year-old boy was in Denver whilst Le Shan stayed in California. The boy had no feeling below his chest after a trampoline accident, and his doctor had put in writing that, 'Medically [he] is where he will be forever.' But at the exact time that the scientist performed his healing attempt (using nothing more than a letter and the boy's photograph to focus), the youngster felt the first sensations in his now recovering legs.[4]

Le Shan and his students give some accounts of what it feels like when they perform this healing. They are the same classic Oz Factor symptoms (calmness, peacefulness, sensory deprivation etc) that we have met many times. They also note that time and space make no difference and that there are often side-effects involving emotions or images transferred between healer and patient. The remarkable correspondence of all these feelings and symptoms with the OOBE, or Near Death Experience, or UFO encounter, is a further demonstration of the crucial point. These seemingly quite different phenomena are *not* different at all. They are movements right across into the psi-event zone of the spectrum of reality. And the Oz Factor is the clue that always tells you that.

This is just what we might expect. The healer and his subject are linked together at the group-mind level. This enables the healer to help the patient cure himself. As Hilary Evans told us, the inner wish must be set on a cure just as much as the patient publicly insists that he wants one. This is where the psychic healer comes in: not in working miracles himself but by transmitting the desire to *want* a cure into the unconscious mind of his patient.

It *is* the patient who does the healing. One of Le Shan's 'best' results proves that. A man in desperate need of surgery agreed to a long-distance healing experiment and the day afterwards was instantly cured. His doctor was so excited that he pleaded with Le Shan to let him write it up for medical literature. The scientist declined. Through much embarrassment he had to explain that, although the man clearly remembered the experiment, he himself had *forgotten* about it. The healing was never performed! It seems that the man's own conviction was enough to foster belief, and this worked entirely on its own.

Near Death Experience (NDE)

'This is a summary of an experience that happens to someone in the United Kingdom every five hours.' With these words Mike Costello introduces the most recent in a long line of detailed surveys of this phenomenon.[5]

We have already discussed this topic at some length, and of all psi-events it is the one receiving most current attention. Costello reviews many possible causes, including hallucinations, drug-induced experiences, birth traumas and epileptic seizures. He finds no pathological answer totally satisfying. But I think we can safely claim that the NDE *is* an altered state of consciousness.

My guess is that it locates on our spectrum in the same sort of area as the OOBE or false awakening, and may happen when a switch into the psi-event zone proceeds further to the right than normal. The real-world environment fades out and is replaced by more and more hallucination content as its percentage rises.

However, it is certainly expressing a consistent message – of all psi-events perhaps the most consistent. The recurrent images of tunnels, bright lights, spirit guides etc are at least as reproducible as alien contacts in the UFO field. Indeed, some psychologists are already exploring the considerable similarities between the OOBE, NDE and alien contact, convinced that a common origin is involved.[6] My argument would be that common (or closely similar) locations on the spectrum of reality are indicated. That is why they seem identical. But the messages are probably quite different.

An understanding of the message in a NDE would certainly be important. It is the only avenue of exploration into the shadowland between life and death. Whilst the NDE is an experience of the last stages of life, and not the first stages of death, it illuminates the direction in which consciousness heads at this point of major upheaval. We may not have a better chance to unwrap the mysteries of post-mortem survival.

It has just been revealed that the actress Stephanie Beacham is the latest in a gathering clan of people willing to talk about their NDEs. Stephanie, star of the Hollywood TV soap *Dynasty II*, explained how she 'died' for a short period whilst in hospital a couple of years ago. 'I was going,' she said. 'I was being led by someone whose face was human but my attention was focused towards the brightest light I have ever known ...' As this makes abundantly obvious, her account of the NDE is just like all the others. And it has had exactly the same effect on a millionairess film star as on thousands of ordinary folk. She has lost all fear of death. 'I realized then that we don't really die. We go on,' she proclaims.[7]

And perhaps we do.

OOBEs

When I first started to assess the out-of-body experience, I wondered if there might not be a simple explanation. I had listened to Dr Sue Blackmore, a professional psychologist but also probably Britain's leading researcher in this field. She had concluded that the OOBE was an imaginary (not real) experience. Of course, in outline I absolutely agree with that. There is a high count on the hallucination scale, because the phenomenon straddles the half-way house on our spectrum. This invades the real-world environment and produces a dreamy psi-event.

Since many OOBEs happen in operating theatres or at times of life crisis (e.g. sudden car-accident), I considered whether the change in state of consciousness might not simply make the person receptive to psi-impressions from other people. In a hospital or a car smash a lot of eyes (and minds) are attending to you. Do we need to believe in some spirit leaving the body? Perhaps all that occurs is a visualization of this attention, flooding into your unconscious mind from all the onlookers. We do not 'see' our own bodies, only other people's view of our bodies at that moment. This idea has superficial attractions, but the problems come quickly when you think it through. Where in the 'mind store' *is* a view of ourselves as others see us, to allow this kind of dramatization?

However, an even worse situation occurs when there are no onlookers to focus attention onto you. The OOBE remains identical. Indeed, my own OOBE falls into this category. I was in bed late at night, and so far as I know there were no 'Peeping Toms'. As it followed the death of my very psychic grandmother, when I was staying at a friend's house the night before the funeral, I suppose it is possible that the onlooker was my grandmother's ghost. But the quite typical OOBE from a Hull woman called Barbara, seems to deny even this extreme option. It was 1962 and she was $7\frac{1}{2}$ months pregnant with her first child. She was dozing in bed, trying to get as much rest as possible, knowing full well there would soon be precious little of that. Suddenly, as she says, 'I got a loud buzzing noise in my left ear and head ... It was just like a dynamo and it was a sound I knew no one else could hear.' By now we have come across this buzzing noise so often, that I doubt you will be surprised by her account. It is obviously a real (even if subjective) phenomenon, as so many people keep on describing it in identical fashion. Notice the remark about the left ear, and thus its connection with the right cerebral hemisphere (where we have suggested psi-awareness may be processed); also her intuitive knowledge that the noise was an internal experience.

Barbara felt a spinning sensation and a rush of speed, to find herself floating 'two feet above and about two feet to the left of my body ... I remember thinking that I wasn't as good looking as I'd always thought I was.' She wondered about 'going up to the ceiling in the corner of the bedroom and I was instantly there'. Then she re-entered her body, just by thinking this. She concludes, 'I have never told anyone about this, as they would say it was a dream. It certainly was not a dream. I was wide awake. I swear this happened, on my mother's life.'

Absolutely. How can we say it did not? The OOBE is a very important psi-event which may be common to everyone. Perhaps the answer to the question of where the 'mind store' image comes from is the many previous OOBEs we have all undergone. They might not be in our conscious awareness but could have established themselves in the 'mind store' by repetition.

In Barbara's case I would guess that we should rate it about forty per cent hallucination, sixty per cent objectivity – towards the left (normal reality) end of the spectrum. The bedroom environment was close to normal. She felt herself awake. So it must have been this side of the half-way house, although in other OOBEs the hallucination content is higher still, and they blend into lucid dreams, on the right side of the spectrum.

The floating and other bizarre elements are a product of the forty per cent hallucination count. In normal reality such things are impossible. But the impossible is all too possible during a psi-event.

Psychokinesis (PK)

Some of the phenomena discussed under 'Hauntings' may well be important here. Psychokinesis means the moving of objects without visible or physical means. It is assumed that the mind achieves it. However, it often happens removed from any alleged ghostly presence. Metal-bending is the classic example.

To illustrate the problem, I was lucky to receive a report from ASSAP investigator Andy Roberts, shortly before I prepared this section, dated January 1986. It involves a twenty-five-year-old hairdresser, Karen Mansley, from Brighouse, West Yorkshire. It is not special in any way, just a typical case of protracted PK.[8]

Many separate incidents are noted between June 1984 and the time of the report. They tend to come in short bursts with long, inactive periods when nothing occurs. That is another common feature of PK. They also appear to need Karen there to manifest. Examples include drawers being opened on their own, cupboard doors banging shut, taps or raps underneath the bed, room lights, alarm-clocks, stereos and other electrical equipment switching itself on, and objects (such as mirrors or photographs) mysteriously moving into unexpected places. Some of the worst experiences came during Christmas Day/Boxing Day 1985 when a barrage of bangs kept Karen and boyfriend Kevin awake all night. At one point a drawer flew out of a bedside cabinet and narrowly missed hitting him.

Karen feels that the events are related to her own mind, although she does not know how. Her mother, Brenda, is much more interested in the possibility of a spirit causing them and believes in life after death. A local medium had been called in to exorcize the influence, and he concluded that both protecting and malevolent spectres were in the house, possibly attracted by Mrs Mansley's spiritual beliefs. However, it must be added that the same medium gave researcher Andy Roberts a 'life reading' which the investigator claims was long and detailed but 'almost totally wrong in every respect'.

One possible clue to Karen's subconscious mind at work came in an incident during this phase of exorcism. One of Mrs Mansley's books on life after death (written by the medium Doris Stokes) disappeared for a time. It turned up later, in the rubbish bin. The symbolism of that is pretty obvious.

PK does seem to be a genuine transfer of energy. The emotions of a subject (young girls are frequently involved) are somehow transformed into physical actions. Science should not scoff at this, if mind or emotion truly is an energy field, because it happens all the time with other forces. The heat that we feel from the sun has travelled 93 million miles across a vacuum as an entirely different type of energy. If it melts some ice, and the resultant water drives a wheel round, physical action has been created in exactly the same way as emotions might turn into PK.

It seems that the energy acts out emotional tantrums deep within the unconscious mind. Almost as if the doorman, tired of not getting some message across by standard psi-event means, decides on a last resort to bring it to notice. Just like the child whose pleas for attention are ignored, it may then go around smashing up the crockery in a frustrated effort to make his point.

Precognition

Precognition is no different from many other psi-events. It involves the detection of a message which gets past the doorman to be visualized by images from the 'mind store'. However, the message relates to what we call the future. Depending upon how little is lost in the various filter stages on route to conscious awareness, the prediction is either close to being accurate or wide of the mark.

We may all experience many inaccurate precognitions, which we then fail to recognize because they are so badly transmitted. Perhaps psychics are nothing more than people better able to spot one when it happens, or with greater skill in this error-ridden translation method.

Even so, a fine line is drawn between success and failure. If the message gets through and is represented by something appropriate from the 'mind store', a remarkable prediction might be the result. If the message only makes it part way as a psi-emotion, the best we may have to show for it will be a feeling of intuition. And if any of these stages fail to work too well, the premonition will probably look like a flop.

British psychic Malcolm Bessent offers us an example.

After the 1966 catastrophe at Aberfan, South Wales, when a whole school of children was engulfed beneath a coal slag, the magazine *TV Times* briefly set up a premonitions bureau. It was not so sophisticated as the one I propose. It was too short-lived, involved too few people, did not take account of the facts about the subject we know, and lacked the modern ability to use computer technology to sift and evaluate precognitions. Now we could do so much better and ascribe probability ratings to any type of event using the computers, but it was a bold attempt to react to the tragedy. I hope that some brave media source will respond to my challenge to create this new, improved version.

Let us look at the outcome of one apparent failure of the original bureau. Bessent, as one of its regular contributors, offered it in 1969, and it was actually published in a 1971 book.[9] So there is no doubt about its veracity.

The dream/vision concerned the US Presidency. It said that Richard Nixon (who had been elected in 1968) would not serve another term. It added that Senator Muskie would win in 1972, but that this year would be crucial for the USA: 'water everywhere, resulting in social upheaval, anarchy and political confusion. The people will be looking for a new leader.'

Of course, the first thing we see is how utterly wrong this prediction was. Nixon *did* get re-elected in 1972. Muskie never made it anywhere near the White House. However, we hardly need a degree in politics to know that Nixon's was a very hollow victory. The seeds of disaster were being sown by the President, whose demise was about to lead to exactly what Bessent predicted, social upheaval, political confusion and even charges of anarchy. The country would indeed be in need of a new leader, as Nixon gained the dubious historical record of impeachment from office.

Remarkably, Bessent chose to interpret his visions of 'water everywhere' as a great flood, though he never explained how this would cause the chaos at the White House his experience foretold. And his dating, 1972, was ever so slightly off. But the symbol of water is astonishingly close to the name Watergate, symbol of Nixon's downfall. It is easy to picture Bessent's 'mind store' detecting this building, which he had likely never heard of (who outside Washington ever had?), and dramatizing it with 'water', 'leaks' and 'floods'.

Treated literally, the prediction is a failure. Remembering that the 'mind store' works on symbols, it turns into a success. Nixon's end did come about because of leaks about taps on phones and bugging in the Watergate complex. One can only marvel at the accuracy with the benefit of hindsight.

But Bessent was wrong about the re-election and a year or so off in his timing. His mistakes, one is tempted to say. Not the fault of the message from his mind. That suspicion is compounded when you add a prediction by another person, Noel Tyl, apparently offered in 1973 and also published in a book (about astrology), *Integrated Transits* (Llewellyn Publications, 1974). About the period 'late 1974 to early 1975', Tyl says of Nixon, 'This will be a terrible time [for him], when heaven and hell will descend. ...' He had a good deal more to add, all pretty gloomy, although there were no absolute predictions of what took place.

Now suppose these predictions by Bessent and Tyl were on our great computer, hopefully with lots of others. The computer programme would sift into categories and those involving Nixon would score highly. A synthesized version, including aspects common to both and an averaged dating, would give a dramatic preview of the impeachment and demise of the president.

This is the sort of thing we could be doing, with very little expenditure. Imagine the commercial benefits of being able to make computer predictions of political events. The Opinion Poll business is a booming and lucrative one, but it would have nothing on this. Perhaps now some media source *will* start taking me seriously!

Malcolm Bessent and Noel Tyl may have just missed out on giving the greatest prediction of this century. But they did their bit. It was our inflexibility that failed them.

Psychometry

This is something else we have met a good deal, as it appears to be one of the best ways to develop your psi potential. There are many approaches you could try. Dowsers, using twigs or even coat-hangers, appear able to find hidden water. Some people dangle pendulum bobs over maps to locate missing persons. Psychiatrists such as Dr John Dale simply pick up an object and read emotions from it. The choice is up to you, the process likely the same.

One of the best demonstrations I have seen from Dr Dale concerned a 'reading' he gave to a middle-aged woman, when immediately he started to talk about France and a man who had died in his early fifties. A good half of the description was based on these things, although there was no reason to connect the woman with any country other than Britain. The psychometrist continued to add fleeting images (e.g. of waddling ducks) which the subject claimed meant nothing to her. But that was after success in the early part of his performance (just like the Zener card guessers who got bored and let their scores drop back to chance). He was holding a ring that belonged to the woman's mother (although Dale had no way of seeing it). There *were* close links with France: the woman had spent much time there. The description of her father's death was also accurate. Whilst the subject was not prepared to go into too much detail with me (she clearly felt it very personal), it was obvious that she had been deeply moved by the experience.

So what happens? Every psychometrist and dowser I have ever met argues that he or she does nothing special. They are using a sensitivity that each one of us possesses. The instrument (e.g. the pendulum or twitching birch twig) just seems like a way to magnify this sensitivity. It is an aid to the dowser, stepping up the small changes in emotion felt inside so that they become externally visible.

Coincidences emerge easily into the world, because it seems less difficult for us to manipulate probabilities than to generate large scale events. So the psychometrist turns the slight trembles of the body caused by psi-emotions into macroscopic movements of the instrument he uses. The same principle is employed by science all the time in monitor equipment. The needle magnifies a tiny current into a huge deflection which can be seen.

It is possible to train yourself out of the need for these aids, as John Dale and Bob Cracknell show. But unless you are very careful, it is easy to make false interpretations. Cruder applications seem much less variable. The narrower your goals, the more accurate the answer is likely to be.

Reincarnation

In the same way as life after death holds a permanent grip on humanity through the group mind, so reincarnation dominates the thinking of many cultures. Millions of people all over the world accept it as fact. Entire civilizations are based on the premise that we *do* return, again and again, to inhabit a sequence of different bodies. It has such remarkable attraction, even to learned scholars, that it could reflect another of those great truths that lurks in the collective unconscious.

Or again it might not. Sceptics ask where the evidence is. They point out that most stories of supposed 'past lives' emerge these days through regression hypnosis. This is a very controversial field, and quite a few cases where someone describes a former incarnation are known to be untrue. We met the phenomenon of cryptomnesia, where memories from the unconscious mind get past the doorman and become conscious. We interpret these as referring to our own previous existence on Earth. In fact, they are fantasies drawing on real forgotten memories from books or television.[10]

However, regression hypnosis is a recent invention and the craze for past-life study a modern artefact of the Hippie cult. All the ancient beliefs in the subject owe absolutely nothing to it. They depend on spontaneous claims of past-life memories – claims that are still made today, which are being carefully documented. Many come from lands where reincarnation is accepted. But there is a secret army of children in the West who, between the ages of three and five especially, also seem to have recall of another existence. If you have a child in this age group and dare ask such a strange question, you might well be amazed at the answer they give. A growing number of parents are making this startling discovery.

Some psychologists think that deep phobias or unexplained traumas could be the result of a hangover from a past life. I have often wondered myself about my terrible fear of water. Despite years of special instruction as a child, no expert could prevent my going into absolute hysterics when I entered a swimming-pool. I have also had many childhood dreams about drowning which come from no real basis. There are times when the idea of a past-life tragedy involving water is the only one that makes much sense to me, silly as I know this should be.

Mrs McGee of Glasgow also never understood why she so disliked any thought of France, until one day she was listening to the Grieg concerto, her mind idling, when a picture flooded in of an upper room looking down onto a sunny street in the South of France. There was little detail of what was happening, but she *knew* the time was about a hundred years ago. A mood of sadness dominated the psi-vision.[11]

This certainly has the feel of a genuine past-life experience. An emotion detected and transformed into a flash picture. Conventionally it is hard to explain why the scene was of somewhere she had never been to, so many miles away, at a time she placed so far into the past. And its relation to her unexplained dislike of France seems important.

This kind of quite common experience tantalizes us about reincarnation. They are rather more significant than the sort of case that gains publicity. For instance, the man who wrote from London about the ghost that came to visit him: this spectre was of his great-grandfather, dressed somewhat unusually as a Viking monarch! My correspondent explained that his relative believed himself to have been a Viking in a former incarnation and had shown him where to dig up his buried longboat and all its treasures. Would I help him to explain to the present owners of the land why we simply had to tear down their property? I treated the request as I had an earlier one to go and excavate Noah's Ark from half-way up Mount Sinai. I declined.

Besides, if reincarnation is a fact, I wonder why the king does not wait a couple of centuries and go and claim the prize himself!

Remote Viewing

I need add little to what I have said already about this important phenomenon. It seems to be clairvoyance without the false assumptions. The subject accepts psi-emotions about a distant location and turns these into visual impressions that are more or less accurate, according to how skilful he is. Visual or artistic people seem better than most, for reasons not hard to fathom.

Hella Hamid is a photographer who fits this description. She is one of Stanford Research Institute's star viewers. In 1981 she took part in a televised experiment with the late, sadly missed Dr Kit Pedler.

Noted for his scripting of *Doctor Who* and for the creation of the famous TV series *Doomwatch*, Pedler became interested in the paranormal towards the end of his life and published a first-rate book about his work, based on a Thames TV series he presented. In this he describes the experiment with Hella, supervised by Dr Liz Rauscher, a Berkeley physicist who has followed the trail of Puthoff, Targ and Harary.

One film crew went with Pedler and Dr Beverley Rubik (a biologist overseeing the experiment) to visit the selected site. Another stayed in a locked hotel room with Dr Rauscher and Hella Hamid. The latter had no idea where any of the potential sites were, nor where Pedler and Rubik had gone at that time. There was no question of trickery here. The entire experiment was filmed from both angles from start to finish.

The selected target was a large outcrop of rock. When this was compared with Hella Hamid's description and sketches, Pedler says, 'We gradually began to convince ourselves that the correspondence was fair to good.' And indeed there were points of comparison. However, when the psychic went to visit the six possible sites for feedback purposes, it immediately became obvious that there was a major success with one of the five sites *not* chosen![12]

This displacement effect is quite common for some reason. We can only assume that when Hella visited the sites *after* the experiment she felt more attached to one that was not the subject of the test. This personal interest crossed through time to the moment when the experiment occurred and was more powerful than the thoughts of either Pedler or Rubik at the time. In other words, personal precognition was more effective than impersonal remote viewing. There are clearly things we still do not understand about Remote Viewing, but its potential for experiment is again highlighted.

Time Slips

There is one psi-event I have not delved into, although it personally fascinates me. The time-slip does not merely involve a visualization of the past or the future. The subject steps into it.

If anything rates the description of a waking lucid dream, this is it.

The phenomenon is not common, but Joan Forman collected a surprising number of hidden cases (using newspaper appeals in East Anglia) when she researched what remains the only book on the subject. One of them shows how the time-slip borders on the psi-vision.

Mr C.H. d'Alessio was walking through a suburban street in London on a warm evening in 1975. It was a familiar road. He knew exactly where he was. But suddenly he began to lose all sense of time and place. The sounds of traffic vanished from around him. Everything became muted. He felt oddly calm and almost in a trance state.

Although neither Mr d'Alessio nor Joan Forman knew this, we can easily recognize that he is describing the Oz Factor. In other words, he must have slid to the right on the spectrum of reality. No longer was he walking the street in the sunshine of Normal Reality mode. He was now in the land of psi-events.

This particular psi-event did not involve seeing a UFO or a ghost, although it just as easily could have done. Instead he reports the environment changing. Strange cars were gliding past as if on cushions of air. There was a kind of automatic guidance system that prevented collisions. And the buildings and roadways had a silvery, synthetic feel to them. Intuitively he was sure that this scene came from the future, maybe a century ahead of 1975.[13]

Time-slips heading in this direction do happen but are less frequent than trips to the past. But would we know a future time-slip *was* to the future? Are some UFO encounters precisely this? There is so much direct comparison between the details of Mr d'Alessio's experience and Mrs Sage's adventure with the unusual helicopter (page 33) that I am tempted to regard them as identical cases.

Clearly visions of future transport are hallucinations which super-imposed themselves onto the Normal Reality background of the street. The messages they represent can only have come from the future, although their precise form will owe most to the individual and his 'mind store' – perhaps from a science-fiction novel he read.

Cases like these, where no inter-action occurs, fit easily into my model. When the witness says he *lived* inside the other time zone and met and talked with people there, things become much more difficult. This is a major challenge to our growing hypothesis, which is why we should look at the best example I have come across.

I met a couple, Geoff and Pauline Simpson from Kent, who described a holiday drive to Spain with their friends Len and Cynthia Gisby. It was 3 October 1979 at about 9.30 p.m., and they were searching the area around Montélimar for a hotel to break their southbound journey. They found one, down a lonely back lane off the main autoroute, and stayed the night. The only problem is that this accommodation does not exist. Not in the twentieth century! All four tourists support the story in an apparently honest fashion. Much as I would like to think that they are teasing, I have no evidence for that view. Their descriptions match and come in some detail, depicting old-fashioned rooms, antique plumbing, no glass in the windows or locks on the door, ridiculous beds and pillows – everything you might expect of a turn-of-the-century rural hotel.

There was some hint of the Oz Factor (a total disappearance of traffic on the road before they found the hotel). However, a psi-event that involves four people and lasts all night long (because they woke up in the phantom hotel!) is virtually unprecedented in the annals. As is the way in which they related to the characters in the hotel (who wore strange, outdated clothing). They also ate breakfast and evening meals of eggs, steak and potatoes. But when the bill came, it was for less than £2, for all four of them! Also a *gendarme* who entered the hotel did not understand the word *autoroute*, when they asked for directions the next day.

A couple of weeks later, when they returned north and decided to have a further taste of this bargain rate, they searched for ages down the back lane. In 1984 Yorkshire TV flew them to Lyons to search with police and tourist officers. The hotel just does not exist.

Only these four people know the truth. Perhaps it was a clever hoax. It has the ring of a spooky story. And there are some major problems that worry me. I do not like the way they claim to have taken three photographs of the hotel (using two separate cameras). Not only did these fail to come out, but the films have no missing frames as they ought to. How come nobody at the hotel found their clothes, or language, or car unusual? If this really was a time-slip, these things would be like a holiday family from 2087 riding into town. Hardly unremarkable. And how come the 19 francs of 1979 currency were accepted without quibble by the hotelier? Surely they would be valueless to someone from the last century.

I put these things to the Simpsons and they maintained a stony conviction. 'You tell us what the answer is. We only know what happened.'[14]

Indeed they do. And, dubious as objectivity makes me, I have to admit this case is not the only one. Others involving direct inter-action exist. Perhaps they are the most extreme form of psi-vision, exceedingly rare but possible. However, before I forsake my model in the light of such accounts, I feel entitled to expect less controversial cases than this one. Even though regression hypnosis and careful questioning have not produced a shred of evidence to disprove the claims of the Gisbys or the Simpsons.

UFO Contacts

As my previous books have shown, I believe there is a good deal to the UFO mystery. In some respects I feel sure that physical phenomena do exist. These are probably natural, atmospheric processes which we are beginning to understand. And I call them UAPs (Unidentified Atmospheric Phenomena) just to make sure we do not get confused.

What I am talking about here are the other UFOs, often called 'Close Encounters' or 'Alien Contacts'. These come when a witness sees a strange craft of undeniably alien design or even meets up with supposed denizens of another world. One or two even presume to ask that we believe in their kidnap and abduction on board the craft.

As with interactive time-slips, such extraordinary cases require special discussion, which there is no scope for here. I am not rash enough to dismiss these things out of hand because they sound incredible. I have learned by experience the stupidity of that. Instead I want to talk about a typical 'close encounter'. And I ask you to remember that, whilst a UAP is an object that can be seen, the 'close encounter' is a psi-event to be experienced.

Eileen Arnold is a retired headmistress. We have corresponded at some length about her encounters, and she was good enough to go to quite some trouble over this. They began with one that happened in February or March 1942.

At the time she was twenty-seven years old and not yet a teacher. Seven and a half months pregnant with her first child (identical with OOBE witness Barbara from Hull, whom we met undergoing her first experience), Eileen lived in Cheltenham, Gloucestershire, and was returning from a pre-natal check-up. The High Street was busy, despite war-time austerity, on a sunny early afternoon.

Many of the things she says about the experience are important, so I will quote Eileen's words direct. She was in 'a particularly sensitive state' and shared what seems like a telepathic rapport with a passing stranger. Then 'on impulse' she turned to look across the road above a house. She knew 'instinctively' that this was 'not anything from this earth'. The object seemed to be sailing across the sky and discharging fins from its side as a porcupine ejects quills. At the same time, while this was happening, there was a time lapse and an environment lapse – which I don't have a name for. Can you have a space lapse?' Time slowed. The extremely busy road altered. 'Traffic and people had completely vanished [but] I didn't even see the road and pavement ... all I "saw" apart from the UFO was the rooftop over which it appeared.'

Of course, Eileen had never heard of the Oz Factor. Nor did the term UFO exist in 1942. She had no way of relating her experience to an accepted phenomenon. (Coincidentally, the very first reported sighting came in the USA on 24 June 1947 from a man who also had the surname Arnold.) Despite her puzzlement she longed for somebody to see the thing with her, felt emotionally attached to it but then (quite inexplicably) forgot it immediately afterwards. 'From the moment of the sighting to the arrival at my flat was a period of total blank.' She also kept the whole thing secret for years. 'I never thought to tell ... It seemed so "privately" mine.'

All these different symptoms have been associated with many UFO cases and other types of psi-event. They tell the knowledgeable researcher loud and clear that there is no real distinction between reports that seem to be separate. Psi-events must be studied together, if they are to be studied at all.

The interpretation of what was seen as a 'flying saucer' seems only to be circumstantial. It is a convenient label that fits the second half of the twentieth century. The nature of what is seen moulds itself to topicality. A hundred years ago it would have been something else. A hundred years from now it will have changed yet again. But the psi-event that underpins them all will continue unabated.

Mrs Arnold uses a lot of words like 'I felt intuitively' and 'it appeared to be for my eyes alone'. The more she told me about herself, the more it was obvious that she was a medium, even though that word might never have occurred to her. She receives something that she calls 'impressions dictation', which others call 'automatic writing'. What this means is that images filter up from her unconscious as feelings or impressions, and by allowing her mind to wander and her hand to doodle on a piece of paper these can be translated into words. It is another method of gaining access to your psi-potential that works for some people. The messages that she writes tell of spirits and such like and are sometimes evidential. She also has visions which she knows to be hallucinatory ('Of course they are all symbolic – what else?')

None of this was spoken in her initial letter to me. If I had not been around long enough to know the truth, it is doubtful I would have asked or that she would have thought to tell me. The UFO in the Cheltenham High Street (which nobody else saw, of course) would be on the files as a near landing by a spaceship. Indeed, Mrs Arnold tells me that in 1975 she *did* report it to a famous UFO group, who were quite uninterested in her other experiences. So she never bothered to describe these. They logged her sighting as a 'mother ship' on their computer – whatever one of those is!

So far as she is concerned, her experiences illustrate how 'the vast network of heightening consciousness is spreading throughout the world.' And I have now met or corresponded with dozens of Eileen Arnolds whose encounters and feelings are virtually identical. There is a dawning awareness of their psychic potential. And this is far more important than the relatively minor differences between their individual psi-events.

Eileen joked with me that, although she had built a respectable career and raised a family without most people suspecting any of the above, and despite her certainty that these things had happened, 'I could still be dotty.'

Somehow I do not think she is.

Conclusions

Conclusions

'If the Russians have it and we don't, we are in
serious trouble.'

Charles Rose, US Congressman,
talking to the science journal *OMNI* in 1979

Every day dozens of new psi-events happen. Sceptics are turned
into believers – not by reading books such as this, but by the
evidence of their own experience.

To round things off, I shall select one case at random. The
report arrived during the week I write these words of conclusion
and is one of five that found their way to me these past seven
days. They come here thanks to my various roles of
investigations co-ordinator. And this is a fairly typical case.

It was collated by David Clarke, who has not long left school
but has already had several years training as an investigator in
the field. It might seem odd that I should use something offered
by an eighteen-year-old, but I know him to be a well-versed
researcher. (This cardinal sin demarking many scientists and
most debunkers is that all they ever do is read about the subject.
They wave away the paranormal from the misguided isolation of
an armchair. Meanwhile, all around them, strange things
continue to happen. If they would only step outside, talk to
people and recognize the scale of this problem, I doubt that they
should fail to share my deep concern.) I regard the work of
David and many others as fundamental to our future. Scattered
around the globe, they are trying hard to be objective, protecting
man's heritage – perhaps even his destiny.

This final, ordinary report concerns the Browitt family from
Sheffield, South Yorkshire. Beryl Browitt, a housewife in her
forties, is its main ingredient, but her decorator husband, David,
and the youngest of three sons, Matthew, have also seen the

'apparition' which brought them to our notice. It is a shapeless mass, like mist or smoke, formed from tiny, pulsating lights. Beryl alleges that 'the thing' first appeared in 1976, when she was pregnant with Mathew and suffering a difficult confinement that kept her awake at nights. The phenomenon has never been seen to appear or disappear but swirls like cigar smoke. However, once seen it is very obvious, and it continues to drift in the air for lengthy periods.

Eventually others said they saw the floating form, although never quite so often as Beryl. It was always in the main bedroom, and the area was also said to have a strange 'feel' to it and be unusually cold. Beryl describes the amoebic nature of the shape as made of 'lights one sees when you close your eyes or go dizzy'. Thinking back to our examination of the sense of vision, you may recognize this clue pointing towards *internal* imagery. However, she adds that whenever she saw the phenomenon she would feel 'a calming effect on me, giving me a feeling of peace'. Once Mrs Browitt even walked *through* the mass, when she did not realize until too late that it was blocking the entrance to the hallway. 'It felt cool and very light of touch' and presented no real barrier to her movement.

Apart from this apparitional experience (which hardly qualifies for the term ghost), many other things have been noted about the bedroom. One woman with fine hairs on her arm felt these stand on end and tingle when she entered, as if there was an electrostatic field present, which is most interesting, because there are similarities between 'the thing' and a collection of dust particles gathered together by electric charges. Perhaps this apparition was, for once, quite real and created by this field of force that somehow congregates in the bedroom.

Supporting this view is the fact that electrical equipment in the house seems to have suffered a number of inexplicable failures. However, we have to set against this Beryl Browitt's other claims, which are not quite so easy to explain. These include a classic UFO encounter, smells of perfume similar to that used by her dead mother, and frequent OOBEs. These begin as straightforward psi-visions in the same bedroom (where she will drift up towards the ceiling) but then tend to become more like fantasy than reality as she flies around the night-time landscape like a witch on an invisible broom. (It is, incidentally, quite possible that this witch legend comes from OOBEs in past centuries, when they were even less understood.)

Beryl says that after the OOBEs she falls immediately asleep. This suggests that, as the hallucination count increases, she passes from the psi-event zone on our spectrum of reality and hovers around the half-way house. Then, as the balance shifts and she enters the right-hand side of the spectrum, the OOBE becomes more hallucinatory than real, she enters a lucid-dream phase and finally drifts into ordinary dream sleep.

Mrs Browitt also demonstrated some ability at dowsing to the investigators, so that, taking all the evidence, it is fairly clear that *she* must be the focus for these events, rather than the bedroom, as might first seem probable.

Unfortunately, the research did not get very far. It began in June 1985 but 'the thing' stopped appearing. It is not known how relevant the placing of a flash camera in the bedroom might have been. Temperature readings also failed to reveal any anomalies, although electric field readings were not taken. Without scientists to back you up, such simple steps are never easy. The only history of the house before the family moved in seems to be its severe damage by a German bomb during World War II. In fact, it lay derelict for a time and was rebuilt in 1947 into its present detached condition.

This kind of case is typical of what the psi-researcher faces all the time. It starts off looking like a routine apparition, but once the right kind of questions are asked, the full extent of the situation resolves. Without such probing few witnesses either think or choose to volunteer the background.

Sadly we are very often left with more questions than answers. Several months into the study the Browitts left the house to live down south. Their experiences were not offered as a reason, but Beryl's apparent desire to move closer to Stonehenge in Wiltshire was. This is an area she has always felt a deep affinity with.

David Clarke's report (which he completed with Gary Taft and Pam Owen) shows that when a psi-event is the subject of investigation it pays to think broadly and ask unusual questions.

Of course, to ignore a case like this will be an admission of failure. A scientist who utters the magic words, 'It must have been imagination', deserves both our admonishment and our sympathy, for in the long run it will be he who misses out.

Science does a lot of things that seem very abstract to the layman. What advantage to us can it be to know the composition of a quasar on the far side of the universe? How can we benefit from calculations, to the tenth decimal place, of the atomic number for some radio-active element which nobody wants and no one can keep stable? The matters that interest people are the ones that impinge directly upon their lives.

Psi-events most certainly do that. There are millions of witnesses and no excuse for denying them a share of the financial cake. The responsibility of science is to take these things seriously. So far it has been largely quite irresponsible.

There are some brave scientists, and we have met many in this book: Blackmore, Bohm, Ellison and Sheldrake in Britain, Jahns, Rogo, Puthoff and Targ in the USA. They are not afraid to look stupid in the eyes of their colleagues for daring to suggest that psi *might* be interesting.

Science, on the whole, still scoffs at the paranormal. It demands material proof for things which are often very subjective in nature. Such demands can be accepted. What is less acceptable is the creation of a team of 'psi-busters' — dedicated to the eradication of anything supernatural.

The main force which psi-researchers must deal with goes by the name of CSICOP (Committee for the Scientific Investigation of claims on the paranormal). The term 'psi-cop' has regularly been given to their members, for they do regard themselves as the police of all things unexplained. Undoubtedly, they do this with sincere motives. But they rarely stop to think of the potential harm their actions can bring to witnesses (who often have no idea what has happened to them and want sympathy instead of ridicule) and serious investigators (who tend to get tarred with the same brush and viewed by CSICOP alongside all manner of credulous fanatics).

It is very easy to dismiss the paranormal out of hand and, by so doing, miss invaluable data that could aid science. Indeed, there have been times when CSICOP have led themselves astray in their quest to ensure that an outcome does *not* support anything unconventional. When they set up an experiment to test a form of astrology, apparently supported by extensive and protracted results obtained by psychologist Dr Michel

Gauquelin, they were utterly convinced that the experiment would disprove his twenty years work. When it did not, and in fact precisely supported his claim that there was a correlation between occupation and the location of planets at the time of birth, they manipulated the figures in such a way as to obscure the outcome. Only when one of their own members left in horror at what had been done was the embarrassing truth slowly and painfully extracted and admitted to.

More recently, journalist Philip Klass made extensive efforts to stop a conference at which I spoke. It was hosted by the University of Lincoln, Nebraska and covered a number of fields which might be termed paranormal – although many of the speakers were scientists. Klass, and CSICOP, were not happy with this endorsement of 'pseudo-science' and endeavoured to persuade the university hierarchy that it was against the interests of mankind to allow the three-day event. In fact the university overturned his appeals, which included the curious suggestion that because some speakers accused the American government of a cover-up of data the conference was fostering the aims of the communist party! The programme went ahead. But, perhaps understandably, the university declined to host the event when the matter next came up for discussion.

In 1979 James McDonnell, of the McDonnell-Douglas Aircraft Corporation, set up a laboratory to experiment into psi-effects. 'MacLab', as it was known, was especially interested in possible interference with aircraft systems that pilots might unconsciously generate should they have the ability to perform psychokinesis. The dangers of this for aircraft safety explain 'MacLab's interest. But in August 1985 the grant was removed, supposedly because after McDonnell's death the project was not considered financially viable. However, one is left to ponder the effect of CSICOP's own 'experiments' on the lab which went as follows.

James (The Amazing) Randi is one of the most outspoken members of the Committee. A professional magician, he considers anyone who claims psychic abilities a challenge to his own skills and sets trials and tests for them to prove themselves. In 1981 he trained two young magicians to pretend to be psychics who could bend metal objects in the style of Uri Geller. The very inexperienced 'MacLab' team were for a brief period fooled by this charade. Peter Phillips, the physics professor in charge of the lab, admitted he was not a true parapsychologist and had no real background in isolating fake psychics. However, even he began to suspect something was awry within a few weeks. As soon as he tightened up controls all positive results with the Randi stooges ceased. As Randi agreed, from that point until mid 1982, when 'MacLab' dumped the jokers, nothing considered to have a paranormal origin was accepted by the research team.

Phillips and his colleagues did not have any idea of the CSICOP 'experiment' and simply forgot about the two failed psychics. They never used or published any of the results previously obtained with them. But some time later, in early 1983, a carefully stage-managed TV exposé was set up. Randi pulled out the two psychics from his conjurer's bag and used them to demonstrate how, in the view of CSICOP, it is remarkably easy to hoax parapsychology. The implication was that all psi-researchers are desperate for any evidence of the supernatural and, thus, their work cannot be given credence.

It is interesting that Klass is a journalist and Randi an entertainer. Many of the most vociferous supporters of CSICOP fall into these categories, although there are some scientists involved. The non-scientists are very aware of how the media love a good story and if it is about the paranormal so much the better. They know exactly how to use this fact to their advantage.

Of course it is right that the paranormal be subject to close scrutiny. We all make mistakes and it is fair that these be pointed out. But there is reasonable criticism and proper testing. What CSICOP gets up to, in the name of science, does on occasion tend to push these definitions to their limit. There are plenty of so-called psi-researchers keen to star in media circus shows but scientists and science groups, including those opposed to the paranormal, have an obligation to behave with dignity.

These deliberate moves to discredit investigation into the paranormal only drive away the already meagre grants from scientists who *do* wish to study psi in a serious manner. This forces the work into the hands of governments and secret service agencies. Already we see this happening in an alarming way. We have encountered Soviet efforts, pumping money into parapsychology for military applications. They have long outgrown the need to prove that psi exists. What matters now is how to utilize it.

Congressman Rose expressed the worries many Western diplomats must have felt when they saw the extent of Russian domination, for they are miles ahead in the study of the paranormal. His words must have furthered the increasing and covert funding of American psi-research.

A few days before MacLab closed, on 12 August 1985, Jack Anderson and Dale Van Alta in the *Washington Post* described some of the work carried out at Stanford, home of the Targ and Puthoff Remote Viewing experiments. A CIA agent was apparently trained to penetrate a secret nuclear facility at Semipalatinsk without leaving the Californian laboratory. His visions were confirmed by satellite photography. But he also 'saw' underground facilities which the CIA experts considered impossible. However, after they had concluded that the test had failed, new evidence reached them by conventional spying methods. This turned on its head their previous judgement. The psi-vision now made perfect sense.

The columnists add, 'Before dismissing this as hallucinogenic hokum, the tax-payers should know that our government has spent – and continues to spend – millions of dollars on this hush-hush research.'

The name coined for all this is predictable: ESPionage. But no government which must justify each penny is going to fund schemes to this extent without every reason to expect success. Indeed, unless it was already showing promise, it would not still be going on.

On 10 January 1984 William Broad, science correspondent on the *New York Times*, passed comment on some of the things we *do* know, care of the American Freedom of Information Bill: 'The Pentagon has spent millions of dollars ... on secret projects to investigate ESP and to see if the sheer power of the human mind can be harnessed to perform various acts of espionage and war.' Doubtless the British Government are no more than their customary few years behind. And if this is what we *do* know, ponder what we do not!

It seems that man has a deathwish. Every time we make some major breakthrough in our understanding of the cosmos, the first thing we do is figure out how it can kill people. Preferably the more the better. As the evidence in this book makes abundantly clear, there are many beneficial ways to put psi into use. This secret take-over by the super-powers worries me deeply. And it obviously worried Russel Targ at Stanford. He abhorred the Pentagon funding and ended his successful partnership with Harold Puthoff.

Targ and psychic Keith Harary teamed up with a San Francisco businessman to run 'Delphi Associates'. They then faced the dilemma of all psi-researchers: if you do not get your money from the CIA or the dwindling number of science institutions awarding grants, where do you get it from? You can write books for the 'occult' shelves, and see your work crop up alongside junk about lost Atlantis or fortune-telling tortoises. Targ and Harary have done this. But it is a sad thing to have to rely on.

So they tried a novel approach. They devised an extension of the Remote Viewing technique where specific (and easily visualized) objects were matched with a multiple-choice outcome in any affair. Then, using psi-ability to scan for one of the representative objects, they could link it back to the affair they were studying and make a prediction about it. This affair could be a horse race or general election, or anything they wished. They applied it to silver on the stock market, and by predicting up and down movements claim they made $100,000 in a couple of months. With this fund it was no problem to launch their research work!

This happened four years ago. One of the first things Delphi have done is to develop a psi-based computer game with Atari. The player improves his score only when he gets more skilful at using psi. The process of feedback is supposed to help train your potential, as well as being good fun.

I applaud any such moves to break the CIA/KGB monopoly. We *must* ensure that our psychic powers are the subject of *free* development, not bureaucratic chicanery. Einstein made his great mistake with the atom bomb. We must never let that happen again.

In this regard I wish to make several appeals, designed to find a way around this obstacle.

To witnesses who experience psi-events: I urge that you try to report them. There are people who will listen without considering you mad. You can write to me if you so desire (see address on page 223). But do write to somebody, quickly, and constructively. Help break the official stranglehold.

To scientists and sceptics who do not believe: I respect your privilege but ask that you take a cool look at the evidence. There are millions of people who disagree with you. Rather than close your mind to what they are saying, think up experiments that can test psi-events. Then, whatever the results, have the courage to publish them. They may seem like nonsense today. But those who sit on fences run the greatest risk of looking foolish.

However, it is the media whom I ask to shoulder the main responsibility. My quotes from the *Washington Post* and *New York Times* show that the most respectable of sources can take stands. This should not be left to the less celebrated tabloids. Television programmes such as *Tomorrow's World* and journals like *TV Times* and the naturally more committed *Unknown* have already proved that it can be done. As the word 'media' actually defines, these news sources stand between progress and the people. Nobody can do better what must be done.

It is possible to devise genuine tests of the paranormal which rely on no beliefs – tests that will either succeed or fail, but will add to our knowledge either way. By promoting these to a large audience, many ordinary people can try out psi for themselves. It will open this up to those who dare not try alone and who remain ignorant thanks to the judgement of the wise; there is comfort in numbers and power too. At the same time as providing 'good copy' or great television, major results will be forthcoming.

An isolated claim of a psi-event is fascinating and useful but ultimately lacking. A dozen media tests all around the world could create a storm of interest impossible to ignore.

This book has made a few suggestions of things that can be done without great expenditure. I am ready to work with any media source in devising and implementing full-scale experiments. There is no need to fear competition. There are plenty of new ideas to go around. And I am sure that many colleagues feel as I do, and will support this appeal to the mass market media.

Here are just three possibilities that seem to have potential:

Telepathy

Television or radio would be ideally suited to this type of work. A test of telepathy that uses emotion, interest and personal involvement would be necessary. Not just trying to figure out a symbol on a playing-card. After doing it over the airwaves in one country (e.g. Britain), or one part of the country, an immediate follow-up of the same experiment should be conducted somewhere else. According to Sheldrake, the second test should succeed better than the first. Indeed, if a whole series (perhaps of five) were carried out across the space of a week or two, the results would be even more significant.

Remote Viewing

This would work well through regional or national newspapers, and the more trials the better. By following the conventional technique to locate someone at a randomly selected position, and have thousands try at once to get impressions, the results should be interesting, to say the least. If psi-exists, half a dozen experiments of this kind could amass sufficient evidence quickly and easily. If they work, it will be very hard for sceptics to deny them. If they fail, the results will be equally important. If those of us who feel that something might be going on are willing to make a call for such a test, are the sceptics willing to gamble on the outcome? The media hold the answer to that question. All it need do is accept my challenge.

Precognition

Or how about the launch of a modern premonitions bureau, perhaps through a monthly magazine? They will not be so worried about the long-term requirements of such a project, although it *could* achieve immediate results, of course. Such a scheme would collect psi-visions and vivid dreams long-term. But as time-spans between dream and fulfilment are often short it must depend on a telephone hotline as well as on written sources. All input should go onto a computer, programmed to sift and take account of what we know, recognizing the symbolism, assigning weightings to incoming reports, and issuing probability percentages based on cumulative totals. If a major event reaches a high level of probability and then *really* happens, the way ahead is clear. Next time, perhaps, we shall be able to stop it.

We have skirted round the issues for too long. We must not be at this crossroads a decade from now. Psi either exists or does not, and we have the means to decide which almost immediately. It must be make-your-mind-up time.

Of course, I suspect what the answer will be. But if I am wrong, I shall say so without reservation. A concerted effort is all we require, and then books such as this will become obsolete. No longer shall we need to ask if it is possible. One way or the other we shall know.

In justifying the need to fund this work at secret levels there are those who talk of psi-wars, instead of star-wars – that World War II has already begun, and the West is losing.

My fear is that, unless we bring back psi into the hands of the people, it will not be the West (or the East) who will lose.

It will be mankind.

Reference Section

Reference Section

Readers who have an experience they wish to share may write to the author at the address below. I shall endeavour to ensure that somebody local follows up the report, unless the writer expresses a wish for confidentiality, in which case the report will be treated as such.
8 Whitethroat Walk, Birchwood, Warrington, Cheshire, WA3 6PQ.

If you are interested in furthering your research into psi, there are many good amateur groups who always need support. The addresses below direct you to some of these. They all have open meetings, and most produce magazines. If you are interested in something more local, a request (plus SAE) to the author, at the address above, will bring assistance in this regard.
ASSAP (Association for the Scientific Study of Anomalous Phenomena)
30 South Row, London, SE3 ORY
BUFORA (British UFO Research Association)
30 Vermont Road, London. SE19 3SR
CUFOS (Center for UFO Studies)
1955 John's Drive, Glenview, Illinois 60025, USA

The following magazines may be useful to readers wishing to develop their interest. Whilst I would not recommend that everything be taken seriously, they have certainly been of assistance to me.
Anomaly, 65 Amersham Road, High Wycombe, Bucks, HP13 5AA
Fate, 500 Hyacinth Place, Highland Park, Illinois 60035, USA(*)

Fortean Times, 96 Mansfield Road, London, NW3 2HX.

Magonia, 5 James Terrace, Mortlake Churchyard, London, SW14 8HB

Quest, 68 Buller Crescent, Leeds, West Yorks, LS9 6LJ

Supernaturalist, 19 St David's Way, Wickford, Essex, SS11 8EX

UFO-Brigantia, 84 Elland Road, Brighouse, West Yorks, HD6 2QR

The Unknown, Sovereign Publications, Brentwood, Essex, CM14 4SE (*)

(*) indicates that the magazine is sold in shops. All other titles are subscription only.

Chapter References

Chapter References

Introduction

1. *Fate*, No.408, March 1984
2. Quoted from Scott's autobiography *The Eye of the Wind* by Heywood, 1964.
3. *Clues to the Unknown*, R. Cracknell (Hamlyn, 1981)

Chapter 1

1. *Beyond the Body*, Dr S. Blackmore (Heinemann, 1982)
2. My own OOBE experience was described in *Beyond Explanation?* p.91
3. *Phone Calls from the Dead*, Dr S. Rogo (Bantam, USA), records many similar cases
4. *Ball Lightning and Dead Lightning*, James Barry (Plenum Press, 1980)
5. For an introduction to the Oz Factor you are advised to read my book *UFO Reality*
6. 'Very Strange Bedfellows', J. Randles in *Destiny* (December, 1985)
7. SPR Proceedings, 1905
8. *Apparitions*, C. Green and C. McCreery (Hamish Hamilton, 1975)
9. *The Story of Ruth*, Dr M. Schatzman (Duckworth, 1980; Penguin, 1981)
10. Pages 128-9
11. *Visions* H. Evans (Aquarian Press, 1984)
12. *Natural History of the Mind*, G. Rattray-Taylor (Secker & Warburg, 1979)
13 A good place to start is *The art and science of Visual Illusions*, N. Wade (Routledge & Kegan Paul, 1982)
14. *Illusion in Nature and Art*, edited by Dr R.L. Gregory and Dr E.H. Gombrich (Duckworth, 1973). See especially section by Blakemore entitled 'The baffled brain'.
15. *The Psychology of Perception*, Dr M.D. Vernon, (Penguin, 1971)
16. 'An experimental study of the effect of language on the reproduction of visually received form', L. Carmichael, H.P. Hogan, A.A. Walter in *Journal of Experimental Psychology*, Volume XV, 1932
17. Vernon, op. cit., pp.82-3
18. 'Children's long-term memory for information that is incongruous with their prior knowledge' S.J. Ceci, R.C. Caves, and M.J. Howe in *British Journal of Psychology*, Volume LXXII, November 1981

19. *The universe within*, M. Hunt (Harvester Press, 1982)
20. See pp.39-42 of *UFO Reality* and pp.83-4 of *UFO Study* for two cases
21. Quoted in *The Infinite Hive*, R. Heywood (Chatto & Windus, 1964; Pan, 1966)
22. Heywood, op. cit., p.211.

Chapter 2

1. Vernon, op. cit.
2. *The Paranormal*, Dr S. Gooch (Wildwood House, 1978; Fontana, 1979)
3. *The Conscious Brain*, S. Rose (Weidenfeld & Nicholson, 1978)
4. For a good survey of the main localizations see Rattray-Taylor, op. cit.
5. *The Dragons of Eden*, Dr C. Sagan (Hodder & Stoughton, 1977)
6. The series began with the book *Shikasta* and is published by Jonathan Cape
7. *The Mind*, A. Smith (Hodder & Stoughton, 1984)
8. *Janus*, A. Koestler (Heinemann, 1978)
9. This is introduced in my book *Beyond Explanation?*
10. See Chapter 7 particularly of my book *UFO Reality*
11. 'Nocturnal wanderings of a little green man', P. Bennett, in *UFO Brigantia*, July 1985
12. A very similar case from Cyprus can be found in *UFO Reality*, pp.114-16
13. 'A report on Mrs P', dated 1 March 1984, Dr M. Clare
14. *Mind out of Time*, I. Wilson (Gollancz, 1981)

Chapter 3

1. *The Roots of Coincidence*, A. Koestler (Hutchinson, 1972)
2. *Psychic Animals*, D. Bardens (Hale, 1987)
3. Dr Lyall Watson discusses this fully in *The Romeo Error* (Hodder & Stoughton 1974), so called because Romeo had one or two problems deciding as well!
4. *Life after life*, Dr R. Moody (Bantam, 1975)
5. *Alien Contact*, J. Randles (Neville Spearman, 1982; Coronet, 1983)
6. *States of Mind*, J. Miller (BBC Publications, 1983)
7. For details of this amazing dream coincidence see 'Literary Assistance of a Curious Kind', J. Randles in *Fortean Times*, 42, 1984
8. 'You may be bringing up a genius', R. Brightwell, *The Listener*, 7 February 1985
9. Dr Justine Sargeant reports in *Mind/Brain Bulletin*, 28 March 1983
10. Rattray-Taylor, op.cit., pp.5–6
11. 'When wishes come true', H. Evans, in *Fate*, No.429, December 1985
12. *Fate*, No.408, March 1984
13. 'Driven crazy by telepathy', C. Bloom in *Fate*, No.427, October 1985

Chapter 4

1. *Fate*, No.338, May 1978
2. *Psychic Nexus*, Dr B. Schwarz, (Van Nostrand, 1980), pp.3–24
3. *UFO Study*, pp.150-51
4. *Earthlights*, P. Devereux (Thorsons, 1982)
5. *When the Snakes Awake*, Dr H. Tributsch (MIT Press, 1983)
6. *Fate*, No.426, September 1985
7. *Premonitions*, H.B. Greenhouse (Turnstone, 1971; Pan, 1975), p.60

Chapter 5

1. *The Human Senses*, Dr F. Geldard (John Wiley, 1972)
2. *Psychic Discoveries behind the Iron Curtain*, S. Ostrander and L. Schroeder (Sphere, 1970), pp.232–9
3. *The Luscher Colour Test*, Dr M. Luscher (Jonathan Cape, 1970, Pan, 1971)
4. 'The nature of the dermo-optic sense', Dr A. Novomeisky, in *International Journal of Parapsychology*, Volume VI, 1964; 'Seeing colour with the fingers', A. Rosenfield in *Life*, 12 June 1964
5. *Memory and Hypnotic Age Regression*, Dr R. Reiff and Dr M. Scheerer, (IUP, 1959)
6. *Fortean Times*, 38, 1982, p.18
7. *American Medical Association Journal*, May 1979
8. *Arthur C. Clarke's World of Strange Powers*, S. Welfare, (1985)
9. *Photographs of the Unknown*, R. Rickard and R. Kelly (NEL, 1980)
10. Report by Dr R. Moody, in *The Lancet*, Volume CCLIV 1948
11. 'Stigmatic Heretic', R. Rickard in *Fortean Times*, 30, 1979
12. Letter ref. *NOW* 6, February 1983
13. See photograph facing p.161 of *UFO Study*
14. *Coventry Evening Telegraph*, 7 January 1986
15. *Clairvoyant Reality*, Dr L. Le Shan (Turnstone, 1980)
16. 'Dowser finds the men who vanished', L. Cortesi *Fate*, No.410, May 1984
17. *Dreamers*, J. Grant (Ashgrove Press, 1984, Grafton, 1986)

Chapter 6

1. *Creatures from Inner Space*, Dr S. Gooch (Rider, 1984)
2. Schwarz, op. cit., p.180.
3. *The Kick Inside*, album (ref. EMC 3223, 1978), song 'Strange Phenomena'
4. Heywood, op. cit., p.139
5. Ibid. p.89
6. Quote from *Chicago Tribune* in *Fate*, No.430, January 1986
7. For a report on the Lawson and McCall experiments see *The Evidence for Alien Abductions*, J. Rimmer (Aquarian, 1984)

8. *The Pennine UFO Mystery*, J. Randles (Grafton Books, 1983) pp.157, 187-8
9. Schwarz, op.cit., p.217
10. *Subliminal Perception: The Nature of a Controversy*; N.F. Dixon (McGraw-Hill, 1971)
11. *Introduction to the Psychology of Hearing* B. Moore (Macmillan Press, 1977)
12. Letter from witness to me, 16 October 1984
13. Various letters, reports, sketches to me between February and July 1978. Summarized in some more detail in *Flying Saucer Review*, 1979.
14. Letters to me dated November 1984. Fuller account in *Northern UFO News*, No.111
15. Letter dated 22 March 1983

Chapter 7

1. *Margins of the Mind*, F. Musgrove (Methuen, 1977)
2. Rattray-Taylor, op. cit., pp.69-77
3. 'The Confounded Eye', Dr R.L. Gregory, in Gregory and Gombrich, op. cit.
4. Heywood, op. cit., pp.99-100
5. 'Spooks are camera shy', J. Randles in *Fate*, No.418, January 1985
6. See review in Chapters 13 and 14 of *UFO Reality*
7. Ibid. pp.44-9
8. *Sky Crash*, J. Randles, B. Butler and D. Street (Spearman, 1984; Grafton, 1986)
9. *An Experiment with Time*, J.W. Dunne (Faber, 1939)
10. For these and other devastating quotes see *Order out of Chaos*, I. Prigogine and I. Stengerz (Heinemann, 1984)
11. Letter dated 14 March 1984
12. *The Tao of Physics*, Dr F. Capra (Wildwood, 1975)
13. Letter to Radio City, January 1983. Jim Feltham case report for ASSAP, March 1983
14. *Fate*, No. 397, April 1983
15. 'Shattered legend of the gods of space', G. Gordon in *Daily Mail*, 13 February 1986

Chapter 8

1. *Long Distance Voyager* album (ref. TXS 139, 1981), song 'The Voice'
2. *Mind over Matter: the Case for PK*, Dr S. Rogo (Aquarian, 1986)
3. Rattray-Taylor, op. cit.
4. *Lifetide* Dr L. Watson (Hodder & Stoughton, 1979), p.266
5. *Mysteries*, C. Wilson (Hodder & Stoughton, 1978; Granada, 1979), p.569
6. *Greenhouse* op. cit., pp.75-6
7. *Earthworks* Dr L. Watson (Hodder & Stoughton, 1986)
8. Letter dated 14 March 1983
9. *Fate*, No.418, January 1985

10. 'The Psychic vs the Killer', R. MacGregor and T. Janeshutz, in *Fate*, No.412, July 1984

Chapter 9

1. Zener cards were offered as part of a package on Rhine's work in *The Unexplained*, Issue 2, Orbis Publications, 1980
2. 'A multi-dimensional approach to the relationship between mood and weather', E. Howarth and M.S. Hoffman, in *British Journal of Psychology*, 1984
3. 'Can weather make you psychic?' Dr S. Rogo in *Fate* No.430, January 1986
4. Musgrove, op.cit.
5. Paper given to the seminar 'Science and ESP', Manchester University, December 1985
6. Schwarz, op. cit., p.29
7. 'The telepathic dolphins', F. Graham in *Fate*, No.340, July 1979
8. 'My best friend's a dolphin', K. Wheatley in *You*, 9 February 1986
9. *The Mind Race*, Dr R. Targ and Dr K. Harary (Villard, 1984; NEL, 1985)

Chapter 10

1. Prigogine and Stengerz, op. cit.
2. *Other Worlds* Dr P. Davies (Paladin, 1980)
3. *Timewarps*, Dr J. Gribbin (Dent, 1979; Sphere, 1981)
4. *Stalking the Wild Pendulum* I. Bentov (Wildwood, 1978)
5. *The Holographic Paradigm*, edited by Dr K. Wilber (Shambala Press, 1982)
6. *Wholeness and the Implicate Order*, Dr D. Bohm (Routledge & Kegan Paul, 1980)
7. *Flying Saucers: A modern myth of things seen in the skies*, Dr C. Jung (Routledge & Kegan Paul, 1959)
8. *A New Science of Life*, Dr R. Sheldrake (Blond & Briggs, 1981)
9. 'Is this the secret of life?' Dr S. Blackmore in *Fate*, No.426, September 1985
10. An in-depth interview with Rupert Sheldrake in connection with psi-events appears in *Fortean Times*, 37, 1982
11. 'Dreamscape', part of the *Everyman* series, BBC1, first shown 10 November 1985
12. *Lucid Dreams*, C. Green (Institute of Psychophysical Research, Oxford, 1968)

Chapter 11

1. 'A visit from beyond the moon', E. Polin, in *Fate*, No.418, January 1985
2. See, for example, *Fortean Times*, 44, 1985
3. Cracknell, op.cit.
4. L. Le Shan, op.cit.
5. *Psi-Eye*, No.1 (17 Langbank Avenue, Rise Park, Nottingham NG5 5BU)
6. See article by Darren Chanter in *The UFO World* (BUFORA, 1986)
7. Interviewed by S. Young in *Sunday Magazine*, 16 February 1986
8. *Mind over Matter*, Dr S. Rogo (Aquarian, 1986)
9. Greenhouse, op. cit., p.29
10. Wilson, op. cit. (especially the paperback version, updated 1983 as *Reincarnation?*)
11. *Mask of Time*, J. Forman (MacDonald & Janes, 1978), p.68
12. Mind over Matter, Dr K. Pedler (Thames Methuen, 1981; Granada 1982), pp.47-53
13. Forman, op. cit., p.214
14. 'A night in a phantom hotel', J. Randles in *Fate*, No.430, January 1986

Index

153-4, 176-7, 188-91, 203, 210
Ossicles, 104
Owen, Pam, 211
Oxford Psi Laboratory, 22, 175
Oz Factor, 20-1, 24, 34, 55, 107-9,
120, 127, 131, 140, 147, 177-8,
188, 200, 201, 203

Pain, 82-5, 87-92
Pattern recognition, 27-30
Pedler, Dr Kit, 199
Perception, factors affecting, 25-31,
63-4, 116-19
Pezze, Linda, 74-5
Pheromones, 67
Phillips, Ann, 151-2
Phillips, Ken, 156
Phillips, Peter, 214
Piddington, J.G., 21-2
PK (Psychokinesis), 60-3, 72, 135-6,
192-3, 213
Placebos, 61
Plato, 162
Poison, taking of, 71
Poltergeists, 72, 91
Pons, 40
Portmadoc, Wales, 131
Pre-lucid dreams, 173, 175
Precognition, 9, 18, 74-5, 121-6,
130-1, 132-3, 135, 139-40, 141-2,
154, 193-5, 218-19
Premonitions bureaux, 132-3, 194-5,
218-19
Prince of Wales, 50
Princeton, New Jersey, 154-5
Prosopanosia, 99-100
Psi, defined, 11, 148-9
Psi-events, defined, 11
Psi-audio defined, 129; 76-8, 100-1,
107, 109-10, 111, 185-7, 192-3
Psi-emotions defined, 129; 9, 10, 18,
64-5, 92-7, 130, 136, 140-2,
146-7, 150-2, 185-8, 192-3,
195-6
Psi-visions, defined, 129; 10-11,
15-18, 19-21, 32-6, 44-6, 55, 72,
74-5, 76-8, 92-5, 106-9, 111,
113-14, 120, 121-7, 128, 130-1,

140-2, 181-5, 185-7, 189-91, 194,
199, 200-5, 209-11
Psychometry, 10-11, 79, 92-7, 168,
195-6
Puerto de la Cruz, Spain, 155-6
Puthoff, Dr Harold, 153-4, 199,
215-16

Quantum Mechanics, 159-63
Quasi-conscious experience, 177
Quinn, Mr, 17

Radio City,, 102-3, 183-4
Randi, James, 213-14
Randles, Lucia, 18-21, 99
Rattray-Taylor, Gordon, 24, 61, 136
Rauscher, Dr Liz, 199
Readers Digest, 100
Reality, nature of, 23-36, 147-8, 158
et seq.
Reality blinks, 31-6, 108
Receptor cells, 81-2
Reincarnation, 48, 197-8
Relativity, Theory of, 159-63
Remote Viewing, 149-50, 152-7,
198-9, 215-16, 218
Repeater witnesses, 107-9
Retina, 115-16
Rhapsody in Blue, 50-2
Rhine, Dr J.B., 144-5
Richards, Charlotte, 130-1
Rides, 15-18
Ridgeway, John, 24
Right brain/left brain, 58-60, 88
Roberts, Andy, 192
Rods, 115-16
Rogo, Dr Scott, 146
Rorschach test, 29-30
Rose, Charles, 209, 215
Rose, Dr Steven, 40
Rubik, Dr Beverley, 199
Russell, Bertrand, 118, 158
Ruth experiments, 22-3

Sage, Mrs E., 33-6, 108, 200
St Thomas Hospital, London, 175
Schatzman, Dr Morton, 22-3, 175
Schering Corporation, 71

Vernon, Dr M.D., 27-31, 37
Vision, sense of, 113 *et seq.*
Visual illusions, 25-31, 63-4, 118
Voodoo, 62

Wales, University of, 50
Wallasey, Merseyside, 72
Warrington, Rosalind and Peter, 32
Washington, University of, 31
Washington Post, 215, 217
Watergate, premonition of, 194-5
Watson, Dr Lyall, 137, 166
Weather and moods, 145-6
Weather and psi, 146
West Kirby, Merseyside, 128-9
West Yorks. UFO Research Group, 44

Wheathampstead, Herts., 10-11
Whiting, F.H., 126-7
Whittaker, Paul, 104
Wilber, Dr Ken, 143, 148
Wiley, Renie, 142
Wilson, Colin, 138
Wisconsin, University of, 89
Wolverhampton, West Midlands, 123-4

X-ray photograph, 106

Yarrington, Robert, 89
Yeats, W.B., 148-9
Yorkshire Television, 201

Zener cards, 144-5, 150, 195